Foreign Trade Regimes and Economic Development: ISRAEL

Foreign Trade Regimes and Economic Development:

A Special Conference Series on Foreign Trade Regimes and Economic Development

VOLUME III

NATIONAL BUREAU OF ECONOMIC RESEARCH
New York   1975

ISRAEL

by **Michael Michaely**

THE HEBREW UNIVERSITY OF JERUSALEM

DISTRIBUTED BY Columbia University Press
New York and London

NATIONAL BUREAU OF ECONOMIC RESEARCH

*A Special Conference Series on Foreign Trade Regimes
and Economic Development*

ᴄ ᴄ

Library of Congress Card Number: 74–77691
ISBN for the series: 0–87014–500–2
ISBN for this volume: 0–87014–503–7

Printed in the United States of America
DESIGNED BY JEFFREY M. BARRIE

Relation of the Directors of the National Bureau to Publication of the Country Studies in the Series on Foreign Trade Regimes and Economic Development

Contents

Tables

Charts

Co-Directors' Foreword

This volume is one of a series resulting from the research project on Exchange Control, Liberalization, and Economic Development sponsored by the National Bureau of Economic Research, the name of the project having been subsequently broadened to Foreign Trade Regimes and Economic Development. Underlying the project was the belief by all participants that the phenomena of exchange control and liberalization in less developed countries require careful and detailed analysis within a sound theoretical framework, and that the effects of individual policies and restrictions cannot be analyzed without consideration of both the nature of their administration and the economic environment within which they are adopted as determined by the domestic economic policy and structure of the particular country.

The research has thus had three aspects: (1) development of an analytical framework for handling exchange control and liberalization; (2) within that framework, research on individual countries, undertaken independently by senior scholars; and (3) analysis of the results of these independent efforts with a view to identifying those empirical generalizations that appear to emerge from the experience of the countries studied.

The analytical framework developed in the first stage was extensively commented upon by those responsible for the research on individual countries, and was then revised to the satisfaction of all participants. That framework, serving as the common basis upon which the country studies were undertaken, is further reflected in the syntheses reporting on the third aspect of the research.

The analytical framework pinpointed these three principal areas of research which all participants undertook to analyze for their own countries.

Subject to a common focus on these three areas, each participant enjoyed maximum latitude to develop the analysis of his country's experience in the way he deemed appropriate. Comparison of the country volumes will indicate that this freedom was indeed utilized, and we believe that it has paid handsome dividends. The three areas singled out for in-depth analysis in the country studies are:

1. *The anatomy of exchange control:* The economic efficiency and distributional implications of alternative methods of exchange control in each country were to be examined and analyzed. Every method of exchange control differs analytically in its effects from every other. In each country study care has been taken to bring out the implications of the particular methods of control used. We consider it to be one of the major results of the project that these effects have been brought out systematically and clearly in analysis of the individual countries' experience.

2. *The liberalization episode:* Another major area for research was to be a detailed analysis of attempts to liberalize the payments regime. In the analytical framework, devaluation and liberalization were carefully distinguished, and concepts for quantifying the extent of devaluation and of liberalization were developed. It was hoped that careful analysis of individual devaluation and liberalization attempts, both successful and unsuccessful, would permit identification of the political and economic ingredients of an effective effort in that direction.

3. *Growth relationships:* Finally, the relationship of the exchange control regime to growth via static-efficiency and other factors was to be investigated. In this regard, the possible effects on savings, investment allocation, research and development, and entrepreneurship were to be highlighted.

In addition to identifying the three principal areas to be investigated, the analytical framework provided a common set of concepts to be used in the studies and distinguished various phases regarded as useful in tracing the experience of the individual countries and in assuring comparability of the analyses. The concepts are defined and the phases delineated in Appendix C.

The country studies undertaken within this project and their authors are as follows:

Brazil	Albert Fishlow, University of California, Berkeley
Chile	Jere R. Behrman, University of Pennsylvania
Colombia	Carlos F. Diaz-Alejandro, Yale University
Egypt	Bent Hansen, University of California, Berkeley, and Karim Nashashibi, International Monetary Fund
Ghana	J. Clark Leith, University of Western Ontario

India   Jagdish N. Bhagwati, Massachusetts Institute of Tech-
                  nology, and T. N. Srinivasan, Indian Statistical Institute

Israel   Michael Michaely, The Hebrew University of Jerusalem

Philippines   Robert E. Baldwin, University of Wisconsin

South Korea   Charles R. Frank, Jr., Princeton University and The
                  Brookings Institution; Kwang Suk Kim, Korea Develop-
                  ment Institute, Republic of Korea; and Larry E. West-
                  phal, Northwestern University

Turkey   Anne O. Krueger, University of Minnesota

The principal results of the different country studies are brought together in our overall syntheses. Each of the country studies, however, has
been made self-contained, so that readers interested in only certain of these
studies will not be handicapped.

In undertaking this project and bringing it to successful completion, the
authors of the individual country studies have contributed substantially to the
progress of the whole endeavor, over and above their individual research.
Each has commented upon the research findings of other participants, and
has made numerous suggestions which have improved the overall design and
execution of the project. The country authors who have collaborated with us
constitute an exceptionally able group of development economists, and we
wish to thank all of them for their cooperation and participation in the project.

We must also thank the National Bureau of Economic Research for its
sponsorship of the project and its assistance with many of the arrangements
necessary in an undertaking of this magnitude. Hal B. Lary, Vice President-
Research, has most energetically and efficiently provided both intellectual and
administrative input into the project over a three-year period. We would also
like to express our gratitude to the Agency for International Development for
having financed the National Bureau in undertaking this project. Michael
Roemer and Constantine Michalopoulos particularly deserve our sincere
thanks.

JAGDISH N. BHAGWATI
Massachusetts Institute of Technology

ANNE O. KRUEGER
University of Minnesota

Acknowledgments

I express my utmost gratitude to Hal B. Lary and to the Co-Directors of the project, Jagdish N. Bhagwati and Anne O. Krueger. Their involvement in the present study has undoubtedly gone far beyond shaping the general outline of the project. Through their comments in oral discussions and their detailed review of several drafts of the study they have made very substantial contributions to the final product.

I have also benefited from suggestions by my colleagues in the project during our periodic meetings as well as from presentations of their own studies; particularly helpful have been comments of Albert Fishlow and J. Clark Leith on an early draft.

Reuven Borkowsky has rendered a most valuable service as research assistant to this study. I am also indebted to Mario Blecher, for help in the calculations involved in Chapter 6; to Ester Moskowitz, for meticulous editing of the manuscript; and to H. Irving Forman for skillfully drawing the charts.

MICHAEL MICHAELY

Principal Dates and Historical Events in Israel

1917–18 Palestine is captured from Ottoman Turkey by the British army.
1921   The League of Nations grants Britain a mandate over Palestine. The Jewish Agency is established under the terms of the mandate. The "Histadrut" is established.
1933–36 Large-scale Jewish immigration to Palestine.
1939   Imposition of exchange control with the opening of World War II.
1947   UN decision to partition Palestine into Jewish and Arab states.
1948   War of Independence; State of Israel established in May 1948.
1949   Armistice agreements between Israel and neighboring Arab countries.
1949–51 Large-scale immigration—doubling of population. Imposition of widespread quantitative restrictions (QRs).
1952   Declaration of "New Economic Policy," starting a process of progressive devaluation from IL 0.36 to, eventually, IL 1.80 per dollar.
1956   Sinai campaign.
1962   Declaration of second "New Economic Policy," consisting of devaluation from IL 1.80 to IL 3.00 per dollar and liberalization.
1967   Six-Day War. Devaluation from IL 3.00 to IL 3.50 per dollar
1970   Imposition of 20 per cent levy on imports.
1971   Devaluation from IL 3.50 to IL 4.20 per dollar.

Foreign Trade Regimes
and Economic Development:
ISRAEL

Chapter 1

The Israeli Economy:
An Overview

i. INSTITUTIONAL AND
POLITICAL FRAMEWORK

Israel was declared an independent state on May 14, 1948. Palestine, part of which became the state of Israel, had belonged for many centuries to the Turkish Ottoman Empire. During 1917–18, toward the end of the First World War, the country had been captured by the British army and remained subject to British military rule until 1921. In that year, Britain was accorded a mandate over Palestine (along with other territories in the Middle East) by the League of Nations. The mandate expired following the decision of the United Nations General Assembly, on November 29, 1947, to partition the country into two separate, independent states—one Arab and one Jewish—with close economic ties (such as a customs union) between the two. In fact, however, following the UN decision, a war (referred to in Israel as the War of Independence) broke out between the Jews and the Arabs of Palestine (joined later, on May 15, 1948, by the neighboring Arab countries). As a result, the intended Arab state in the parts of Palestine outside Israel did not come into existence; instead, most of this territory became part of the kingdom of Jordan. Since 1948, the state of belligerence has continued between Israel and the Arab countries; there are, therefore, no economic relations between Israel and the countries immediately bordering on it.[1]

During the period of the British mandate, Palestine was governed, for most purposes, as a British colony. The local sovereign was the British High Commissioner, but all principal decisions were made in London. In the economic sphere, the degree of local autonomy was rather small. The annual budget of the government, as well as any decision on specific taxes, had to be approved by the British government in London. The Palestinian currency (legal tender after 1927, when it replaced the Egyptian currency) was managed by the Palestine Currency Board (run, again, from London), and had 100 per cent coverage (in fact, slightly more) in British short-term assets in the form of Treasury bills. Thus, no fiat money was issued in Palestine, and there was no equivalent of a central bank. Israel's central bank, the Bank of Israel, was not established until 1954. From August 1948 until that time, Israeli currency (the pound) was issued, through a special treaty with the government of Israel, by the Issue Department of Bank Le'umi Le'Israel, the country's largest commercial (but publicly owned) bank. The treaty specified, first, a 50 per cent coverage of currency by foreign assets. But a change, introduced very shortly thereafter, made Israeli Treasury bonds and bills equivalent to foreign assets, thus in effect freeing loans to the government by the Issue Department from any legal ceiling. Under the Bank of Israel law, lending to the government may not exceed 15 per cent of the size of the annual budget and must be fully repaid by the end of each fiscal year. But this regulation has been circumvented by special legislation permitting frequent funding of current government borrowing from the Bank.

During the British mandate, the country as a whole lacked the mechanisms needed to conduct a discretionary economic policy. However, the Jewish sector had begun to develop, according to the popular phrase at that time, as a "state in the making." Its political and economic autonomy was partly the result of traditions inherited by the British government from the Ottoman Empire and partly the outcome of special circumstances applying to the Jews in Palestine. The Turkish Empire, particularly during the last century of its existence, had granted a large measure of autonomy to members of various religious groups and sometimes to ethnic or national groups. Thus, an autonomous Jewish community already existed during the period of Ottoman rule and further developed its institutions under the British mandate. Among the most important aspects of this development was the maintenance of a separate system of elementary education (not financed out of the government budget) which, while lacking the compulsory status a state law might have given it, was still almost universal. The other important source of autonomy was the recognition—first by the British government itself, in the "Balfour Declaration" of 1917, and then by the League of Nations—of the special status of the Jewish people in the affairs of Palestine. Under the terms of the 1921 mandate of the League of Nations, the Jewish Agency for Palestine was established. Its membership included representatives of both the world Zionist movement and (most of the time) other, non-Zionist elements of world Jewry. Under the terms of the mandate, the Jewish Agency was recognized as the political body representing the Jewish sector in Palestine, a body which the mandatory government was supposed to consult with continuously. Although the contact between the government and the Jewish Agency was rarely as harmonious as had been intended under the terms of the mandate or anticipated at the time of its granting, the Jewish Agency nevertheless became a very powerful institution, probably even more so in the economic than in the political sphere, since it became the channel for economic aid from world Jewry to the Jewish sector of Palestine. In particular, it was responsible for establishing most of the Jewish agricultural settlements in Palestine, and for promoting some (but not the major part of) industrial development.

When the state of Israel came into existence, the Jewish Agency of course lost most of its political functions. But, though most aspects of economic policy are conducted by the government of Israel itself, a few important economic functions have been left to the Agency. Relations between the Agency and the Israeli government were determined by a special treaty concluded a short time after the establishment of the state. The Jewish Agency is still the vehicle through which most donations from world Jewry are channeled. These funds are intended to finance the transfer of immigrants and, primarily, their resettlement in the country, functions still performed by the Jewish Agency. For the most part, resettlement of immigrants has been in agricultural settlements. Consequently, the task of establishing new settlements and supporting them financially for a time has been left primarily to the Agency. Other important areas of activity of the Agency have been housing and education.

Another very important economic-social (and, to some extent, political) organ is the Histadrut, the general organization of workers, which was established in 1921. It is, first, a comprehensive labor union, much more universal and centrally organized than most other labor union movements outside the Eastern bloc; the majority of the workers have always belonged to the Histadrut. The organization as a labor union is subdivided primarily into local (city or town) "councils," rather than being a federation of unions. Countrywide unions, within the Histadrut, are only a recent phenomenon. Due to the circumstances in which it operated under the British mandatory government, the Histadrut has grown, however, into much more than a labor union. It has developed a social security system, the most important part of which is its health service, which provides medical care for over half the Jewish population.

The Histadrut is also the roof organization of a widespread cooperative movement, which has a variety of forms of cooperative in production, distribution, and services, although in practice the connections between elements of this movement are rather loose. In production, cooperatives are found chiefly in agriculture, where they are the chief form of production unit. These have either the form of a "kibbutz," a collective settlement in which all pro-

duction and most of the consumption are done jointly, with no private owner-
ship of capital; or a "moshav," a settlement of separate farm holdings with
a large measure of cooperative organization of production and distribution.
Histadrut cooperatives also account for most passenger transportation and a
large fraction of cargo transportation. In addition to its functions in the cooperative movement, the Histadrut owns a large number of manufacturing
firms outright, through a wholly owned holding company. This direct involvement of the Histadrut started in the 1920s, in the construction industry, chiefly
as a means of providing and assuring employment; but it has gradually spread
into practically all branches of production.

Although it is likely that the Histadrut would not have been developed
in the same way had it begun under the aegis of an independent Jewish state,
the establishment of the state of Israel in 1948 has not radically changed the
form, functions, or relative size of the organization. It has been estimated that
in each of the years from 1953 to 1960 the share of the Histadrut sector in the
widest interpretation of its involvement in the economy—including, among
others, the health service, all cooperatives, and plants owned directly—
amounted to about one-fifth of the net domestic product.[2]

On the whole, the British mandatory government of Palestine restricted
itself to the "classical" roles of government. Its direct handling of productive
activity was limited to two major public utilities, the postal services and the
railways. The government of Israel, on the other hand, has interpreted its
functions in a much broader sense, along the lines of a "welfare state." In
addition, the Israeli government is heavily engaged, through a multitude of
public corporations it owns either wholly or partly (very often jointly with
the Jewish Agency or the Histadrut), in various aspects of the economy's
productive process.[3] As a result, the share of government in the Israeli economy also exceeds the share of government usual in most Western-type economies, although the difference is probably not substantial. In the 1950s, the
share of the public sector in the net domestic product is also estimated to
have been about one-fifth. Of this, roughly three-quarters (that is, some 15
per cent of the domestic product) are accounted for by the government's general activity; and the other quarter (that is, 5 per cent of the product) is due
to the productive activity of public corporations.[4]

The Israeli economy may thus be characterized as a "mixed" economy,
in which roughly three-fifths of the product originates in the private sector,
one-fifth in the public sector, and the other fifth in the Histadrut sector. As
will be noted shortly, however, the impact of governmental activity on the
economy is considerably greater and more pervasive than would be indicated
merely by its share in the national product.

Despite enormous changes in all other aspects of Israel's economy and
society, the country's political structure has been remarkably stable. Ever

since the establishment of the state, the government has been run by a coalition of parties whose precise combination may vary, but which is always dominated by the country's main labor party (called "Mapai" until 1968 and since then the "Labor party"). In fact, since 1933, this coalition has also run the Jewish Agency, the main political organ before the establishment of the state. Thus the coalition has been in power for some forty years. The Labor party is also the dominant party in the Histadrut where, unlike in the country as a whole, it has been the majority rather than the largest minority party, and thus been exempted from the need of aligning itself with others to form a coalition "government." [5] The country's political conduct has thus been determined all along by the Labor party, which is a largely heterogeneous and nondogmatic grouping roughly similar to the main social-democratic parties of western Europe. As in most other aspects of Israeli political life, changes in economic conduct and economic policy have, therefore, been brought about almost exclusively through decisions by the organs (or individuals) of the same party, never by a complete transfer of power from one party to another, and only to a small extent by the changing nature and identities of the minor partners in the coalition government.[6]

Ever since the establishment of the state, economic policy has been conducted in a strong spirit of governmental interventionism. This is partly explained by the ideological background of the governing party, as well as that of a few other elements of the population. Partly, however, it is the consequence of the circumstances prevailing both before and after the establishment of the state. Under the British mandate, economic activities were to a large extent undertaken because they were conceived of as enhancing and furthering the national cause of the Jewish community, rather than as yielding maximum remuneration to the enterprises and people involved. This attitude was especially significant in agriculture, but it was evident in other sectors as well. Not only the community immediately involved, but the Jewish people everywhere, acting through institutions created for these express purposes, were expected to furnish financial and organizational support as well as much of the initiative for these enterprises.

The expectations inherited from that period were not only that the central organs of the community would play a major role in economic activities, but also that these activities would not necessarily be undertaken for the sake of profit making. Sometimes, the latter notion has even taken the extreme form of an implicit assumption that when profits are made, the national cause must have been subverted. Similarly, a substantial fraction of the population as well as many policymakers maintained at the beginning that "economic laws do not hold in Israel."

After the state was established, mass immigration began (see section ii, below), and its absorption was obviously a major economic effort which could be undertaken only by public organs (the government and the Jewish Agency); thus, again, the role of the government was stressed. Other evidence of the same process is that not only since the establishment of the state but before that time as well, the government (including under this term the Jewish Agency) has been a major recipient of capital transfers from abroad. This has led, again, to the assumption of additional roles by the government and has contributed to the idea that the economy should not be "left free" but should be managed by the government. One way, though, in which economic relations with the world—particularly with world Jewry—worked to mitigate this tendency was the perception that an overly managed economy would not be looked upon favorably by Jews in the Diaspora, particularly by the Jewish community in the United States; and would be likely to discourage private investment from abroad. Yet, to repeat, the government's economic policy has been determined throughout, although with diminishing force through time, by the notion that the government's impact should be pervasive and widespread, and that economic activities should be directed by governmental decisions rather than by general and nondiscriminatory policies. The area of foreign-exchange and foreign-trade policy, with which the present study will deal, is one of the more important manifestations of that interventionist spirit.

Interventionism in Israel has never approached the stage of etatism, in which the state is the main organ for carrying out economic activities. Moreover, even the common milder form of binding long-term investment planning—by way, say, of four- or five-year comprehensive plans—has been entirely absent. Even indicative plans, which have been prepared on occasions, have not generally been used as a guide to policy. Planning of large sectors has sometimes been more meaningful; but that, too, has been the exceptional case—found mainly in agriculture—rather than a common phenomenon. On the whole, then, the economy may be referred to as "managed" but not as "planned."

ii. POPULATION AND IMMIGRATION

At the end of 1948, the population in the area which eventually constituted the state of Israel [7] was roughly 900,000, consisting of about 750,000 Jews and 150,000 Arabs and other minorities. By the end of 1972, the population had reached about 3.2 million (see Chart 1-1), of which over 2.7 million were Jews and close to half a million, Arabs.[8] This is an increase of more than 250 per cent over this period of twenty-four years, or an average annual rate of increase of population of about 5.5 per cent, undoubtedly one of the highest rates of increase of population to be found in the modern world.

However, the rate of increase of population was far from uniform. The increase in the Arab population was determined almost entirely by the rate of natural increase, which was rather stable over the years (being, incidentally, the highest recorded rate in the world during the last generation). By contrast, for the Jewish population, who are the majority, less than one-third of the increase in population over the period as a whole is the result of natural increase; over two-thirds is accounted for by (net) immigration, the size of which has varied widely over the period. A sharp distinction must be made between the period of 3½ years from May 1948 to the end of 1951 and the rest of the period. In the second half of 1948 immigration amounted to about 100,000; in 1949, to 240,000; in 1950, to 170,000; and in 1951, to 175,000. Over this period of about 3½ years immigration thus amounted to roughly 700,000 people, more than the entire Jewish population in Israel in mid-1948. By the end of 1951, the total population of the country was almost double its size of three years earlier. Then an abrupt change took place, largely because the main sources of immigration were exhausted, but to some extent also due to establishment of a policy of selectivity in financing the transfer of immigrants. In 1952 immigration tumbled to less than 25,000; and in 1953 it was only 11,000. Since then, annual immigration has fluctuated mostly within a range of about 20,000 to 60,000 people. Consequently, the average annual rate of increase of population between 1951 and 1972 was less than 3½ per cent, in contrast to an average rate of over 20 per cent during 1949–51. Very roughly, the increase in Jewish population from 1952 on was provided for in equal shares by immigration and natural increase.

When the state of Israel was established, the educational level of the population was unusually high in comparison with other countries within the same range of per capita income. This was due primarily to the high level of education of immigrants: at that time, the large majority of the adult population had acquired all or most of its education abroad. In particular, the level of education was high among immigrants from Germany, who formed a large fraction of total immigration during the 1930s. The system of almost universal elementary education in the Jewish community in Israel also contributed to the high educational level. Thus, the rate of literacy in the Jewish segment of the population in 1948 was about 94 per cent (it was only some 20 per cent in the Arab segment); and about one-third of the adult Jewish population had completed secondary or higher education.

The great wave of immigration which followed the establishment of the state acted to lower educational standards. At first (in 1948 and early 1949) immigration consisted mainly of the East-European Jews who had survived the World War II holocaust, mostly in concentration camps, and had obviously been denied any education for many years. There followed, beginning in 1949, mass immigration from Asian and African countries, primarily Iraq, Yemen, and Morocco. The educational level of these immigrants was substantially lower than that of the mostly European immigrants of the 1920s and 1930s. Thus, the median number of years of schooling for people aged 14 and above was about 10 for immigrants who came before 1948 and only 7.7 for immigrants who came during 1948–51. By 1954, the degree of literacy of the adult Jewish population had fallen to 85 per cent, and the proportion of graduates of secondary and higher education, to 25 per cent. From then on,

CHART 1-1
Key Economic Variables, 1949–72

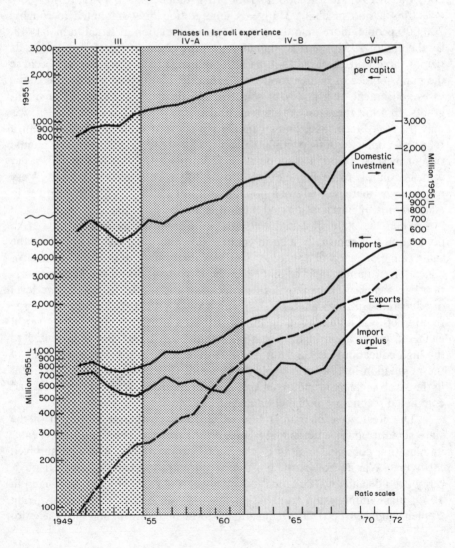

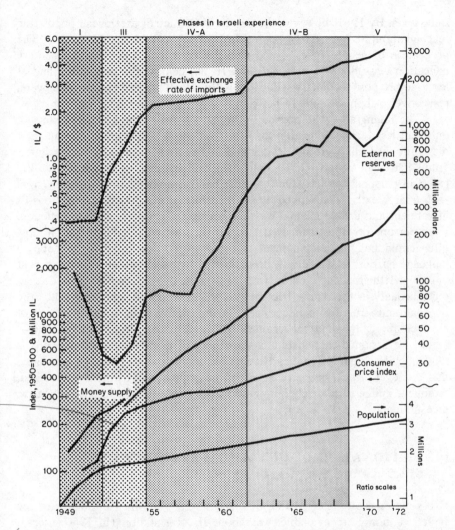

SOURCE: Effective exchange rate of imports—Table 4-3; external reserves—Table 2-2; money supply—Table A-16; consumer price index—Table A-17; population—Table A-1; GNP per capita—Table A-2, col. 2, divided by end-of-year population, Table A-1, col. 1; domestic investment—Table A-4; imports, exports, and import surplus—based on Don Patinkin "The Economic Development of Israel" (unpublished; January 1970), App. Table 5, with several modifications and with extensions based on Bank of Israel, *Annual Report*, 1972.

as immigration subsided, the educational system in Israel itself became a major factor. At first, the raising of educational levels by this means was offset by the declining number and weight of the better-educated veteran immigrants; therefore, for a few years, average standards remained at about the same level. By 1961, however, the degree of literacy of the Jewish population reached about 88 per cent (it approached 50 per cent among the Arabs). The proportion of people aged 14 and above with at least some post-elementary education was about 45 per cent, and 10 per cent of the population had at least some post-secondary education. By 1971, these proportions were, respectively, about 55 and 14 per cent.

The immigrants who arrived in the mass wave of the first few years not only had less formal education than the resident Jewish population, but their occupational skills were not in demand in Israel. The majority of the immigrants had been traders, clerks, craftsmen, and artisans, or they had been engaged in personal services. On the other hand, employment demand in Israel —to a large extent determined by governmental decisions about directions of investment and development—was in agriculture, industry, and construction. Even persons previously engaged in areas such as public administration most often could not find employment in the same occupation in Israel, due to language barriers. As a result, the majority of new immigrants—60 per cent —changed their occupation in Israel (even though "occupation" is defined quite broadly in the data), becoming in effect unskilled laborers.[9] Since the occupational structure in Israel itself, in the twenty years following, has not changed radically—and the changes which did take place were gradual— it may be assumed that involuntary mobility of labor among occupations is now much less than in those early years. As a result, it may safely be assumed that the level of skill and proficiency of the population has greatly increased, although, unlike formal schooling, this is not easily subject to comprehensive measurements.

iii. NATIONAL PRODUCT AND EXPENDITURES: SIZE AND COMPOSITION

Gross national product in 1950, the earliest year for which estimates for the Israeli economy are available, was about IL 460 million (in 1950 prices). With an average population of 1.27 million in that year, the per capita annual product is about IL 370. At the formal rate of exchange of that year (IL 0.357 per dollar) this would be approximately $1,000. There is no doubt, however, but that use of the 1950 formal rate of exchange for international comparisons grossly exaggerates the size of Israel's product. Thus, although estimates of per capita national product at constant prices show a substantial increase from 1950 to 1954 (as shown in Chart 1-1), the application of the 1954 formal rate (IL 1.80 per dollar) to the 1954 data on product and population would yield a per capita product of only about $570 per year. It appears that, for comparative purposes, per capita annual product in Israel around the time of its establishment was roughly $400 to $500. By this criterion Israel at that time would probably be classified as being in the border zone between developed and underdeveloped economies—in the same range, say, as the higher-income countries in Latin America.

From 1950 to 1970, the GNP increased (at constant prices) by 615 per cent—over sevenfold—an average annual rate of increase of about 10½ per cent. This is a rate rarely equaled or surpassed by any other economy during the last generation, Japan being the only other case which comes to mind. Part of this spectacular increase in the national product is, of course, due to the unusually large increase of the population and labor force. But even per capita GNP tripled between 1950 and 1971, at an average annual rate of increase of about 5.8 per cent, which is again outstanding (although not a rare exception) by current international standards. For international comparisons, again, per capita annual product in 1970 could be roughly estimated as being $1,500; that is, about the middle of the range of countries that would be normally classified as "developed."

Along with the expansion of population and labor force, growth of the stock of physical capital was another important source of the substantial and consistent increase in the national product. The average annual rate of growth of capital stock during the period 1950–65, for which estimates are available, was 13.1 per cent on a gross basis or 13.5 per cent on a net basis.[10] The increase was particularly rapid at the beginning of the period: in 1950–55 the annual rates of growth were 17.4 per cent gross or 19.5 per cent net. Yet the increase in both labor force and capital stock accounts for only a part of the increase in the national product. Beyond the expansion of the two factors of production, there was a substantial increase in productivity. For the period 1950–65, the average annual growth of "total-factor productivity" was estimated to be within a range of 2.5 to 3.3 per cent depending on the concept of productivity adopted.[11] If residential structures are excluded from the stock of capital, the annual growth of productivity of the private economy is about 4.2 or 4.3 per cent. Per capita product thus increased both by the rise of the stock of capital per capita and by the growth of productivity in the use of resources.

The rapid increase in the capital stock must, in turn, be due to a substantial investment. Indeed, relative to the size of the economy, investment in Israel has been apparently among the highest in the world. For the period 1950–71 as a whole, the ratio of gross domestic investment to GNP was 29 per cent. Although it declined somewhat over the period, the downward trend was rather slight. Thus, the average ratio was 31.7 per cent during the early years, 1950–55, and 27.7 per cent during the latest years, 1969–71. Only in the recession years 1966–68 was this ratio substantially below the trend line.

Normally, such a high ratio of investment would indicate a similarly high ratio of saving to income. This, however, is not the case in Israel, where the saving ratio has been low, the gap between saving and domestic investment being made up by an unusually large flow of capital imports, which will be noted shortly. During the period 1950–71, the average ratio of gross saving[12] to GNP was 7.3 per cent, with no noticeable trend of change over the period. Since this is roughly the ratio of depreciation to GNP, net saving in the economy appears to have been nil, on the average, or even slightly negative. This particularly low rate of saving in the economy is apparently due to the flow of capital imports. The relationship between the two can be explained in three primary ways. First, although the rate of household saving out of disposable income is quite similar in Israel to the rate in other economies at similar levels of development, an important segment of disposable income in Israel consists of unilateral transfers from abroad to the private sector (such as restitution payments from Germany or, mainly in the first few years, private gifts in cash or in kind). Since such transfer payments are treated as part of the national income and product of the paying country, rather than of Israel, consumption out of such income is recorded as negative saving in the Israeli accounts. Second, and similarly, transfers from abroad to the public sector (the government and the Jewish Agency) are, to a minor extent, spent on consumption, and these also are recorded as negative saving. Third, financing of private investment is available on easy terms from governmental sources. Funds are provided largely through governmental borrowing and from unilateral receipts from abroad. As a result, the need of the business sector to save has been reduced.

As the industrial composition of its product indicates, Israel has since its establishment possessed the structure usually associated with a highly developed economy. Agriculture, as has been mentioned, was particularly boosted both before 1948 and during the first few years after the establishment of the state, when a large fraction of the mass immigration was directed to agricultural settlements. But even at its peak, in the middle and late 1950s, agriculture contributed only about 12 or 13 per cent of the national product. This share has gradually declined since then, and by 1970 it was down to 6 per cent. Similarly, the share of agriculture in employment went down from about 17 per cent in the 1950s to less than 9 per cent by 1970. The share of manufacturing in the national product, on the other hand, increased gradually, from about 20 per cent in the first few years after the establishment of the state to about 26 per cent twenty years later. The share of manufacturing in employment increased, too, in roughly the same proportions. About half of the labor force, more than that in more recent years, has been employed in construction and services (close to 10 per cent of the labor force in the former, 40 per cent and more in the latter). The extremely large share of services—in comparison to its share in other economies with the same level of per capita income—is partly explained by the structure of demand (including, among other factors, the share of the public sector in the economy), and by the distribution of proficiencies and previous occupations of immigrants. But a great part of the explanation lies again in the size of the import surplus, which satisfies a large portion of local demand for goods and thus tends to direct local production toward services (which are, on the whole, much less tradable than goods).

iv. FOREIGN TRADE AND CAPITAL IMPORTS

Israel, and Palestine before it, have had a large import surplus ever since exports and imports have been recorded, and probably for many years before that. In Palestine, exports of goods were normally about one-third the size of imports. The Jewish sector of the population accounted for the major part of both exports and imports, and the ratio of exports to imports was even lower for that sector than for the country as a whole. The gap between the two was covered by capital imports. These consisted primarily of transfers by the Jewish Agency and other major public Jewish institutions, transfers of immigrants, and, to a much smaller extent, private investment from abroad. During the years 1940–47, from the beginning of World War II to the evacuation of the country by the British army, sales to the armed forces—recorded as exports of services—were a major source of earnings[13] and were just equal to the gap between imports and exports of goods. The continuation of large capital imports during these years thus led, as a net result, to a large accumulation of foreign assets, primarily short-term investments of the banking system and of the Currency Board in London. These external reserves, which by the end of World War II amounted to over £ 100 million sterling, were first frozen by the British government and then, near the end of 1949, released for gradual use by agreement between the two governments.

In the first few years after the establishment of Israel, the ratio of exports (of both goods and services) to imports was extremely low, lower than the ratio for Palestine as a whole before World War II, or probably even lower than that for the Jewish population in that period. In 1949 and 1950 exports were only about 15 per cent as large as imports. This ratio increased gradually, particularly during the 1950s, with many fluctuations along the upward trend. By the late 1950s or early 1960s the ratio of exports to imports was roughly 50 per cent; and by the end of the 1960s it was fluctuating around 60 per cent.

The increase in this ratio kept pace, however, with the increase in total imports; and the *absolute* size of the import surplus thus kept rising, as may be seen in Chart 1-1, albeit not monotonically. The annual import surplus (again taking both goods and services) was about $300 million in the late

1940s and early 1950s and, with fluctuations, remained around this level until 1960. During the 1960s, on the other hand, the import surplus rose substantially, especially with the increase in imports of military goods following the Six-Day War of 1967. In the mid-1960s the import surplus fluctuated around $500 million; in 1968 it was about $650 million; and in the early 1970s it was about $1,200 million. Similar trends would appear if trade in goods alone were considered, in order to eliminate the direct impact of military imports (which are recorded as services). On this basis the surplus of imports was about $250–$300 million in the late 1940s and early 1950s, and fluctuated around this level until the late 1950s. In 1965 this surplus was roughly $400 million; it approached $500 million in 1968 and averaged close to $800 million during 1970–72.[14]

Over the period as a whole, autonomous capital inflow from abroad, including both unilateral transfers and long-term borrowing, was roughly equal to the import surplus: by the end of 1971 Israel's external reserves amounted to about $600 million—about $500 million more than the size of reserves (mostly frozen sterling balances) at the end of 1949. This is low in comparison with the accumulated amount of capital imports over this period; and even most of this would be canceled out if short- and medium-term indebtedness to the outside world were offset against it. The over-all rough equality between autonomous capital imports and the import surplus does not mean, of course, that they were equal in any given year: year-to-year fluctuations in the (positive or negative) gap between the two were considerable, as may be seen from the movements of external reserves depicted in Chart 1-1. On this score, a few subperiods may be clearly distinguished. From 1949 to 1951, foreign-exchange reserves were drawn upon extensively and virtually disappeared; they began to recover in 1954, and increased substantially between 1958 and 1967. Between the end of 1967 and early 1970 reserves declined sharply. The trend was reversed again in mid-1970, with a substantial accumulation of reserves in 1971 and 1972, despite the unusually large import surplus in those years.

Over the period from 1950 to 1971, total autonomous capital inflow—including unilateral transfers, long-term (and a minor amount of medium-term) borrowing, and foreign direct investment—amounted to about $11.6 billion. The importance of the various sources of capital imports varied over the years. The most important, and most permanent, single source was contributions from abroad (primarily from the Jewish community in the United States) to Israeli institutions, mainly the Jewish Agency. Since 1951, the Jewish community abroad—again, primarily in the United States—has also provided capital by purchasing issues of a special governmental loan, termed first the "Independence Loan" and then the "Development Loan." In the early 1950s the U.S. government was a relatively important source through two

Export-Import Bank loans. Since 1970 it has again become important through large-scale lending primarily for military purchases. The German government has been another major source. First came the reparations agreement, by which the German government paid the Israeli government about $800 million during the period 1953–63; since 1954, Germany has also been making restitution payments to individuals in Israel, the annual amount of which has been rising continuously. Other important sources of capital imports have been private unilateral transfers, both gifts and transfers of capital by immigrants, and direct investment from abroad, which was substantial mainly in the first half of the 1960s and again in the early 1970s.

Of the above-mentioned total of $11.6 billion for 1950–71, about 23 per cent has been provided by contributions to Israeli institutions, another 10 per cent from the (net) sale of Independence and Development bonds, about 13 per cent through loans and grants in aid from the U.S. government, about 23 per cent from reparation and restitution payments by the German government, some 14 per cent from private unilateral transfers, about 8 per cent from direct private investment, and the rest (about 9 per cent) from an assortment of long- and medium-term loans. Alternatively, about 62 per cent of the total capital inflow consists of unilateral transfers, and 38 per cent, of transfers on capital account. The latter, although the smaller part of the total, have nevertheless left the country by the end of 1971 with a long-term indebtedness to the outside world of about $3.4 billion, in addition to an accumulated value of close to a billion dollars of foreign private direct investment. The combined size of this outstanding indebtedness, about $4.4 billion, was about 2½ times the size of Israel's exports in 1971. By way of a very rough comparison, it was almost as large as the country's national product in 1971, or equal to about 40 per cent of the value of the gross national physical capital at the end of the year. By these or similar yardsticks, Israel's national foreign indebtedness has apparently become by the early 1970s one of the world's highest.

In view of the rapid rise of the economy's product, the rising trend in capital imports and in the import surplus was still consistent with a decline in the relative importance of the import surplus for the economy, as measured, say, by the relation of the size of the import surplus to that of the national product. But, once more, this trend has been far from uniform over the period. Measured in constant (1955) prices, the ratio of the import surplus (excluding from it imports of military goods) to GNP fell from about 43 per cent in 1950–51 to around 14 per cent in 1960.[15] From then on, the average ratio has remained at about that level, with no noticeable trend (although with substantial year-to-year fluctuations). It was lowest during the years 1966–68— mostly a recession period, as will be noted later—when it averaged only 10.5 per cent; but in later years it climbed back to 15 or 16 per cent.[16]

The ratio of foreign trade to the national product, the simplest and most common index used to indicate the importance of the former to an economy, varies radically of course in the case of Israel, according to whether imports or exports are considered. To make these ratios more meaningful, the import component in exports (that is, in essence, reexported imports) is omitted on both sides, leaving only imports for domestic use on the one side and value added in exports on the other. Imports so defined (and again excluding military imports) amounted to 50 per cent of GNP in 1950 and 47 per cent in 1951. The ratio then fell by almost one-half, to 26 per cent, in 1954. From then on no trend appears: the ratio of imports to GNP fluctuates roughly around 25 per cent, reaching its highest level, close to 30 per cent, in the most recent years.[17] It may be presumed that the ratio of around one-fourth of GNP for most of the period is high by international standards, although similarly adjusted measurements for other economies are not readily available. The more conventional method of comparison—the ratio of total imports of goods and services to GNP, where imports include the import component in exports and military imports, GNP is estimated at current prices, and the import surplus is converted at the formal exchange rate—fluctuates most of the time around a level of 40 per cent.[18] This ratio is about the same as in other small, industrial economies. In distinguishing among major categories of national expenditure, it is seen that imports are the least important in private consumption, where the import component (whether direct or through the use of imports in domestic production of consumer goods) has been slightly over 20 per cent. The ratio is somewhat higher in public consumption, particularly in recent years, due to the large increase in military imports; still higher in investment; and highest in the production of export goods, where the import component approaches half of the gross value of exports, leaving only somewhat over half as value added.

The ratio of value added in exports to the economy's total value added, its gross national product, is a rough indication of the share of the country's productive resources involved in production for exports. This ratio, again valued in 1955 prices, was at first negligible: in the first half of the 1950s, it fluctuated around a level of 5 per cent. From then on, a rising trend is clearly visible: in the early 1960s the ratio was about 10 per cent, and by the early 1970s it approached 15 per cent. With time, then, a significant share of the national economy was accounted for by exports, although even in recent years that share has been less important than in other small economies.

The growth of exports was accompanied by a considerable change in their structure. In the early 1950s almost half of total exports of goods consisted of citrus fruits (mainly oranges). This category had a predominant share indeed of total exports when measured in terms of value added (the share of value added in total value of citrus fruits is particularly high—about 70 to 75 per cent). Of the rest, mostly industrial exports, about half were polished diamonds, in which the value added is only about 20 per cent of total value. Thus, all other industries accounted for only about one-quarter of total exports of goods (slightly less in terms of value added). Exports of services were at that time negligible. Since then, a few strong trends appear in the development of exports. The share of citrus fruits has fallen sharply, amounting in recent years to only about 12 per cent of the gross value of exports of goods or about one-fifth of value added. The share of polished diamonds has been roughly maintained, amounting to about a quarter of the gross value of exports of goods but less than 10 per cent of value added. In recent years, two-thirds of exports (in both gross and value-added terms), compared with a mere one-quarter in the early 1950s, have consisted of an assortment of industrial goods and some agricultural products other than citrus fruits, chief among the former being textile products, chemicals, and metal products. Valued in current dollar prices, exports of goods other than citrus fruits and diamonds increased between 1950 and 1970 from $7.5 million to $446 million, an average annual rate of growth of close to 23 per cent. Even in the latter part of the period, and starting from a higher base, the rate of growth of this group is still impressive: in 1960, for instance, these exports amounted to $108 million, and the average annual growth from then to 1970 has been about 15 per cent.

In addition to goods exports, a particularly rapid growth has occurred in exports of two services: tourism and transportation (both sea and air). While in the first few years these exports were negligible, even in relation to the size of exports of goods, by 1970 they amounted to $257 million for transportation and $103 million for tourist services. This is the equivalent of about half of the total of $730 million yielded by exports of goods; in terms of value added, which is high in the sale of tourist services but low in transportation, the fraction of services in total exports would probably not be much lower.

The structure of imports, too, has undergone a considerable change. At first, imports of consumer and investment goods were roughly equal, each amounting to close to one-quarter of the total value of imports of goods. Raw materials made up 40 to 45 per cent; and the rest, some 10 per cent, was fuel. Investment goods have approximately maintained their share over the years; but the share of consumer goods has been declining throughout, and that of raw materials rising. Thus, by 1970 imports of consumer goods constituted less than 10 per cent of the value of imports of total goods; imports of investment goods, about 24 per cent; imports of fuels—declining relatively over time despite spreading industrialization—about 5 per cent; and raw materials, over 60 per cent of the total. In imports of services, a noticeable relative increase has occurred since 1968 in imports of military material. These items are not appropriately termed "services," but are accounted as such (under the item "government, n.e.s.") in the balance of payments. Another noteworthy increase has been in the service charges for capital (interest and profit remittances), which in recent years have risen to about $200 million annually, a reflection of the country's growing indebtedness to the outside world.

v. THE INFLATIONARY PROCESS

Inflation has been a permanent attribute of the Israeli economy, although the rate has varied substantially. The increase in the consumer price index between 1949 and 1971 was about 560 per cent, an average annual rate of about 9 per cent. The implied GNP price deflator rose slightly more: from 1950 to 1971 it increased by close to 630 per cent, an annual increase of about 10 per cent. Roughly speaking, therefore, an annual price increase of 10 per cent has been the long-term norm in the Israeli economy.

The inflationary forces were strongest from 1949 to 1951, the first few years after the establishment of the state. But during this period inflation was severely suppressed. Consequently, inflationary pressure was only partially reflected in official prices. From the end of 1948 to the end of 1951, the official consumer price index increased by a mere 16 per cent; but from estimates of the inflationary potential, it would seem that, had prices been free to change, the increase in the index would have exceeded the recorded increase by at least 30 or 40 per cent. The result of the strong suppression of the inflation—accomplished by fixing constant ceiling prices and instituting severe rationing—was the development of widespread black markets, in which prices were often many times the official ones.

During the period 1952–54 the process was reversed. The basic sources of inflation were eliminated. Had price movements not been repressed earlier, price increases in this period would have been very small. In fact, however, prices were freed during this period, with the result that movements of the official prices reflected the preceding inflationary pressure, and with the further result of a closing (from both ends) of almost the entire gap between official and black-market prices. The increase in the official consumer price index from the 1951 to the 1954 average was 127 per cent (in 1952 alone, it increased by 58 per cent!). This was the highest rate for a (recorded) price increase in any period of some length in Israel's history, although at that time basic inflationary forces were weaker than ever. Since 1954, prices have been relatively free, and recorded price changes have probably reflected, by and large, the extent of inflationary pressures.

During the period 1955–61, inflation was relatively modest. Consumer prices rose somewhat less than 5 per cent per year on the average (the record low being achieved in 1959, when prices increased by only about 2 per cent).

From then on until 1965, inflation accelerated again: the average annual change in consumer prices between 1961 and 1965 was somewhat over 7 per cent.

By the fall of 1965, the inflationary trend was reversed, and Isarel's only severe recession started. At first, prices kept increasing. Indeed, consumer prices increased by about 6 per cent during the first half of 1966, when all the phenomena of recession were already obvious. But from then on, prices stabilized: from mid-1966 to the end of 1968 the increase in the consumer price index was less than 4 per cent (it was nil during 1967, the only year with complete price stability in Israel's history).

While the turning point toward renewed expansion probably came in early 1967, prices started to increase again only in early 1969, when the recessionary slack was exhausted. At first, these price increases were mild: the average annual change in the consumer price level from 1968 to 1970 was less than 4.5 per cent. But beginning in the fall of 1970, inflation assumed very substantial proportions: from August 1970 to December 1972, the consumer price index increased by 36 per cent, an average rate of increase of about 14 per cent per year. At the time of writing, it appears that in 1973 this rate of price increase will even be greatly surpassed. The rate of inflation in recent years thus approaches that experienced during the state's first few years, although the forms of inflation are radically different.

As in many other countries, it has very often been debated in Israel whether inflation originates from demand or whether it is of the "cost-push" variety. While the issue probably cannot be resolved with complete certainty, it appears to me that by and large the inflationary process in Israel has been determined by demand forces. Cost factors—increases in the exchange rate, price increases abroad, or autonomous increases in wages—can very rarely be blamed for having started an inflationary development, or having extended its magnitude significantly beyond what it would have been solely as a result of an autonomous increase in demand. More often, cost factors may have accounted for the precise timing of major price increases, increases which would otherwise have started somewhat later or stretched out over somewhat longer periods. A case of this nature which serves probably as the clearest example is the substantial price increase which followed the imposition of a 20 percent levy on imports in August 1970.

A clear association appears between price increases and increases in the money supply in Israel.[19] Over the period from 1949 to 1971 as a whole, money supply increased at an average annual rate of around 19 per cent, slightly less than the combined (and compounded) increase of the real GNP and its price level, which came to about 22 per cent.[20] More important, however, is the apparent association of movements of prices and the money supply over time: usually, the price level follows movements in the money supply with a time lag of about ten or twelve months. Another important factor in determining demand has been the government's deficit, both in its own right, as a direct source of demand, and in its effect on liquidity and money supply. Excess demand by the government has been a constant feature of the Israeli economy. During the "normal" years 1956–66,[21] the excess of purchases of goods and services by the government over net tax collections averaged about 2.5 per cent of the GNP. If net domestic lending by the government is added to it, the provision of liquidity by the government appears to be over twice this size. Other important determinants of the creation of liquidity and of demand have been credit expansion (the rate of which has been more stable than that of other major monetary variables) and, particularly since the late 1950s, the accumulation of external reserves.

It is consistent with the persistent expansion of demand and the inflation that Israel has only rarely experienced mass unemployment. In the first few years, structural unemployment was very substantial: the mass of new immigrants constituted a major addition to the labor force. If they were to be effectively absorbed, they required radical changes in labor qualifications (including changes in their attitude toward various professions). Also needed were major additions to physical capital, changes in the techniques and organization of production, and mass provision of housing for workers, all of which did not (and probably could not) match the rate of immigration and the virtual doubling of population within about three years. As a result, a high fraction of new immigrants (but not of the resident population!) remained for a long time either unemployed or occupied in relief work, a phenomenon which became gradually less important until its virtual disappearance by the late 1950s. As distinguished from this form of structural unemployment, unemployment attributable to insufficient demand appeared only twice. The first time was in 1953, when additional unemployment over that of the preceding years amounted to about 4 per cent of the labor force.[22] This is reflected also in the national product, which in 1953 increased in real terms by only about 1 per cent, compared with 7 per cent in 1952 and 22 per cent in 1954 (and with a long-term average of over 10 per cent).

The other episode of unemployment, which was more severe and lasted longer, was the recession that started in the fall of 1965. The bottom of this recession may be placed in late 1966 or early 1967, but full employment did not return until the end of 1968. Based on semiannual manpower surveys, unemployment in the second half of 1965 amounted to about 40,000 persons (this was nearly a "full-employment" situation); it then went up to a peak of just over 100,000 (more than 10 per cent of the labor force) in the first half of 1967. The number of unemployed then fell to about 60,000 in the first half of 1968; and by the first half of 1969 it was back to somewhat over 40,000, again a full-employment position (although a slight further reduction in the number of unemployed may be seen even in later years). This course is also reflected in the national product estimates: GNP increased in real terms by 6.8 per cent in 1965, 2.2 per cent in 1966, and 1.3 per cent in 1967, an annual average of less than 3.5 per cent compared with an average of close to 11.5 per cent in the four preceding years or with the long-term average of 10.5 per cent.

vi. FOREIGN TRADE AND FOREIGN-EXCHANGE POLICY: DELINEATION OF PHASES [23]

Except in the very early years, Israel's trade and payments policy has developed progressively from restriction to liberalization. The absence most of the time of major shifts in policy makes the delineation of phases difficult and sometimes rather arbitrary. In fact, as will be indicated below, the description of Israel's payments policy as belonging to Phase IV is applicable throughout most of the period, though the nature of this policy did undergo considerable change during that phase. With this qualification in mind, the phases of policy development are as follows:

1948: The Background.

When the state of Israel was established, it inherited a situation and a history of mixed attributes. During the British mandate period, the government's foreign trade policy was probably one of the most liberal. This was, in part, a reflection of the generally conservative way the government looked upon its functions. But it also reflected the conflict of interests between the two population groups in Palestine: the Arabs were mostly engaged in agriculture, which they dominated, whereas manufacturing was predominantly Jewish. Any encouragement of a specific industry by tariff protection or otherwise was likely to favor one nationality at the expense of the other, and was interpreted in this way by the two groups. The easiest way to avoid this issue was, of course, to follow a completely liberal trade policy. A very heavy dose of "natural" protection was introduced by World War II. The overwhelming difficulties in overseas transportation, almost completely isolating the Middle East for a few years, increased not only local demand but demand from the region as a whole for goods produced in Palestine. To this was added a heavy demand by the armed forces stationed in the Middle East. This gave a tremendous boost to manufacturing, which as noted was predominantly Jewish. With the end of the war, as transportation gradually eased, and wartime exchange-control regulations were gradually relaxed, much of this war-born industry disappeared. Thus, the industry still existing by 1948 was mostly competitive; but the memory of what industry had been when not faced by foreign competition remained vivid and was apparently a strong factor in steering trade policy toward protectionism. In addition, it should be recalled that the explicit policy of the institutions of the Jewish sector was always to encourage specific enterprises or economic sectors, and that the general approach of the community was one of interventionism.

By 1948, the foreign-exchange-control machinery was still maintained by the mandate government in its wartime form, although controls were much less severe than during the war. The legal framework of the machinery was adopted by the state of Israel when it came into existence. But the payments situation of the country was much more serious than in 1946 or 1947. In February 1948, as part of a complete "hands off" policy which Britain adopted following the UN partition decision, Palestine was expelled by the British government from the sterling area, and the country's sterling assets were for a time frozen. In addition, exports declined radically as the fighting spread: citrus plantations, the country's main export source, could not be cultivated for the most part, nor could the fruit be exported. The demand for imports, on the other hand, was particularly heavy, due both to the requirements of the war and to the wave of mass immigration which started immediately. Foreign-exchange control thus became much more restrictive as soon as Israel was established.

1949–51: Phase I.

During the period from the establishment of the state to the end of 1951 controls became rapidly more stringent. The foreign-exchange-control system was the vital component and focal point of the system of repressed inflation. The foreign-exchange rate was kept fixed all this time (aside from a slight adjustment in September 1949, when the pound sterling was devalued). With the accumulation of inflationary pressures, the gap between the actual rate and its equilibrium level kept growing, and imports approved under the licensing system as a proportion of the demand for imports kept falling. The major assumption on which policy at that time was based was that a free market for imports (at an equilibrium exchange rate) would result in the importation of luxuries, while low-income groups would remain without necessities; that is, the foreign-exchange policy was deemed to play an essential part in assuring an adequate level of equality in the distribution of real income. Another basic tenet of the system was that imports of final consumer goods should not be allowed if their domestic production was at all feasible.

As the degree of disequilibrium in the system grew, and rationing became more severe and more inclusive, the system started to deteriorate. Black markets became widespread, and production of various goods was often stopped for lack of imported raw materials. Foreign-exchange reserves were completely exhausted. Discontent with the economic policy gradually became widespread. The faith of the leaders of economic policy in the potential of intervention by the state and in the feasibility of directing the economy by orders weakened, as did their mistrust of the price mechanism. In 1951, it became obvious that a change in policy was due. This change came first in the summer and fall of 1951, with a shift from an expansive to a restrictive monetary-fiscal policy. But the major part of the switch came in February 1952 with the declaration of the "New Economic Policy." The departure from the preceding policy was radical; so Phase II of the exchange system may be said to have been bypassed altogether, with the economy moving directly to Phase III. From then on, the process of liberalization proceeded almost without interruption.

1952–54: Phase III.

The most important element of the policy introduced in February 1952 was a major devaluation. A system with three different exchange rates was introduced. The highest of these rates (IL 1 per dollar) was almost three times the previous rate (IL 0.357 per dollar), and the average of the three was set at more than twice the predevaluation rate. From then on the process of moving to an equilibrium exchange rate was rapid and progressive, through the introduction of new rates and the shifting of transactions from lower to higher rates. The process was almost completed by mid-1954, when most transactions were already subject to the rate of IL 1.80 per dollar, the rate which remained in force for a long period thereafter. Thus, within less than three years, the rate of exchange rose fivefold, compared with only about a doubling of domestic prices during the same period.

In addition, as already observed, monetary and fiscal policy was quite restrictive for about two years. This, together with the devaluation, resulted in a gradual reduction in the degree of disequilibrium in the system. By the end of 1954 the rate of exchange was roughly in equilibrium. Likewise, as has been mentioned earlier, domestic prices were allowed to rise. Consequently, rationing became gradually less severe, black markets became less widespread, and black-market prices and official prices moved closer to each other. Although by the end of 1954 foreign-exchange reserves were still very small, the balance-of-payments position with the new rate of exchange ceased to be the major basis for trade and payments restrictions.

1955–68: Phase IV.

This long period is best divided into two stages: 1955–61 and 1962–68. During the first stage, liberalization of imports proceeded gradually but along a very clear guideline: the system changed from one intended to regulate the balance-of-payments position into one intended primarily to protect local production. There was a rapid de facto liberalization of imports of raw materials of which local production was not feasible, although licenses were still required. Such products made up the greater part of total imports, owing partly to the control system itself. Imports of final consumer goods, on the other hand, were practically prohibited in almost all instances in which domestic production either was actually taking place or was contemplated by a potential entrepreneur. Policy toward imports of investment goods sometimes had to face conflicts of interest arising when the encouragement of local production of a particular investment good handicapped another branch of local production which required the use of that good. In effect, imports of most investment goods were also liberalized, but not to the same extent as raw materials.

The second stage started in February 1962 with the announcement of another "New Economic Policy." The currency was devalued, for the first time since the end of the progressive devaluation of 1952–54: the rate of exchange was raised from IL 1.80 to IL 3.00 per dollar. The net devaluation was, however, much less than the 67 per cent indicated by the formal change, since almost all export subsidies, which had increased gradually during the first stage, were abolished; and the rates of many import tariffs were lowered. The devaluation was intended, in fact, to be an act of unification of the effective exchange-rate system at least as much as an increase of the general level. This step was combined with the other major component of the new policy: a declaration of an intention to liberalize the imports of consumer goods (and some investment goods) which until then were excluded by quantitative restrictions (QRs). Procedures were set up to carry out this process. Most of this liberalization took the form of replacing the QRs by tariffs, at different rates for each good, which were intended to be approximately prohibitive—though some (relative) increase of liberalized imports did take place. The work of the liberalization machinery ended in 1968, and the process was supposed then to be completed.

1969 and After: Phase V.

By 1969, almost all imports were liberalized in the sense of not being subject to effective quantitative restrictions (although licenses were still required). The declared policy, since that time, has been gradually to lower the level of protection afforded by the tariff system by reducing all tariffs by a given (small) proportion at the beginning of each year. Such reductions have indeed been performed, and their cumulative effect has been a significant lowering of protective rates. Formal devaluations were undertaken twice after the 1962 devaluation: in November 1967 the rate of exchange was increased by 16.7 per cent, from IL 3.00 to IL 3.50 per dollar; and in August 1971 it was increased further by 20 per cent, to IL 4.20 per dollar. Conclusions about general attributes of this period would obviously be premature. It seems likely though that this period will be characterized by a chain of relatively minor devaluations, with the average of the effective rate of exchange being maintained, most of the time, close to its equilibrium level, and by a tendency toward unification of tariff rates and a reduction of discrimination in levels of protection.

NOTES

1. This has changed slightly since the Six-Day War of June 1967. A nearly free movement of goods (and, to a large extent, of labor) exists between Israel and the West Bank, the part of Palestine annexed to Jordan after 1948 and held by Israel since 1967. Due to the "open-bridges" policy of Israel and Jordan, goods flow rather freely between Jordan and the West Bank. As a result, some trade takes place indirectly between Israel and Jordan and, through the latter, with other Arab countries as well.

2. Haim Barkai, "The Public, Histadrut, and Private Sectors in the Israeli Economy" (in English), Falk Project for Economic Research in Israel, *Sixth Report 1961–63*, Table 1.

3. By 1972, the number of such corporations exceeded 200.

4. Barkai, "The Public," Tables 1 and 2.

5. The central organs of the Histadrut are elected by its members, periodically, by voting for party lists in proportional elections. This is similar to the system by which the country's parliament (the Knesset) is elected—and the parties running in both elections are by and large the same.

6. The only important exception was the municipal elections of 1950, in which a major shift from the Labor Party to the main Liberal Party was interpreted as a protest against current economic policy, and may have had an effect on the future course of this policy.

7. The de facto borders of Israel were determined in the series of armistice agreements concluded between Israel and its Arab neighbors during the period from March to August 1949.

8. Since June 1967, the data include the population of the eastern part of Jerusalem, roughly 70,000 people.

9. This is discussed in more detail in Nadav Halevi and Ruth Klinov-Malul, *The Economic Development of Israel* (New York: Praeger, 1968); see especially pp. 75–84.

10. See A. L. Gaathon, *Economic Productivity in Israel* (New York: Praeger, 1971), Chap. 3.

11. Ibid., Chap. 4.

12. This is derived as a residual: gross domestic investment minus the import surplus.

13. Estimates of the size of trade in other services are not available for the period of the mandate, but the trade was probably small enough to be ignored for most purposes.

14. These figures are based on a c.i.f. evaluation of imports. An f.o.b. evaluation materially changes the allocation of the import surplus between the goods and services account, lowering the import surplus in the former account and raising it in the latter.

15. This sharp downward trend largely disappears if the import surplus and the national product are measured in current rather than constant prices. The question whether, for this purpose, constant or current prices are appropriate was for a while a lively topic of discussion among academic economists in Israel; the use here of a constant-price measure is consistent with my position in that debate.

16. The addition of military imports would, of course, increase the weight of the import surplus, particularly in these recent years.

17. These ratios are computed with national product and imports taken in constant (1955) prices.

18. This ratio would exceed 50 per cent if effective rather than formal rates of exchange were used. See definition of concepts in Appendix C.

19. See, for instance, E. Kleiman and T. Ophir, "The Effect of Changes in the Quantity of Money on Prices in Israel, 1955–1965" (in English), Bank of Israel *Economic Review* (forthcoming).

20. Even in money terms, the import surplus increased substantially less than the national product. When this is taken into account, the rate of increase in the value of resources used by the economy would appear to be more similar to the rate of increase of the money supply.

21. Comparable data for earlier years are not available; however, in the years following the Six-Day War of 1967, the government's excess demand has been much larger.

22. The absolute figures—about 7 per cent of the labor force in 1952 and 11 per cent in 1953—are probably less meaningful than the change between the years. The rate fell to about 9 per cent in 1954, and to around 7 per cent in 1955.

23. See Appendix C for definitions of the phases distinguished in the project of which this study is a part. Note, however, that Phase IV is here divided into two subperiods designated IV-A and IV-B in Chart 1-1.

Chapter 2

Comprehensive Control and Partial Liberalization: The 1950s

In the main, this chapter contains a detailed description of the machinery and attributes of the comprehensive restrictive system of Phase I, the years 1949–51. It also includes an explanation of how the radical policy changes introduced during 1952–54 (Phase III), as well as the milder and more gradual changes of 1955–61 (first stage of Phase IV) have altered the nature of the system.

i. ORGANIZATION OF THE SYSTEM OF QUANTITATIVE RESTRICTIONS [1]

The legal and institutional framework for quantitative restrictions on foreign trade was inherited by the government of Israel in 1948 from the mandatory government of Palestine. Administrative regulation of trade was first introduced in 1939 when World War II broke out. The Ordinance of Imports, Exports, and Customs, by which the regulation was imposed, was originally meant to prevent trade with the enemy during the war. Yet it has served since then as the basis for intervention which, during most of the time, has had nothing to do with trade relations during wartime. The main feature of the ordinance, which made it the legal basis for the regulatory system, was the prohibition of any imports unless licensed by the "competent authority" appointed by the government for this purpose.

During the first few years of the state's existence—the late 1940s and early 1950s—import licenses were issued by several competent authorities, without any central regulation, although most import items were the domain of one ministry. This ministry has changed its name, as well as its structure and some of its functions, several times; but since 1951 it has remained the Ministry of Commerce and Industry. Along with an import license from the relevant competent authority, an importer had to obtain a currency allocation from the Controller of Foreign Exchange in the Ministry of Finance.

During 1952 the concept of the "foreign-exchange budget" was introduced into the regulatory system. In early 1952 an experimental budget was prepared for 1952–53.[2] Later in the year, a Department of the Budget was established within the Ministry of Finance, and it undertook the preparation of a foreign-exchange budget, starting with the budget for 1953–54. From then on until 1964, an annual foreign-exchange budget was prepared and submitted for cabinet decision, along with the conventional parts of the government's budget. The government's basic policy decisions on the allocation of foreign exchange were thus made in the adoption of the annual foreign-exchange budget.

The preparation of a foreign-exchange budget followed normal procedure for budgetary planning. Some six months before the new fiscal year, the department of the Budget would issue directions to the competent authorities within the various ministries, providing them with rough guidelines for presentation of foreign-exchange requirements.[3] At the same time, the Budget Department, with the help of the Foreign Exchange Department of the Ministry of Finance, would make an estimate of forthcoming foreign-exchange receipts. These receipts included export proceeds, unilateral cash transfers to Israel, and long-term and some medium-term loans. The selection of medium-term loans to be included was left to the discretion of the Department of the Budget. Short-term loans and the use of foreign-exchange reserves were not included in estimated receipts. Most transfers in kind, whether unilateral or on capital account, were included in the budget. This applied, among other things, to some major items such as German reparations or U.S. food surpluses. Minor transfers in kind, such as personal gifts or immigrants' personal effects, were excluded.

When estimated requirements of the various competent authorities were in hand, they were compared with estimated receipts and, not surprisingly, the former were found to exceed the latter. The Budget Department, following the normal course of budgetary negotiations with the ministries, then cut the allocations to the various authorities and proposed a foreign-exchange budget. This proposal was submitted by the Minister of Finance to the Cabinet Committee for Economic Affairs and then to the cabinet as a whole. The adoption of the budget by the cabinet made it an operational administrative directive. In this last step, the foreign-exchange budget differed from the conventional parts of the budget, which the cabinet had to submit to the Knesset for approval.

Once a foreign-exchange budget was approved by the cabinet, it provided a general allocation plan for the competent authorities. Within the limits of the quotas allocated, each authority was empowered to issue import licenses for the various items which it handled. An import license thus issued had to be approved by the Controller of Foreign Exchange, whose function—parallel to that of the government's controller in authorizing normal budgetary expenditures—was to check whether the license indeed fell within the authorized budget. The approval by the Controller of Foreign Exchange made the import license valid and also automatically resulted in commitment of the required foreign exchange, which was then provided when payment for the import was due. An exception to this rule was for import licenses labeled as "without allocation of foreign exchange"; these included substantial categories of import transactions, some of which will be mentioned later. Also subject to the approval of the Controller of Foreign Exchange were the terms of payment (cash, supplier's credit for a certain duration, etc.) and the currency of payment: the Controller could, and very often did, specify that only one currency and no other could be allocated for the import for which a license had been granted. This provision was mostly used to turn away imports from "hard currency" countries to countries with which Israel had payments and clearing agreements.

The foreign-exchange budget allocated licensing quotas among *functions and purposes* of the imports, rather than explicitly to competent authorities. The most general classification specified four categories: consumption, imports for exports, investment, and debt servicing (starting with the 1958–59 budget, services were separated from consumption and made into another category). These were subdivided into a three-digit classification, corresponding to the main industrial branches. The latter were then further divided by a five-digit classification, and this was the one with effective meaning: each five-digit item was handled by a particular competent authority. Five-digit items could be physically similar but classified as separate items if intended for purposes which were within the domains of separate authorities. For instance, a truck would fall under one item if intended for use in an industrial plant, another if intended for agricultural use, and still another if purchased for the use of a port authority.

As mentioned, 1952–53 was the first year for which a foreign-exchange budget was prepared, and the budget-making process in its entirety became effective in 1953–54. The last year for which such a budget was prepared was 1964–65. The budgets for all these years, by major classifications of receipts and expenditures, are presented in Table 2-1.

TABLE 2-1

Foreign-Exchange Budgets, Fiscal[a] 1952–64
(millions of dollars)

	1952[b]	1953[b]	1954	1955	1956	1957	1958	1959	1960	1961	1962	1963	1964
Approved budgets													
Receipts	215	233	310	346	480	519	587	590	685	795	910	1,030	1,190
Exports of goods and services	32	35	66	88	139	186	216	225	305	365	435	530	610
Other receipts	183	198	244	258	341	333	371	365	380	430	475	500	580
Expenditures	185	233	310	346	480	519	587	590	685	795	910	1,030	1,190
Consumer goods	141	138	184	229	250	294	184	176	198	207			
Capital goods	22	37	85	77	119	98	140	140	170	204	550	620	660
Imports for exports	21	21	40	38	69	87	80	80	92	115			
Services	—	—	—	—	—	—	130	143	177	207	260	325	420
Debt servicing and reserve	—	—	—	—	42	38	47	51	48	63	100	85	110
Budgetary performance													
Receipts	181	260	345	357	516	548	608	668	796	884	1,008	1,170	1,207
Expenditures	185	191	356	396	529	570	574	631	734	865	879	1,081	1,023

SOURCE: Nadav Halevi, "Exchange Control in Israel," in Pierre Uri, ed., *Israel and the Common Market* (Jerusalem: Weidenfeld and Nicolson, 1971; in English), p. 45.

a. Fiscal year begins in April.

b. In 1952 and 1953, the budgetary data are for the first nine months only of the fiscal year.

The aggregates presented in the table reveal some interesting phenomena. First, it appears that actual receipts were consistently underestimated in the budget. Therefore, since the principle of a balanced foreign-exchange budget was always maintained, budgeted expenditures were always below actual receipts for the year.[4] This was apparently not a coincidence, but resulted from a deliberate policy of leaving in the budget some concealed, or implied, reserve or safety margin. It could even be guessed, from the figures in Table 2-1, that this was done by the use of some particular naive model, which was known always to yield an underestimate. It may be observed that with the exception of the comparison of 1956–57 with 1955–56, the *planned* (i.e., anticipated) receipts of one budgetary year were remarkably similar to the *actual* receipts of the preceding year; there is definitely a much closer similarity than can be observed in comparisons of anticipated and realized receipts for the same year. One may speculate that the budgetary planners used estimates of receipts in the current year in which they were working as a projection, perhaps with a few adjustments, of receipts for the next year, realizing (or, at least, correctly hoping) that normally this would yield an underestimate of receipts.

It also appears that in the large majority of the budgetary years, actual expenditures were higher, mostly by a substantial margin, than planned expenditures. This was made feasible partly by the availability of the surplus of actual over anticipated receipts. Even so, it is worth inquiring what made expenditures reach the higher levels, since automatic adjustments of expenditures to receipts are obviously not provided in the budgetary mechanism.

The gap between actual and planned expenditures is explained in a number of ways. One is that supplementary budgets were very often presented and adopted during the course of the year (a procedure, incidentally, often practiced in Israel with regard to the conventional parts of the government's budget). In this way, the surplus of realized foreign-exchange receipts could be allocated for expenditure. Thus, the foreign-exchange budget was, in effect, quite flexible and subject to changes during the course of the year, a purpose which was served by the practice of underestimating receipts.

Supplementary budgets were often prepared retrospectively. Expenditures exceeding the sums allocated in the original budget were commonly made without the sanction of a supplementary budget. The office of the Controller of Foreign Exchange, which was in charge of supervising the execution of the budget through the authorization of import licenses, without which the licenses were not valid, did not, as a rule, adhere too closely to the budget. It authorized expenditures over the planned quotas, in amounts which were determined by something close to supply and demand forces, that is, by the amount of pressure of potential importers (expressed through the various competent authorities) and the size of the flow of foreign-exchange receipts. It also appears that the Controller assumed, from experience, that import licenses might not be fully utilized: some of them did not result in imports even after many months. The Controller therefore issued import licenses beyond the amounts allocated in the import plans, even without having an extra supply of foreign exchange, anticipating that since the licenses would not be fully used, there would be no extra pressure on the supply of foreign exchange.

In contrast to the case of foreign-exchange allocation among goods or competent authorities, for which procedures existed, a mechanism or a set of rules for allocating import quotas for goods among users or importers was lacking. At the beginning, the "past trade" principle was apparently applied most often; but according to the available evidence its importance declined as time passed. Instead, in many cases, particularly when imports of raw materials were concerned, the decision on allocation was placed in the hands of trade or manufacturers' associations: the entire quota would be turned over to the association, which would allocate it among its members. This practice, of course, granted an instrument of considerable power to the associations, a factor which undoubtedly contributed to the prevalence of cartel-type agreements at the time when QRs were strongly effective.

ii. THE SCOPE OF THE SYSTEM OF QUANTITATIVE RESTRICTIONS

One ideal measure of the severity of a QR system is the amount of excess demand for each imported good at the controlled prices; or, more precisely, the proportion of total demand that remains unsatisfied. A second measure is the degree by which official prices underestimate the value of imports at prevailing quantities to actual or potential buyers. With demand elasticities varying over time (in temporal comparisons) or among goods (in cross-sectional comparisons), these two measures would not necessarily, of course, yield the same ordering in the system in measuring the severity of controls for each imported good, or the same answer in the analysis of developments over time. Both, however, are conceptually legitimate measures, and, when large differences or large changes in the degree of restrictiveness are involved, the differences in demand and supply elasticities become relatively less important and the two measurements would tend to yield similar results. Quantity measures are discussed in this section; price indicators are taken up in the next two sections.

The measurement of excess demand is, unfortunately, not feasible, and there is probably no reliable information anywhere on this point. Even if consumers or other potential buyers of imports were asked to estimate their shortages, the results would be unreliable. In any case, no such field survey has ever been made in Israel. It has sometimes been suggested that the amount—size or value—of unsatisfied applications for import licenses could be used instead. But this measurement suffers from some serious flaws, even overlooking the immense practical difficulties in any attempt to collect data on such applications.[5] On the one hand, many applications for import licenses did not reflect any actual demand for imports. In a QR system, where it is well known from experience that a certain fraction of applications will get a negative response, importers are naturally motivated to apply for licenses for amounts larger than they actually need or intend to buy; this resulted, among other things, in the phenomenon that a significant fraction of import licenses was not utilized.[6] On the other hand, there is no doubt that some of the demand for imports was not reflected in requests for import licenses, since potential applicants for licenses may have decided that their applications stood no chance. When, for instance, licenses were in effect allocated by a trade or manufacturing association, trying to bypass this procedure in applying for an import license would be pointless. The competent authority would appear, in such cases, to grant practically all the import licenses for which it received applications, since applications would be restricted by the trade association to the total quota available.

Thus, there does not seem to be a feasible way of estimating excess demand for imports directly, or even by proxy. Instead, a few indirect indications will be mentioned, starting with data on the foreign-exchange budgets.

As I pointed out earlier, the data in Table 2-1 show, as a rule, an excess of foreign-exchange expenditures over the levels of planned expenditures and anticipated receipts. During the earlier part of the period covered, actual expenditures also usually exceeded actual foreign-exchange receipts. The budgetary year 1958–59 appears, on this score, to have been a turning point. From that year on, actual expenditures, while continuing to exceed planned expenditures—often by a substantial margin—always fell short of actual receipts, again often by a significant margin. The two gaps combined are one of the indications of the changing nature of the system of foreign-exchange controls. The acute shortage of foreign exchange seems to have disappeared in the late 1950s, and the system was not designed any longer to serve the major purpose of adjusting foreign-exchange expenditures—specifically on imports—to receipts. Indeed, by all available indications, the foreign-exchange budget ceased to play any serious role during the early 1960s; its discontinuation after 1964–65 was only a recognition of this fact.

Beginning in the late 1950s, the continuing system of administrative regulations was designed for purposes other than that of general adjustment of foreign-exchange flows. One such major purpose, which will be discussed later at greater length, was the protection of local industries from competing imports. Another purpose was the regulation of capital transfers. It should be pointed out that during the later years, this meant not just prevention of capital outflows, but also regulation of capital inflows. In time, the government's objection to capital inflows strengthened, and regulations were made (although not always strictly adhered to) to prevent capital inflows of short duration and high interest rates. One source which was particularly discouraged was foreign suppliers' credit: the terms of the import license normally specified payment in cash, rather than on credit. One of the major motives of this rejection of foreign credit, besides the avoidance of interest payments (whether explicit or implicit in the terms of purchase on credit) was the fear of the effect of capital inflow on domestic liquidity. With a contractive domestic monetary policy and tightening credit conditions, importers (as well as banks or other domestic borrowers) tended to turn to credit from abroad. In Israel's circumstances—a country with a high ratio of imports to production and good access to foreign capital markets—unrestricted short-term capital inflows could thus defeat any contractive policy. Indeed, the possibility of abolishing foreign-exchange controls, which was contemplated on a number of occasions, most seriously right after the devaluation of February 1962, was rejected mainly on such grounds.

A similar indication, supporting (and to some extent repeating) the observation made on the basis of the foreign-exchange budget, is the movement of foreign-exchange reserves. The higher the reserves and the more they tend to increase, the less severe are restrictions expected to be. The position of Israel's external reserves is shown in Table 2-2.

This table shows that foreign-exchange reserves declined rapidly during 1949–51, and then remained close to zero during 1952 and 1953. In 1954 some reserves were re-established by a special operation,[7] but remained at a low level until 1958. From then on, Israel's external reserves rose markedly and almost without interruption for a whole decade—until the middle of 1968.

Another indication of the severity of restrictions may be found by asking what proportion of imports were in effect free, that is, suffered from no unsatisfied demand. Such a measure does not indicate the degree of severity of controls on imports which were *not* free; but it gives some idea of how important these unsatisfied amounts could be in relation to total imports. In an experimental study on this subject, Rom tried to answer this question by asking the persons in charge of each import item at the various competent authorities whether that item was *effectively* restricted or free.[8] Rom's study relates to a single period of time, and so throws no light on the development of the system over time. In addition, the method of inquiry could, at best, yield only tentative results. Yet, it is worth looking into the findings of the study, mainly for the impressions gained about the structure of the system.

Rom's study originated in an examination of the desirability of Israel's joining the Common Market (the European Economic Community) when it

TABLE 2-2

External Reserves,[a] End of Year, 1948–72

(dollars in millions)

Year	Reserves[a]	Rates of Change	Year	Reserves[a]	Rates of Change
1948	$141		1960	$ 270	60.7%
1949	117	−17.0%	1961	376	39.3
1950	66	−43.6	1962	506	34.6
1951	34	−48.5	1963	615	21.5
1952	31	−8.8	1964	643	4.6
1953	39	25.8	1965	748	16.3
1954	81	107.7	1966	756	1.1
1955	90	11.1	1967	968	28.0
1956	87	−3.3	1968	916	−5.4
1957	84	−3.4	1969	729	−20.4
1958	130	54.8	1970	849	16.5
1959	168	29.2	1971	1,278	50.5
			1972	2,134	67.0

SOURCE: For 1948–59, Michael Michaely, *Foreign Trade and Capital Imports in Israel* (Tel Aviv: Am Oved, 1953; in Hebrew). For 1960–72, *Statistical Abstract of Israel*, 1973, Table VII/6.

a. Gross reserves, including deposits abroad of commercial banks and of the government and foreign assets of the Bank of Israel.

was formed. Since joining the Market would have involved an Israeli liberalization, the aim of the study was to discover the goods which would not be affected because they were already either formally or effectively liberalized. The examination was concerned in principle with *private* imports only, and excluded import items handled mainly by the government. The proportions reported obviously related to total actual imports as influenced by restrictions, a fact which raises problems too well known to be dwelt upon here. Rom also asked officials at the competent authorities whether the liberalization of import items which were effectively controlled was "possible" if duties were levied on them. A negative answer to this question was most often based on the assumption that the duty required would be, according to the person asked, "too high." While all these are very crude estimates, based on personal judgments, they may provide a tentative indication of the relative severity of restrictions. On this basis, and with this limited and tentative interpretation, imports are divided, in Table 2-3, into three groups: effective liberalization, moderate restrictions, stringent restrictions.

TABLE 2-3

Effectiveness of Import Restrictions, 1956

(proportions of total value of imports)

Import Category	Formally or Effectively Liberalized	Moderately Restricted	Severely Restricted	Total
Foodstuffs and fodder	40%	4%	56%	100%
Raw materials	60	32	8	100
Finished goods	35	33	32	100
Total imports of goods	45	31	24	100

SOURCE: See accompanying text.

The indication provided by Table 2-3 is that close to half of total imports in 1956 were effectively liberalized, and roughly a quarter were subject to stringent restrictions. An earlier point must be emphasized here: these percentages are for the actual distribution of imports; weighting by shares of industries in local production, or by hypothetical imports in the absence of controls, would, of course, have resulted in a much higher degree of restriction. It should be further noted that 60 per cent of raw materials were liberalized, and that most other imports in this category were subject to only moderate restrictions; that is, by 1956, imports of raw materials were by and large not subject to severe controls, effective restrictions being mainly confined to other categories of imports. Note also that the category of foodstuffs and fodder, in contrast to the other two categories, was characterized by either full liberalization or severe restriction. This impression is compatible with the views prevailing at that time, which tended to classify imports of foodstuffs as either "essential" and to be imported relatively freely or as "luxuries" and to be discouraged. Data on effective exchange rates, which will be studied later, also show a similar concentration of imports of this category at the extreme ends of our classification.

iii. THE "IMPORTS-WITHOUT-PAYMENT" MARKET

A very interesting feature of the QR system in its earlier years was the institution known as the "imports-without-payment" (IWP) market.[9] It was the most important attempt during the early 1950s to establish or regulate a private foreign-exchange market parallel to the official one.

Supply in the IWP market originated from three acknowledged sources: foreign capital transfers, immigrants' capital, and gifts from abroad.[10] At the

end of 1948 the government allowed foreign investors to transfer their capital
in the form of goods from a specified list, on condition that foreign exchange
amounting to 30 per cent of the import license be sold to the Treasury at the
official rate. In effect, import licenses thus issued became, to a large extent,
marketable, although not in a sanctioned market. In July 1949, both the list
of categories exempt from the obligation of selling to the Treasury and the
list of goods which could be imported were extended. Most of the imported
goods allowed were "nonessential." This, plus a steep rise in the black-market
rate of foreign exchange, led the government to reverse course. In December
1949 and January 1950 new regulations were issued, narrowing the list of per-
mitted imports and prohibiting transfer of the right to import (by no longer
permitting an Israeli importer to deposit money in the restricted account of a
foreign investor). Likewise, in April 1950, IWPs from the United States and
Canada were disallowed altogether, although a few large transactions did
receive ad hoc permission. The level of imports covered by these regulations
fell considerably thereafter. This, together with rapidly mounting shortages,
led the government to reverse course once more.

In October 1950, this reversal and the regulations which followed during
the next two months led to what may be viewed as the classic form of imports
without payment, in which imports were made accessible to the original
owners of foreign capital as well as to Israeli residents; that is, transferability
of the right to import became legal. The Israeli importer became free to buy
foreign exchange from the transferer of capital at a rate determined by the
partners to the transaction. Import items eligible under this scheme were determined by the government, and embraced nonessential as well as essential
goods. If imports belonged to the former category, foreign currency at a specified proportion of the value of the import license was to be submitted to
the Treasury at the formal rate of exchange; imports of essential goods were
exempt from this obligation. In effect, the government allocated licenses for
"imports without payment" during this period in the following way: 70 per
cent were allocated for the importation of construction materials; 20 per cent,
for importation of rubber tires; and 10 per cent, for other essential goods,
mainly construction materials for schools and hospitals. Licensees in the first
category were required to sell half the foreign exchange they bought in the
IWP market to the Treasury at the formal rate of exchange, using the other
half to finance their imports. The other two groups of licensees were exempt
from the currency-selling requirement.

Within a few months the policy was changed again. The rate of exchange
in the IWP market rose rapidly along with the black-market rate. This led
the government to intervene in the market by establishing a consortium of
importers, which became the only agent entitled to buy foreign exchange in
the market. Under terms of a regulation issued in April 1951, the rate of

exchange for these transactions was determined by the Treasury. The latter first stabilized the existing rate and then actually lowered it. Initially, this had little effect on the size of the market. But within a few months, the disparity between the black-market rate, which was rising sharply, and the rate in the IWP market became wide enough for the supply of foreign exchange in the latter market to fall drastically. In the latter half of 1951, the IWP market therefore came to be confined again, in the main, to various transactions approved ad hoc by the government.

"Imports without payment" originated in response to a number of circumstances, and were intended to satisfy several governmental goals. The latter were not always consistent, and the inconsistency (as well as changes in circumstances) contributed to the many fluctuations in the nature and operation of the market. Basically, the conflict was between two objectives. On the one hand, the government wanted to use the IWP market as a vehicle for encouraging various kinds of capital inflows by giving them a premium over the official exchange rate. This was accomplished by using these capital imports for the importation of goods that commanded high domestic prices: the premium involved would be the excess of the prevailing domestic price over that yielded by the official rate of exchange (allowing for transportation, marketing, etc.). Reaching this target thus called for high premiums and, hence, importation of goods with high local prices. Another objective of the government, leading in the same direction, was to provide an outlet for spending some of the involuntary accumulation of money by making available some goods not provided by the controlled market. On the other hand, the government was particularly anxious to increase imports of "essential" goods, which were usually subject to low ceiling prices. In addition, the government was reluctant to let effective exchange rates in the IWP market rise very high, lest the credibility of the official rate be impaired.

After the formal devaluation of February 1952, no attempt was made to reestablish a regulated IWP market. From then on these imports consisted to an increasing extent of gifts, bona fide or otherwise. The market for gifts of food packages became increasingly organized, and much of the capital transfer to the country was illegally channeled through this market. Instead of transmitting actual parcels of food prepaid abroad, a few companies were established that provided food items to local recipients in exchange for scrip certificates which were paid for abroad (mainly in the United States). Within a short time these certificates became transferable, first illegally and then, after bearer certificates were allowed, in effect with official approval. The scrip companies were entitled to import food, having committed themselves to transfer a given proportion (42.5 per cent) of their foreign-exchange proceeds at the formal rate to finance local purchases of food, a commitment which was not strictly observed. During 1955 the scrip arrangements were abolished and the IWP market lost its importance as a channel of imports except for imports in kind by immigrants or through bona fide gifts, which, of course, went on. The size of the IWP category during its years of significance is shown in Table 2-4.

TABLE 2-4
Imports Without Payment, 1949–54

	1949	1950	1951	1952	1953	1954
Total imports of goods (millions of dollars)	253.1	302.0	383.7	324.1	282.1	290.3
Imports without payment (millions of dollars)	38.6	51.2	71.3	65.1	59.8	42.7
Source of financing of imports without payment (per cent):	100.0	100.0	100.0	100.0	100.0	100.0
Capital transfers	42.8	40.9	44.3	44.7	40.2	22.5
Immigrants' transfers	39.5	29.1	17.0	14.6	5.0	3.6
Gifts	17.7	30.0	38.7	40.7	34.8	48.8
Other	—	—	—	—	20.0	25.1

Source: Michael Michaely, *Israel's Foreign Exchange Rate System* (Jerusalem: Falk Institute, 1971; in English), Table 2-3.

For most of the period, data on prices paid in the IWP market are scarce. In studies of that period it is mentioned that during the first half of 1949, when IWP licenses were in effect largely transferable, they were sold to importers at a price ranging from 20 to 25 per cent of the import value. Since the importer at that time was obliged to sell foreign exchange equivalent to 30 per cent of the import value to the Treasury at the formal rate and presumably bought the currency in the black market, at a rate which was about 25 per cent above parity at that time, this price meant a premium of over 30 per cent for the import license. This seems to be a rather modest premium.[11] Later data show a rapidly growing disparity (see Table 2-5).

The observations in Table 2-5 for 1949 and 1950 may be viewed as illustrative, tentative samples. The data for 1951, on the other hand, are complete and precise: they refer to the uniform, publicized rate that applied in the organized market at that time. Special attention should be paid to the period of January–March 1951, during which the rate of exchange in the IWP market was completely free.[12] During that period the implied rate of exchange for imports of construction material[13] was about six times the formal rate of exchange. This ratio is quite close, as will soon be seen, to the size of disparities between free and official prices of foodstuffs, as well as those of other

TABLE 2-5

**Foreign-Exchange Rates in the
Imports-Without-Payment (IWP) Market, 1949–51**

Period	Exchange Rate in IWP Market (IL per $) (1)	Implied Exchange Rate for Imports of Construction Materials[a] (IL per $) (2)	Ratio of Col. 1 to Formal Rate[b] (3)	Ratio of Col. 2 to Formal Rate[b] (4)
1949: October–November	.446–.500	—	1.3–1.5	—
December	.666–.900	—	1.9–2.5	—
1950: April	.625–.645	—	1.7–1.8	—
1951: January	1.250	2.143	3.5	6.0
February–March	1.300	2.243	3.6	6.3
April	1.100	1.843	3.1	5.2
May–June	0.990	1.623	2.8	4.5
July–December	0.930	1.503	2.6	4.2.

SOURCE: Based on Michaely, *Foreign Exchange System*, Table 2-4.

a. It will be recalled that an importer of construction materials had to surrender to the Treasury, at the formal rate, half of the foreign exchange bought by him in the imports-without-payment market. If r_o is the formal rate, r_s the rate in the imports-without-payment market, r_i the implied rate for construction materials, and p the fraction surrendered to the Treasury, then $r_i = (r_s - pr_o)/(1 - p)$; if $r_o = 0.357$, and $p = 0.5$, then $r_i = 2r_s - 0.357$.

b. The formal rate of exchange was IL 0.333 per dollar until November 1949, and IL 0.357 per dollar from then on until February 1952.

goods, during this period. This similarity may be assumed to be even closer for later periods, for which direct information about the market rate is not available. It will be recalled that from 1952 to 1954 the scrip certificates were the main instrument of the semiorganized IWP market. Purchases by scrip arrangements were apparently the main source of supply of foodstuffs in the black market at that time. With a considerable degree of perfection and arbitrage in the markets, it may be presumed that the foreign-exchange rate implied by the price of the scrip certificates was related to the formal rate of exchange in about the same ratio as between free-market and official food prices.

iv. PRICES IN OTHER "BLACK" AND FREE MARKETS

The IWP market yielded some price data by which the severity of the QR system can be inferred. This is, of course, rather fragmentary evidence. While no data are available to provide a full measure of the severity of controls, as would be reflected by the gap between actual and demand prices for the imports allowed by the system's quotas, a few other fragments may be found which taken together serve as additional indicators. These are prices paid outside the control system—either legally where free markets existed in addition to the controlled, rationed markets, or illegally in black markets, or in the so-called grey markets where transactions were made at freely determined prices without official sanction but presumably with the knowledge of the government.

At the peak of the control system, during the early 1950s, entirely free markets were few and mainly confined to services. Imports, or goods with a high import content, were almost universally rationed and subject to price ceilings, the most important exception once more being imports made under the IWP plan. Noncontrolled prices were thus usually prices paid in black markets. While it was a matter of common knowledge that these markets were widespread, and that prices paid in them were far above the official prices, actual data about black-market commodity prices are quite scarce. Aside from wanting to avoid the difficulty involved in collecting price data in unorganized, widely fluctuating, and illegal markets, the government was reluctant to encourage the collection of such data, because its doing so might have been interpreted as giving some legal sanction to these transactions. Furthermore, by governmental direction, the Central Bureau of Statistics based cost-of-living index calculations only on official prices. It was reluctant to investigate black-market prices, or even the few free legal prices that existed alongside the (lower) official prices. This inhibition was due to the attempt to keep the cost-of-living index from rising (and even, during part of the period, to lower it), mainly in order to mitigate pressure for wage increases.

By way of exception, the Central Bureau of Statistics did collect free-market data on food prices; these were not published or publicized at the time but were made available for later investigations. In one study, these data were used to construct an index of free-market food prices for comparison with the index of official prices.[14] Since these indexes exclude fruits and vegetables from the food category, the remaining food items include (particularly in earlier years) a very high import component—certainly much over 50 per cent on the average—and are, therefore, relevant in the present examination. The results, presented in Table 2-6, are quite revealing and clearly indicate the developments over the period.

For several years controls grew increasingly severe. They reached a peak in 1951, when free-market prices were seven times higher than official ceiling prices.[15] Beginning in the first half of 1952 the severity of controls declined consistently and rapidly, a movement clearly associated with official price trends, which will be surveyed later in this chapter. This downward movement

TABLE 2-6

Ratio of Free-Market to Official Prices of Food, 1949–58

(half-yearly averages)

	Period	Ratio		Period	Ratio
1949	First half	3.1	1954	First half	2.7
	Second half	4.2		Second half	2.9
1950	First half	5.3	1955	First half	2.5
	Second half	6.1		Second half	2.6
1951	First half	7.0	1956	First half	2.5
	Second half	6.8		Second half	1.6
1952	First half	6.1	1957	First half	1.8
	Second half	5.2		Second half	1.5
1953	First half	3.9	1958	First half	1.5
	Second half	2.9		Second half	1.7

SOURCE: Compiled from data in Yoram Weiss, "Price Control in Israel, 1939–1963" (M.A. diss., Hebrew University, 1964; in Hebrew), Table C-1. Weiss used estimates of family expenditures as weights in his index of free-market prices. The indices include sixteen food items.

became very slight from the second half of 1953 to the first half of 1956, a period in which the severity of controls seems to have been virtually stable at a level substantially lower than during the early 1950s but still significant. In the second half of 1956, the severity of controls, as measured by the ratio in Table 2-6, declined perceptibly. The excess of free-market over official prices was only about 50 to 70 per cent from then on, indicating a system of controls of limited "bite" by comparison with the system of the early 1950s.

It is interesting to compare the relationship of these price indicators to indicators of quantities. Again, actual estimates of quantities of excess demand in the controlled markets are obviously not available. Table 2-7 shows the proportion to all food expenditures of expenditures for foods subject to ceiling-price regulations and rationing. These data (available only on a yearly basis) show the same movements as those of Table 2-6, and the association of the two could hardly be a coincidence.[16] The severity of controls must have increased until 1951, and then decreased because of changes both in the number of items controlled and in the strictness of the regulations affecting them, and the two components were probably closely correlated.

The series for food prices, just discussed, is apparently the most complete and organized set of data available on free-market prices of goods. Other pieces of information are only casual examples a few of which are presented in Table 2-8. The first two sections of the table show results quite similar to

TABLE 2-7

**Controlled Food Items as a Proportion of
Total Food Expenditures, 1948–59**

Year	Proportion	Year	Proportion
1948	15.6%	1954	69.0%
1949	62.1	1955	67.1
1950	89.7	1956	55.7
1951	94.6	1957	47.9
1952	89.4	1958	43.0
1953	80.8	1959	21.6

SOURCE: Weiss, "Price Control," Table C-4.

those derived from the data on food prices. Free-market prices were much higher than official prices, generally three to ten times as high. Also, although these two parts are not strictly comparable, it appears that the disparity between the two prices grew between September 1950 and January 1951, as indicated particularly by the free-market price movement of certain construction materials; this again agrees with the indication provided by food prices. The data in the third part of Table 2-8 also show a substantial disparity between free-market and official prices; but it is considerably lower than in the earlier series, ranging only between 1.4 and 2.5. In part, this is probably a reflection of the general movement toward reduced disparity, which started early in 1952 with major boosts of official prices. But it may well be that in the clothing industry, to which the data of this part of the table refer, the excess of free-market over official prices was indeed generally lower than in categories such as food or construction materials.[17]

Finally, a most interesting price for the purpose at hand is the black-market rate of foreign exchange. In principle, this price does not necessarily reflect price disparities in the import of goods. Foreign exchange might be bought in the black market not in order to finance current purchases, but as an asset to be held for some length of time, either for its direct yield or in anticipation of a future rise of the black-market rate itself or of the local price of imported goods and services which the foreign exchange could buy.[18] Indeed, in later years, when the scope of the foreign-exchange black market was small, much of the demand in this market was most likely due to such motivation.[19] In the earlier years, on the other hand, most of the foreign exchange bought in the black market was probably intended for the purchase of imports of goods and services. The IWP market discussed above was probably the most important channel for imports of goods. When the black-market rate is compared with estimates of the IWP rate, for periods when the latter was uni-

TABLE 2-8

Free-Market Versus Official Prices, Specified Dates, 1950–52

(prices in Israeli pounds per unit)

Commodity	Official Price (1)	Free Price (2)	Ratio of (2) to (1) (3)
September 1950			
Plywood (m³)	110.0	330.0	3.0
Soft wood (m³)	22.5	70.0	3.1
Construction iron (ton)	55.0	500.0	9.1
Cement (ton)	10.0	25.0	2.5
Wool, locally woven (m)	2.8	10.0	3.6
Wool, English (m)	4.5	20.0	4.4
January 1951			
Cotton thread (kg.)	1.05	6.00	5.7
Wool thread (kg.)	2.00	20.00	10.0
Wool yarn (m)	5.00	10.00	2.0
Linen, low quality (m)	0.26	1.30	5.0
Linen, high quality (m)	0.78	2.50	3.2
Cement (ton)	11.00	85.00	7.7
Construction iron (ton)	100.00	500.00	5.0
Soft wood (m³)	33.00	160.00	4.8
Pipes, 1/2 in. (m)	0.15	0.95	6.3
Glass (m²)	0.60	5.00	8.3
August 1952			
Men's wool suit (pr.)	45.00	100.00	2.2
Wool "utility" trousers (pr.)	17.00	35.00	2.1
Men's underwear (pr.)	0.51	1.25	2.5
Nylon stockings (pr.)	1.75	3.00	1.7
Silk (unit not specified)	3.00	5.00	1.7
Men's pajamas (pr.)	10.36	23.75	2.3
Sheet	3.27	8.00	2.4
Bath towel	0.73	1.50	2.1
Diaper	0.66	1.50	2.3
Men's shoes (pr.)	10.05	15.00	1.5
Women's shoes (pr.)	8.34	12.00	1.4

m = meter.   m³ = cubic meter.
m² = square meter.   kg = kilogram.

SOURCE: September 1950 and January 1951—Weiss, "Price Control," Table C-16 (based on newspaper reports); August 1952—internal memorandum of the Ministry of Finance approximately September 1953.

form and freely determined in the market, the two rates are indeed found to be very similar (although the number of such observations is rather small). It may thus be presumed that for the first few years, black-market foreign-exchange rates reflect quite well the excess of free-market prices over official prices. The black market for foreign exchange was always well organized, with rather uniform rates prevailing.[20] The black-market rate was, therefore, well known and well publicized.

The impression gained from the quarterly data on exchange rates in Table 2-9 is quite strong and rather similar to that conveyed by the other pieces of evidence presented previously. The ratio of the black-market to the formal rate was at first, in 1949, only slightly above unity, and was rising only slowly. But in 1950, and even more significantly in 1951, the disparity between the two rates grew rapidly and very substantially. At the peak in late 1951 the black-market rate was roughly seven times that of the formal rate—a ratio quite similar to the disparity shown earlier between free-market and official food prices as well as to disparities in prices of other goods. For a number of years beginning in early 1952, the black-market rate was roughly stable, while the formal rate climbed steadily. The disparity between the two thus went down, gradually but considerably, until in 1955 it again reached the same low level as in 1949. From then on, the black-market rate rarely exceeded the formal rate by more than 20 to 30 per cent.[21] Considering the other sources of demand for foreign exchange in the black market—mainly for speculation—this small disparity probably indicates that only a small portion of demand at the existing formal rates (combined, of course, with the effect of tariffs and similar levies on imports) was left unsatisfied by the government's allocation mechanism.

v. THE POLICY SHIFT: FROM QUANTITATIVE RESTRICTIONS TO USE OF THE PRICE MECHANISM

All the available indications thus show the same time pattern: a system of quantitative restrictions growing in severity in 1949 and the early 1950s, and reaching a peak in late 1951 and early 1952, when QRs, as measured by the gap between official and free-market prices, were very severe indeed. Beginning early in 1952, this trend started to reverse itself, until by about 1956 the system of QRs had almost been ended as an instrument for regulating total imports and keeping them substantially lower than they would have been otherwise.

The changing nature and intensity of the QR system could conceivably be explained by accidental circumstances, such as the appearance and disappearance of sources of capital imports. To some extent, it might have been so, but there seems to be little doubt that the pattern of development of the QR system is to be viewed primarily as a change in *policy;* it is one side of a coin, the other side of which was a switch (to which occasional references have

TABLE 2-9

Black-Market Rate of Foreign Exchange, Quarterly, 1949–56
(Israeli pounds per dollar)

Period[a]	Black-Market Rate (1)	Formal Rate (2)	Ratio of (1) to (2) (3)
1949: I	0.379		1.1
II	0.425	0.333	1.3
III	0.419		1.3
1949: IV	0.498		1.4
1950: I	0.573		1.6
II	0.635		1.8
III	0.748		2.1
IV	0.862	0.357	2.4
1951: I	1.349		3.8
II	1.221		3.4
III	1.183		3.3
IV	2.402		6.7
1952: I	2.583	0.460	5.6
II	2.663	0.700	3.8
III	2.544	0.800	3.2
IV	2.240	0.790	2.8
1953: I	2.511	0.770	3.3
II	2.400	0.800	3.0
III	2.314	0.880	2.6
IV	2.442	0.890	2.7
1954: I	2.763	1.240	2.2
II	2.613	1.420	1.8
III	2.553	1.680	1.5
IV	2.495	1.710	1.4
1955: I	2.300		1.3
II	2.225		1.2
III	2.263		1.2
IV	2.423		1.3
1956: I	2.407	1.800	1.3
II	2.379		1.3
III	2.476		1.4
IV	2.748		1.5

been made) to reliance on the price mechanism for regulating the balance of payments. A detailed description and analysis of this change will be presented in Chapter 5. Here it will be only briefly outlined.

From the establishment of the state of Israel until early 1952, the effective price of foreign exchange in the import trade was almost constant. Aside from a slight increase of a few percentage points in the formal rate in September 1949, no formal devaluation was undertaken. Customs duties and other levies on imports also changed very little during these years. Thus, the effective rate of exchange with the dollar in the import trade, which includes these duties, changed between 1949 and 1951 (yearly averages) from IL 0.386 to IL 0.395 per dollar—an increase of just about 2 per cent. The stability of the rate was probably due to the notion prevailing in the government at that time that cheap imports were essential to maintain a minimum standard of living for all segments of the population and to keep the general price level stable—a purpose which came to be regarded as a target in itself.

The policy switch occurred in early 1952, and the execution of the new policy took close to three years. On February 14, 1952, the New Economic Policy was announced—a name fully justified by the events. The essence of this policy was a process of progressive devaluation, accompanied by a parallel increase of domestic (controlled) prices and undertaken within a context of restrictive demand policy. A multiple exchange rate system was introduced, and the average rate kept rising by the shifting of transactions from lower to higher rates. While the formal rate on the eve of this process was IL 0.357 per dollar, by its end, around mid-1954, almost all transactions were conducted at a rate of IL 1.800 per dollar. The formal rate thus increased about fivefold within this period. At the same time, import duties and other levies were also raised; these actions contributed to the increase in the effective rate of exchange, although the contribution was minor by comparison with that of the formal devaluation. The effective rate of exchange in import transactions thus increased, from 1951 to the end of 1954, by about 450 per cent. From then on until the devaluation of 1962, changes in the effective exchange rates, which were introduced only through changes in import duties or in export subsidies, were very moderate—on the average, just a few percentage points per year.

The recorded increase in domestic prices, which reflects primarily changes in controlled (legal) prices, was also very substantial: from 1951 to 1953 this price level about doubled, and it further increased by some 10 per cent from 1953 to 1954. The "true" price level increased substantially less: free-market (or black-market) prices not only failed to rise to the same extent as did official prices, but sometimes they actually declined. But even in comparison with official prices—though they closely reflect changes in import prices, introduced primarily through changes in the exchange rate—the relative level of the rate of exchange (PLD-EER)[22] increased substantially during the period of progressive devaluation. From 1951 to 1955 the PLD-EER increased by about 170 per cent—an average annual (compounded) rise of close to 30 per cent.

The substantial rise in the relative level of the exchange rate—and, through it, of the level of import prices in relation to domestic prices—would be expected to lead to a reduction of demand for imports. This indeed appears to have happened on a very large scale; and, although any statistical inference based on simple comparisons of various time series must be regarded as suggestive rather than firmly conclusive, the chronological association of the series in this instance is too striking to be dismissed as accidental. Imports actually declined after 1951, measured at constant prices, and only in 1955 did they again reach the 1951 level. In proportion to GNP, the decline of imports during these years was striking—from over 52 per cent in 1951 to 33 per cent in 1954.[23]

The decline in imports during 1952–54 is all the more spectacular when considered in conjunction with the development of the QR system. It has been shown that after the first half of 1952 the degree of severity of the controls declined rapidly. The very bold use of the price mechanism, by which relative prices of imports were almost tripled, thus led to the simultaneous achievement of two purposes: the reduction in the size of imports (in relation to the level of the national product); and the scrapping of QRs as a major policy instrument for the regulation of imports. Altogether, the New Economic Policy of 1952–54 and related developments may be considered an outstanding example of the substitution of the price mechanism for regulation through quantitative restrictions.

vi. LIBERALIZATION AND THE NATURE OF THE REMAINING QRs

By the mid-1950s, then, the QR system no longer served as a major instrument of balance-of-payments correction. In late 1956 and early 1957, following the near exhaustion of external reserves due to the cost of the Sinai campaign of October 1956 and the economic sanctions imposed by the United States government, the reimposition of more stringent controls was extensively debated within the government, but finally rejected. From then on the use of this instrument was not seriously contemplated, although during episodes of particularly strong balance-of-payments pressure it has occasionally been advocated in the press or by individual government officials.

The relaxation of restrictions was, however, not uniform: it applied mostly to raw materials and, to a smaller extent, to finished investment goods, rather than to finished consumer goods. This pattern of liberalization was indicated by the data in Table 2-3. It is also supported by the data in Table 2-10, which show the changing structure of imports during the late 1950s. The

TABLE 2-10

Distribution of Main Categories of Imports, 1951–59

	1951	1952	1953	1954	1955	1956	1957	1958	1959
Value (millions of dollars)									
Final consumer goods	87.6	73.3	59.1	49.1	50.4	50.1	50.0	53.1	42.7
Raw materials	127.0	118.7	127.4	150.6	173.0	181.9	211.3	211.8	233.0
Investment goods	100.4	91.4	64.9	64.3	76.7	101.5	116.1	112.2	112.2
Fuel	31.9	40.3	31.3	31.4	33.0	32.9	53.9	40.4	34.7
Total	346.9	323.7	282.7	296.0	333.6	367.0	432.0	417.9	423.1
Percentage of total imports									
Final consumer goods	25.3	22.6	20.9	16.6	15.1	13.7	11.6	12.7	10.1
Raw materials	36.6	36.7	45.1	51.0	51.9	49.6	49.0	50.7	55.1
Investment goods	28.9	28.2	22.9	21.8	23.0	27.7	26.9	26.9	26.5
Fuel	9.2	12.4	11.1	10.6	10.0	9.0	12.5	9.7	8.2
Total	100.0	100.0	100.0	100.0	100.0	100.0	100.0	100.0	100.0

SOURCE: Michaely, *Foreign Trade*, Table 28.

decline in the share of finished consumer goods and the rise in the share of raw materials can be clearly seen: the former category declined over the period from about one-quarter of total imports to less than half of this fraction, while the latter increased from over a third to over a half of the total. Put differently, imports of final consumer goods declined over the period in absolute (dollar) terms, and very markedly so in relation to national income, while imports of raw materials almost doubled in absolute terms, rising at approximately the same rate as the national income and product. This change in the composition of imports might conceivably have been due to other factors, particularly to relative price movements. However, data presented later in this study, on sectoral movements in exchange rates, do not support this hypothesis. Higher elasticities of demand for imports of consumer goods than for other imports, which again will be indicated later in this study, do probably provide a partial explanation for the decline in the share of final consumer goods. But this decline was so substantial during this period that it must in all probability reflect the concentration of quantitative restrictions in this sector.

Liberalization of imports of raw materials was carried out gradually, without specific policy declarations, by increasing the ratio of allowed imports to total import applications. Accompanying the rise of this ratio were accommodating changes in the administration of the system, such as a gradual shift from ad hoc grants of specific import licenses for each individual shipment to general import licenses. The only liberalization explicitly announced during the 1950s took place in early 1956 and involved the importation of a few major raw materials, such as lumber and hides and leather. These imports were declared unrestricted, although the government still retained the right to dictate the source of purchase. In practice, this meant that the government could direct the importer, when this seemed feasible, to buy from one of the countries with which Israel had at that time a trade surplus under a bilateral clearing agreement. At the same time—and this was a specific example of the replacement of QRs by the price mechanism—special levies were imposed on these liberalized imports.

By 1957, most imports of raw materials were, in effect, liberalized. The nonliberalized items belonged mainly to two categories. One, quite substantial in size, consisted of raw materials for the food industry. Imports of these goods were concentrated largely (about 70 to 80 per cent) in the hands of the government, and private imports of items purchased by the government were not allowed at all. This practice started during World War II, when food imports were handled by the British Middle-Eastern Supply Center in Cairo. For several reasons, the practice has to a large extent continued to this day, although the list of governmental import items has narrowed down. One reason for its continuance is a belief that the government, as a single purchaser, would do better than private traders in these import markets, due to the value of its monopsonistic position. Likewise, local consumers of these essential goods would be better protected from monopolistic exploitation if the government were the seller of the import in the local market—by virtue of which role, the government also regulates the price of the final product (such as bread, edible oil, or sugar). A further alleged consideration is that the government must maintain substantial stockpiles of foods for emergencies. For largely similar reasons, the government has also always been the sole importer of fuel oil, which is the largest single import item. By the second half of the

1950s, the handling of imports by the government was exclusively due to such reasons and had almost no connection with the general balance-of-payments situation: excess demand for these raw materials in the local market was the exception, rather than the rule.

The other category of nonliberalized imports of raw materials may be characterized not by the nature of the goods but by the motivation for restrictions, which are found not on the import but on the export side. As will be explained in Chapter 4, during most of the 1950s, a principal means of encouraging exports was the linking of the right to an import license for raw materials to production for export. In order for this system to be in any way influential, such imports must have involved quota profits. Although the generation of such profits was not an original purpose of the imposition of restrictions, it quite often was the reason for not removing effective restrictions on the raw materials involved. During the late 1950s and early 1960s, restrictions motivated by this purpose mostly disappeared, although it is not entirely clear whether imports were liberalized because the linkage of imports to exports was discontinued as an export policy, or whether the policy was discontinued since the spreading of liberalization of imports of raw materials made it ineffective; quite possibly, it was a double-edged movement in this direction.

By the mid-1950s, therefore, imports of raw materials were largely liberalized, and by the early 1960s this liberalization—in the sense of an absence of excess demand at existing prices—was almost complete. This was by no means the case, however, with other imports. Imports of final goods, particularly final consumer goods, were restricted very effectively, and importation of many items was prohibited. These restrictions were due not to balance-of-payments considerations, but to the policy of protecting import-competing domestic industries. Consequently, this policy also applied to imports of certain raw materials which competed with local production, although these imports were not very sizable.

From the very beginning of the operation of foreign-exchange controls and the QR system, the general directive given to the competent authorities was to prohibit any imports of goods which were produced domestically. A declaration by a local manufacturer to the Ministry of Commerce and Industry that he was producing a given item was usually sufficient basis for the ministry to prohibit imports of that item. During the 1950s a public commission "for the protection of local industries," which was associated with the ministry, operated with the announced purpose of deciding on requests for protection. In effect, it served exactly the opposite purpose: since protection by total import prohibition was afforded almost automatically, the commission handled applications of importers who argued that in their specific cases, imports should be allowed even though they competed with existing local production. The commission was willing to consider such applications on the grounds that local production did not meet necessary quality specifications; that it could not be provided on time; or that its prices were excessive. The commission had a rule for deciding upon the last ground: a gap of over 50 per cent between the local and the foreign price was declared to be excessive.[24] If the good concerned was an input to an export good, a gap of over 25 per cent was considered as the limit. Later, in 1958, an advisory council recommended changing this rule so as to grant local production which competed with imports an *effective* protection rate equal to the premium rate given to value added in exports (at that time, roughly 50 to 60 per cent) *plus* an additional rate that would vary according to the type of good—from a minimum of 15 per cent for raw materials to a maximum of 40 per cent for finished consumer goods.[25] In effect, however, these rules were far from serving as operational policy directives. Decisions were made ad hoc, and occasions on which imports were allowed because local prices were found to be excessive were rare indeed.[26]

The policy of total protection by import prohibition was comprehensive in its application to final consumer goods. With respect to raw materials and investment goods, on the other hand, the principle of protection of local industry could not lead to a clear-cut policy, since the protection of one local industry in these categories was necessarily at the expense of other industries using the raw materials or the machines and tools. Most raw materials could not, in any case, be replaced by local production or a local substitute within a relevant price range. Of those which could, some indeed became subject to import prohibition or restriction, although each case, facing strong opposition, was decided only after much discussion rather than in an automatic fashion; raw materials for the plastics industry are a case in point. Most investment goods, too, particularly imports of heavy industrial equipment, could not, during the 1950s, be feasibly replaced by local products; yet many goods, such as tools or replacement parts, could technically be produced locally. In these instances no automatic protection was granted. Although reliable quantitative estimates are not available, the general impression gained from students of Israel's industry and officials administrating the machinery is that, as a rule, the policy was *not* to protect such local industries by import prohibition. This impression is also borne out by data on effective exchange rates, presented later in this analysis.

On the whole, then, it seems that a clear distinction among categories can be made: protection of industries producing final consumer goods by import prohibition was comprehensive and almost universal; protection of industries producing raw materials and investment goods was sporadic, and probably applied only to the minority of instances in which local production was technically feasible.

vii. GEOGRAPHIC DISCRIMINATION

On the whole, geographic discrimination was never a very important trait of Israel's import policy and of the system of quantitative restrictions. When the QR system was at its peak, during the late 1940s and early 1950s, there was only a minor attempt at governmental restriction of the source of purchase (although, technically, each import license designated the currency of payment and the country of supply, and was not valid for purchases under other circumstances). The reason for this surprising largess was a *relative* abundance, even at that period, of "hard" currencies. Exports in these years covered only a small fraction of imports, which were mainly financed by capital transfers. The latter, in turn, comprised mostly convertible or, at least, semiconvertible currencies. At the beginning, one important source of capital imports was the relatively large frozen sterling reserve (over $100 million), which was freed for use in early 1950 by agreement with the British government and was mostly exhausted during the following two years. Although sterling was not then a perfectly convertible currency, its convertibility within a wide area—in addition to the potential importance of the United Kingdom itself as a source of supply in a free world market—was sufficient to insure that the importer was not normally hampered by having to pay in sterling.

More important over most of the period were capital transfers from the United States, by way of loans and grants from the U.S. government and American Jewry. The dollars received were partly used to finance import surpluses from other countries, where the specific imports required (or allowed) were cheaper. Later, beginning in 1953, reparations payments from the German government became one of the major sources of capital imports. By the reparations agreement, purchases financed from this source were confined (except from a certain fraction used to pay the United Kingdom for oil imports) to German goods in agreed-upon categories. While the goods purchased in this way were not normally more expensive in Germany than elsewhere, the restriction on the use of these funds certainly led to some shift in the commodity composition of imports, although this effect diminished with the years. Beginning in 1954, German restitution payments to individuals were added as still another major source of capital imports. Except during a very short period at the beginning, these payments were made in a currency which was convertible for most practical purposes. All in all, the availability of convertible capital transfers obviated the need for any extensive geographic redirection of the import trade by the government.

Paradoxically, significant geographic discrimination started only in 1953, when the general restrictiveness of the system was already rapidly diminishing. This discrimination clearly originated on the export side. In those years, as some capacity for industrial exports developed, it was assumed that such exports would flow provided there was access to protected foreign markets, the instrument for protection being bilateral trade and payments agreements. Consequently, Israel entered into a number of such agreements, in which the partner country was to purchase from Israel mainly industrial products while Israel would buy in exchange mainly foodstuffs and raw materials. The most important partner country to such an agreement was Turkey, with Yugoslavia coming next. Stated in terms of convertible currencies, Israel's imports from these countries were clearly more expensive than similar goods in the free world market. Obviously, each of the partners to such an agreement tried to sell to the other its most expensive goods and to exclude exports which could compete freely in convertible-currency markets. Although Israel used a specific price mechanism designed to compensate importers for these price differences, as will be pointed out later in this study, this mechanism in itself was quite often inadequate; so the government resorted to the QR system as a means of directing Israel's import trade toward its partner countries.[27]

The share of Israel's trade within the framework of payments agreements in the country's total trade during the 1950s is shown in Table 2-11. The bilateral trade flows with each partner country were roughly in balance most of the time, since autonomous capital transfers from these countries were relatively unimportant. (And since, of course, neither Israel's nor the other partner's currency was convertible, trade surpluses would be something of a waste.) In Israel's over-all trade, imports were several times

TABLE 2-11

**Share of Exports and Imports of Goods
Under Bilateral Payments Agreements, 1950–59**
(percentages of total exports or imports)

Year	Exports	Imports
1950	16.2	6.8
1951	18.3	8.9
1952	18.0	8.1
1953	39.7	13.5
1954	40.5	18.3
1955	40.7	18.6
1956	33.0	17.6
1957	31.4	12.5
1958	23.8	15.0
1959	18.7	14.5

SOURCE: Michaely, *Foreign Trade*, Table 47.

the size of exports; therefore, trade under payments agreements made up a much larger share of Israel's exports than its imports. During the years 1953–55, which appear as the peak period for trade under payments agreements, exports to partner countries under trade agreements constituted about two-fifths of Israel's total exports (and, it should be mentioned, the greater part of its exports apart from the two traditional export items of citrus fruit and polished diamonds); whereas imports from these countries reached only about one-sixth of its total imports. While the latter fraction is not insignificant, it seems that even at the peak, geographic discrimination in imports was not a major factor. From 1956 on, trade under payments agreements declined rapidly, although this was felt more in Israel's exports than in its imports. This decline was due to a combination of factors. One was a more effective use of the aforementioned price mechanism, which helped to direct exports—and to a smaller extent, imports—from the payments agreements countries to the open world market. Another factor was the move of the partner countries toward freer trade and currency convertibility; some important examples were the Netherlands, Norway, and Denmark. Turkey, the single most important partner country throughout the years, did not switch to complete convertibility; but this country, too, moved to rely considerably less on payments agreements after its substantial devaluation of 1958. Thus, beginning in the late 1950s, trade under payments agreements, and therewith administrative interference in the geographic allocation of imports, ceased to be a factor of much significance in Israel.

NOTES

1. In this section I draw substantially on Zvi Zussman, "The Foreign-Exchange Budget as a Forecast of Imports of Goods to Israel" (M.A. diss., Hebrew University, 1959; in Hebrew).

2. The budget year of the government of Israel runs from April to March.

3. Competent authorities for import licensing existed within the following ministries: Finance, Commerce and Industry, Health, Post (Communications), Agriculture, Labor, and Transportation. The division of authority among the ministries was determined according to the purpose of the imports. Thus, for instance, hospital equipment was handled by the Ministry of Health, tractors by the Ministry of Agriculture, etc. Sometimes, naturally, the dividing lines were not entirely clear-cut.

4. The principle of balancing the budget should not be taken too seriously. It should be recalled that the Department of the Budget had wide discretion in determining whether to include various categories of loans as receipts. Likewise, projected expenditures could include additions to foreign-exchange reserves. Such inclusions or exclusions could thus substantially alter the nature of a supposedly "balanced" budget.

5. The government did occasionally report the *number* of unsatisfied applications; for instance, out of a total of 5,435 applications made from May 1949 to February 1950, 1,726 were approved and the rest were either rejected or "remained under con-

sideration." There is no estimate, however, of the size (indicated value of imports) of each category of applications.

6. Partly to increase the proportion of licenses actually used, and to discourage applications intended as "safety margins," the government decided in later years to make applications more costly. After April 1956, an application had to be accompanied by a commitment to utilize the license within a specified time after it was granted, or pay a fee amounting to 10 per cent of the value of the license. This procedure did not work out very well and in March 1958 it was replaced by a requirement to deposit 10 to 20 per cent of the value of a license when it was granted. This requirement was also meant, however, to make imports more expensive and to tighten credit.

7. In a rather involved scheme, and with aid of the Jewish Agency, the government raised a special consolidation loan in the United States which was to be repaid from future contributions of the Jewish communities in the United States. The money was intended for the repayment of hard-pressing short-term foreign loans, and for the establishment of some minimum level of reserves. Since this loan was undertaken not directly by the government, but by the Jewish communities, it appears in balance-of-payments data as a unilateral transfer to Israel.

8. The study was conducted by Michael Rom (Rosenberg), and was summarized in a memorandum entitled, "A Report of the Sub-Committee for the European Common Market and Free-Trade Area on the Possibility of Israel Joining the E.E.C." (in Hebrew). The report was circulated in a few typed copies at the end of 1957.

9. "Imports without payment" was the term commonly applied to this category of transactions. Due to its popularity, it is used here too, although in effect, most of the imports concerned were *not* "without payment." The official term for this category was, indeed, more accurate and appropriate: "imports without allocation of foreign exchange."

10. If and when another source was illegally involved, such as repatriated foreign-exchange holdings of local residents, it had to be disguised as originating from one of these three legal sources.

11. In his budgetary speech of May 1950, the Minister of Finance estimated the rate of extra profits in imports of supposed "gifts" at 60–70 per cent.

12. After April, it will be recalled, the rate was determined by the government. As a result, very few transactions were conducted during the second half of the year in the organized market, to which the data refer.

13. As noted above, these imports constituted at that time 70 per cent of total imports via the IWP market.

14. Yoram Weiss, "Price Control in Israel, 1939–1963" (M.A. diss., Hebrew University, 1964; in Hebrew). Part of this study has been published in English: "Price Control in Israel, 1949–58," Bank of Israel *Economic Review* 37 (March 1971): 68–88.

15. Likewise, by all available accounts—which are obviously casual impressions rather than precise estimates—the quantitative extent of the black market reached its peak in that year.

It should be noted that the ratio of seven, mentioned in the text, is an average around which there was substantial variation. The most extreme item was sugar, for which the black-market price in 1951 was reported to be 25 times the official price.

16. On the strength of this association, it may be inferred that in 1959, a year in which the list of controlled items was reduced to half its size in 1958, the excess of free over controlled food prices must have become very small, perhaps insignificant. This inference would be supported by all available casual impressions: by the late 1950s black markets were rarely mentioned.

17. The ratio between the indices of free-market and official food prices was still over 5 in August 1952, the date to which this part applies.

18. In principle, a black-market rate higher than the formal one could thus exist even with a completely free movement of goods when controls are imposed on capital movements alone. This, indeed, has roughly been the situation in Israel since the late 1950s; during all these years, the black-market rate has been only moderately above the official rate, rarely exceeding the latter by more than 30 per cent.

19. Since the mid-1950s, transactions in the foreign-exchange black market are thought to be only in the neighborhood of $5 million–$10 million annually. The major component of net demand in the market is generally believed to be demand by emigrants, who have not been allowed foreign-exchange allocation for transferring their capital. Another important source—up to the late 1950s—was demand by Israeli tourists, because foreign-exchange allowances for travel were then nil.

20. This applies to the market in Tel Aviv. The rate in the Zurich market, confined mainly to currency notes, was sometimes substantially different, although major movements were similar in the two markets.

21. The substantial rise of the black-market rate in the last quarter of 1956 most probably reflects speculative demand due to the Sinai campaign in October of that year. The rate went down again a short time later. During the rest of the 1950s and 1960s, excluding short-term episodes when the black-market rate obviously rose owing to expectations of imminent devaluation, the excess of the black-market rate over the formal rate normally fell within a range of 10 to 25 per cent.

22. That is, the price-level-deflated effective exchange rate. The index used for the deflation abstracts from illegal markets.

23. For this calculation, defense materials are excluded from imports, since their somewhat erratic behavior has had little to do with economic forces, and may be misleading in the case of conclusions based on year-to-year comparisons.

24. This refers, of course, to prices of the finished product. Since imports of raw materials were mostly free of duty, this gap of 50 per cent could have meant, in some instances, very high protection rates. For industry as a whole the value added in the economy during the mid-1950s was below 50 per cent. With the average level of duties on raw materials being not more than a few percentage points, the 50 per cent gap would have meant an average effective protection rate of at least 100 per cent.

25. On average, this would have determined an effective protection rate quite similar to the 100 per cent effective protection rate implied (on average) in the former rule, in which a 50 per cent difference was allowed in the price of the final good.

26. For some evidence on this point, see Tsvi Goldberger (Ophir), "Protection Policy in Israel" (M.A. diss., Hebrew University, 1957; in Hebrew); and Alex Rubner, *The Economy of Israel* (London: Cass, 1960).

27. As was mentioned earlier, even imports which were presumably liberalized required import licenses, by which the importer could be required to purchase the good in a country other than the one of his choice.

Chapter 3

Liberalization of Protective Restrictions: The 1960s

In this chapter I will deal primarily with the second stage of Phase IV which falls in 1962–68, and which constitutes a distinct episode in the development of Israel's policy of liberalization. This will be followed by a description of the policy pursued during Phase V, beginning in 1969—a policy still too recent for an analysis of its outcome; and by a summary of the liberalization process in Israel.

i. THE POLICY PACKAGE OF 1962

By the late 1950s or early 1960s, we recall, the setting of quantitative restrictions had little to do with general balance-of-payments considerations; the QRs were intended instead to serve as a protective device. Imports of raw materials and intermediate goods were by that time mostly unrestricted. Imports of final goods, on the other hand, particularly of consumer goods, were prohibited whenever they were considered competitive with local production, whether actually under way or merely contemplated.

In the absence of balance-of-payments considerations to stimulate or justify the QR system, much more attention started to be paid to its allocative effects. This concern gathered momentum after the mid-1950s, and by the early 1960s most policymakers were convinced that the protection system led to a substantial misallocation of the country's resources and would have to undergo a radical transformation. This conviction resulted in another "New Economic Policy" [1] (referred to officially as "the program for stabilizing the

58

economy"), which was formally declared by Levi Eshkol, the then Minister of Finance, on February 9, 1962. The policy consisted of eighteen separate points, of which two constituted its backbone: formal devaluation and import liberalization.

The devaluation of 67 per cent, from IL 1.80 to IL 3.00 per dollar, was described as being intended both to help in adjusting the balance of payments and to lead to a unification of the exchange-rate system by the abolition of various other charges or subsidies. The liberalization was described in the following words: "The government will gradually lower the walls of overprotection of domestic industry against imports. In order to make manufacturing and agriculture stand on the basis of cheap and efficient production, the government intends to restrict the ceiling on rates of protective tariffs and to eliminate the quantitative restrictions of imports. Local production will have therefore to compete with imported goods." [2]

The devaluation itself, together with other price adjustments which accompanied it, was clearly used to lower the degree of diversification and discrimination involved in the exchange-rate system. Indeed, it seems that this was the purpose of the devaluation, at least as much as the effective increase in the rate of exchange. While the formal increase in the foreign-exchange rate was close to 67 per cent, the increase in the average effective rate of exchange for exports (that is, in the reward per dollar of value added of exports) was only about 13 per cent. The effective rate for imports increased more substantially—by about 37 per cent—but was still considerably less than the increase in the formal rate of exchange.

On the export side, the difference between the formal and effective rates of devaluation was achieved by the abolition of most export subsidies. Since the subsidies had been applied partly in a discriminatory fashion, their abolition resulted in greater uniformity of the effective-rate system in exports. From the 1962 devaluation date until 1966, the effective rate of exchange applied to most exports was roughly equal to the formal rate of IL 3.00 per dollar. Even when export subsidies were reintroduced, in 1966, the system remained much more uniform than it had been before the 1962 devaluation.[3]

In imports, the lower rate of increase of effective rates—compared with the rate of formal devaluation—was due to the lowering of many tariff rates (as well as the automatic decline of rates which were specific rather than ad valorem—although this factor was not very significant in Israel). The result of this adjustment of tariff rates was a considerable increase in the uniformity of the exchange-rate system, similar to the development in exports—although the import system remained much more heterogeneous and discriminatory than that for exports. The coefficient of variation of effective rates for imports went down from 0.435 in 1961 to 0.268 after the devaluation in 1962. Another impression of this lowering of dispersion in the rate system can

CHART 3-1

Distribution of Importers' Exchange Rates, 1951–54 and 1959–62

(Lorenz curves)

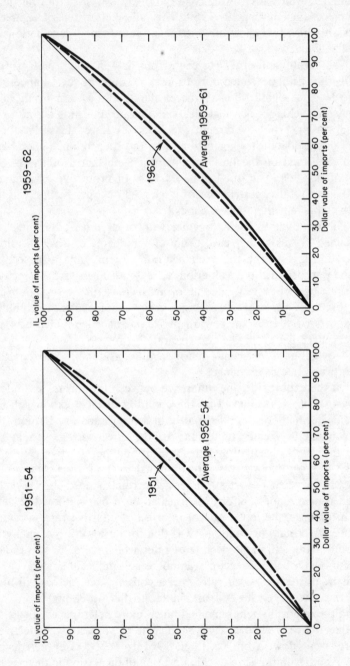

SOURCE: Michael Michaely, *Israel's Foreign Exchange Rate System* (Jerusalem: Falk Institute, 1971; in English), p. 103.

be seen in the Lorenz curves presented in Chart 3-1. The 1962 curve is materially closer to the diagonal than the curves applied to the three years preceding the devaluation—1959, 1960, and 1961 (in which the curves were similar enough to be represented by a single curve). An interesting point is that this pattern is quite contrary to the one observed for the preceding formal devaluation (1952–54). As the Lorenz curves presented in Chart 3-1 show, the earlier devaluation served to widen the dispersion of the rate system, rather than to narrow it.

It is thus clear that changes in the price system—the devaluation itself and the adjustment of tariffs and subsidies which accompanied it—led toward greater uniformity in the exchange-rate system. These changes were not relevant, however, to those imports which were effectively regulated not by tariffs or other price components but by administrative quantitative controls. That category was the object of the liberalization plan, which was the second major policy step declared, the first being devaluation. But, here, it appears that the government was not immediately prepared to state how the declared policy would operate. It evidently had no clear idea of what steps it wanted to take, what the time schedule would be for the introduction of liberalization, or what mechanisms and processes should be involved. As soon as the policy declaration was made, a considerable amount of interministerial negotiations, and even bickering, started over these issues. Within a few months, the following machinery was established.

Liberalization was to be governed by a "Public Commission," consisting of representatives of several government ministries (primarily the Ministry of Finance and the Ministry of Commerce and Industry) and a few organizations (primarily the Histadrut and the Manufacturers Association). The commission, which started its work in May 1962, was to discuss each good separately on the basis of data and recommendations prepared by subcommittees. The latter were to consist of government representatives only, and their work was to be coordinated by the Ministry of Commerce and Industry. The Public Commission was not to initiate discussions, but to consider cases as they were presented by the subcommittees (i.e., by the Ministry of Commerce and Industry). No a-priori time schedule was set for these deliberations. The commission would in each case make a decision on both the quantitative restriction and the tariff level. With regard to the first aspect, the commission could decide to lift restrictions, leave them intact, or leave them intact temporarily pending further discussion on a predetermined date. The commission could *not* mitigate the degree of severity of the restriction, that is, it had to make an "all or nothing" decision, and could not go part of the way. However, the commission was free to determine tariff levels as it saw fit. It could make a once-and-for-all decision on the tariff level; or decide to reconsider the rate within a specified period; or—as it did in a few rare cases—determine a priori a scale of duties decreasing with time. All the commission's decisions were subject to appeal before (jointly) the ministers of Finance and of Commerce and Industry, a recourse which was used only rarely.

The machinery for the introduction of liberalization contained an obvious bias against the declared intention of the liberalization. It assigned a prominent role to the Ministry of Commerce and Industry by giving its representatives a leading position on the Public Commission, including its chairmanship; by yielding only to the ministry the initiative for bringing items before the commission; and by leaving to the ministry the decisive function of preparing all the material for the commission's deliberations. Given the fact that the Ministry of Commerce and Industry stood rather openly against liberalization (and even more emphatically against the devaluation), its prominent position in the machinery must have been very relevant to the process. Moreover, as has been mentioned, no time schedule was set for the introduction of liberalization. In addition, representatives of some of the bodies which were bound to be damaged by each step of liberalization were given a place on the commission and a voice in its deliberations. The machinery in itself was thus not conducive to rapid liberalization.

Liberalization came to be interpreted, at that time, as a process consisting of two stages. The first, which may be termed "nominal liberalization," was a change in the form of protection rather than in its degree or structure: the replacement of the QR system by a system of tariffs or other levies which maintained imports at the same level as under the QR system. The second stage was the reduction of the level of protection through the lowering of tariffs imposed during the first stage of the process. The Public Commission was implicitly or explicitly expected, at least by the Ministry of Commerce and Industry, to handle the first stage only, and to carry out a primarily nominal liberalization.

The commission's work was for the most part completed by the end of 1966—more than four years after this mechanism of liberalization was put in motion. During 1967 and 1968, a few more goods were liberalized. By then, the process of conversion of the system from use of administrative controls to protection by tariffs was supposed to have been concluded. Since then, the second stage of lowering protective import duties has been carried out. The following analysis relates only to the process during the nominal stage, which was carried out by the Public Commission. Later in this chapter, the lowering of duties following this stage will be surveyed.[4]

ii. GUIDING PRINCIPLES IN THE INTRODUCTION OF LIBERALIZATION [5]

In the debate—mainly within the government—which preceded the establishment of the Public Commission, a few principles for the introduction of liberalization were suggested. None of these, however, was formally adopted, and the terms of reference of the commission did not specify any guiding rules or principles for its work. However, the very structure of the mechanism suggested some principles. Others became clear as the commission's work started and progressed. The following is a summary account of the main principles thus revealed.

First, the nature of the mechanism dictated a separate discussion of each good. Thus, the commission was not supposed—nor did it try—to form any general policy or policy rules. No efforts were made, for instance, to determine any over-all protection level leading toward (or away from) uniformity of tariff rates, and so on. It was not bound—and, as a rule, probably did not try—to consider each good within the general context of the economy. From this basic fact, many of the other principles followed.

One guideline, quite often stated explicitly, was "efficiency rather than elimination." That is, the commission's decisions about each industry were supposed to lead to greater efficiency and cheaper production in the industry, but not to its abolition. The commission's concern was thus with technical efficiency, as expressed in the operation of each plant or industry, but not with the economy's efficiency in allocating its resources. The major outcome to which free (or freer) trade would have led thus could not be expected to result from this process of liberalization.

From the rule on efficiency, there followed obviously one that tariffs should not be uniform. This appeared both from the commission's decisions, as will be demonstrated soon, and from explicit statements of the commission's members.[6] The commission appears to have adopted the following procedure in its work: it would try to establish the cost of production of the good, on the assumption that production was handled in an "efficient" way, and then determine a tariff level such that, given the local cost, domestic production would be competitive with imports.[7] Very often, when the tariff level thus required appeared to be extraordinarily high, the commission preferred to leave the administrative prohibition intact rather than replace it by a tariff. On the other hand, in accordance with the preceding principle, in no case did the commission decide that local costs were so high as to justify the admission of imports with an accompanying substantial reduction or elimination of the local industry.

Still another principle, less clear-cut, was that the level of protection depended to some extent on the promised intentions of the industry (this was relevant, of course, mainly when the industry consisted of a single firm). "Good behavior" merited a higher level of protection. Such behavior could be demonstrated in a variety of ways. One was the promise to lower local prices. Another was the submission of plans, usually for technological modernization, which were supposed to reduce the cost of production. A third was, quite often, a plan—sometimes prepared on the initiative of the government—to organize an industry that consisted of several firms into a cartel, on the assumption that this would lead to greater efficiency and lower costs. In other words, determination of the level of protection was often used by the government as a tool to lead the industry to take steps which the government wanted it to adopt.

Another prevalent rule was to tie the level of protection to some extent to the level of exports. A high proportion of exports of the industry's output presumably gave the industry a claim to enjoy a higher level of protection of its domestic sales against imports.

Still another principle was the prevention of "unfair" competition by

TABLE 3-1

Number of References to Guiding Factors in Specific Liberalization Decisions, by Industry, 1962–67
(total number of decisions involved: 179)

Industry	Infant Industry	Protection Against "Brand Name"	Protection from Dumping	Encouragement of Development Regions
Meat, fish, oil, and milk products		1		2
Other food		6	3	5
Textiles	3	6	2	9
Clothing	1			5
Wood and wood products	2	1	2	4
Paper, cardboard, and their products	1		1	3
Leather and leather products	5	2	1	5
Rubber and plastic products	5	9	10	1
Chemicals	3	10	12	8
Nonmetallic mineral products	7	6	5	6
Metal products	2	2	2	1
Machinery	6	9	10	1
Electrical and electronic equipment	4	5	2	6
Transport equipment	5	7	4	9
Total	44	64	54	65

SOURCE: Based on data compiled by Imry Tov from minutes of the Public Commission.

imports. This rule had a few variants. One of the best known concerned compensation for the "good will" of imports; sometimes good will was understood to reflect not just the reputation of a specific imported good but the general "snob value" of imports. It was claimed that an inherently equal local good was judged by the Israeli consumer to be inferior and would merit extra protection to balance this factor. Another significant aspect of this rule was the prevention of "dumping," either by retaining quantitative restrictions or by determining a tariff which would compensate for the dumping element. Dumping tended to be interpreted, in this context, in a fairly broad fashion. Sometimes it even took the form of statements that comparisons of local costs with foreign prices should not be made with the lowest-priced foreign imports, but with some average price abroad (very often, a statement such as "it is good enough if we can compete with European imports, and should not subject the industry to competition with imports from a highly industrialized country like the United States" was made and was accepted).

The major principles involved were not, as a rule, repeated in each of the commission's discussions. On the other hand, the factors relating to good behavior and unfair competition, were usually mentioned specifically in the commission's deliberations and decisions, when they were deemed relevant. The extent of references to these factors is indicated by the data in Table 3-1 which is based on the commission's reports.

iii. THE EXTENT OF LIBERALIZATION

Liberalization was to have been introduced gradually but was to apply, once the process was completed, to all imported items. One sector, however—agriculture—was left out of the process from the start. Since Israel at that time could not have any trade relations with its neighboring countries, all fresh agricultural produce, which made up much of the output of this sector, could not, in any event, be subject to import competition within any relevant price range; consequently the inclusion or exclusion of these goods could not be of much significance. Another important segment of agriculture was of the opposite variety: goods such as wheat, oil beans, animal fodder, and the like could not be produced locally within the relevant price range (at least in the marginal sense, i.e., where domestic production existed, it could not be increased significantly). These were semiliberalized all along: their importation was mostly handled by the government itself; but they were sold locally at something close to the formal rate of exchange and no unsatisfied demand was left. However, still other agricultural goods, such as milk products, sugar, or meat, were at neither extreme, and for these, the issue of liberalization was definitely relevant. After a heated debate on the issue, it was decided to exclude these goods from the scope of the Public Commission. Indeed, to this day (1973), liberalization has not been extended to these agricultural products. The process was thus confined to manufactured goods—admittedly, a much more important sector in its weight in the economy.[8]

TABLE 3-2

Extent of Liberalization, 1962–67

(Israeli pounds in millions)

	Total Value of Industrial Product[a] (1)	Value of Product of Items Added to Liberalization List During Year (2)	Col. 2 as Per Cent of Col. 1 (3)	Cumulation of Col. 3 (4)
1962	IL 3,785	IL 183	4.8%	4.8%
1963	4,469	475	10.5	15.3
1964	5,262	406	7.7	23.0
1965	5,744	692	12.1	35.1
1966	5,767	331	5.7	40.8
1967	5,721	45	0.8	41.6

SOURCE: Data from Imry Tov, "Protection of Domestic Production in Israel, 1962–1967" (M.A. diss., Hebrew University, 1971; in Hebrew).

a. Excluding diamonds.

Table 3-2 is an attempt to summarize the extent of liberalization; it requires, however, a few words of explanation. Column 1 is derived from industrial censuses but column 2 is based on estimates prepared for the discussions of the Public Commission. Comparability and consistency of the two columns are thus not ensured, although errors cannot be very large. It should also be noted that, strictly speaking, a comparison of the two columns is meaningful only if it is done for each year separately. On the other hand, a cumulative series based on column 2, and its comparison with the size of product indicated in column 1, is of very little significance, since both quantity and price changes which took place from year to year in the product of "liberalized" industries would be excluded. Column 3, on the other hand, can be made into a cumulative series if it is assumed that the *proportion* of the product of each good (or at least of the total of liberalized goods), in total manufacturing production, remains unchanged. Where large aggregates are involved such an assumption probably does not lead to grossly misleading estimates.

It appears from column 3 that most of the liberalization process took place between 1963 and 1965, that is, from a year to four years after the declaration of the liberalization policy. By the end of the period, local production in industries competing with liberalized imports amounted to roughly 40 per cent of the total value of the product of the manufacturing sector (excluding diamonds).

It thus seems that a very high proportion of domestic manufacturing—probably over one-half—remained outside the liberalization process.[9] Of these, some had been liberalized before 1963; but the overwhelming majority were still controlled, and thus remained free from import competition when the liberalization process was supposedly completed. Among these nonliberalized industries were the food processing industries classified in the censuses as "manufacturing" rather than "agriculture." The latter sector, as was mentioned earlier, had been explicitly exempted from liberalization when the machinery was set into operation. Also included—again by explicit decision—were all branches of the motor vehicles and motor parts industries. In numerous cases, exemptions from liberalization were granted by ad hoc decisions, owing to binding promises by the government to (usually foreign) investors to give them complete protection from imports for specified (sometimes, rather long) periods.[10] Other industries, estimated to have accounted for 10 to 15 per cent of total manufacturing production in 1967, were candidates for liberalization by the yardsticks used but, in fact, remained subject to administrative regulation (that is, usually, to import prohibition). Still another important segment, amounting to roughly 20 per cent of total manufacturing, consisted of industries which were labeled "irrelevant" for liberalization by the government and which, therefore, were not presented at all before the Public Commission.

The argument of irrelevance is open to doubt. There are obviously many goods which, due to high transportation costs, may be deemed nontradable. Examples often mentioned in the present context in Israel are industries such as clay and sandstone or repair services provided by small shops. A decision to liberalize imports of such goods would be immaterial—from the viewpoint of the local industries involved. Since definitions of goods and industries are usually quite broad, it is likely that in any "industry," some fraction would face import competition within the revelant price range. If the intention of policymakers was indeed to lead the economy toward liberalization, it would be rational to declare such imports free, rather than leave them restricted on the argument that the restriction is "irrelevant." It is therefore quite possible that a fraction of the supposedly irrelevant sector is indeed relevant and that these industries are effectively protected from import competition by quantitative restrictions. There does not seem to be, however, any feasible way of estimating the size of this fraction without undertaking an unduly large amount of very detailed work.

Table 3-3 contains, first, data for 1962–68 on the value of actual im-

TABLE 3-3

**Imports of Goods Subject to Liberalization, by Industry and in Relation
to Other Aggregates, 1962–68**

(imports in millions of dollars)

Industry	1962	1963	1964	1965	1966	1967	1968
1. Food products	0.2	0.2	0.2	0.3	0.5	0.4	0.8
2. Textiles and textile products	8.5	6.8	6.7	6.1	7.1	8.9	11.6
3. Wood and wood products	0.1	0.3	0.5	0.4	1.9	1.3	1.9
4. Paper, cardboard, and their products	0.5	0.5	0.6	0.3	5.7	6.8	12.0
5. Leather and leather products	0.6	0.5	1.2	1.4	2.2	2.1	2.7
6. Rubber and plastic products	1.6	1.3	1.6	1.8	1.6	1.8	1.9
7. Chemicals	1.8	1.0	0.9	1.7	2.8	2.9	2.8
8. Mineral products	1.1	0.8	1.0	1.5	2.1	1.8	1.6
9. Base metals and metal products	6.5	10.4	11.9	11.8	29.1	25.1	24.3
10. Machinery and electric equipment	8.9	13.7	20.2	21.7	28.8	28.7	39.5
11. Optical and scientific instruments	0.5	0.6	0.6	0.8	0.9	0.7	0.8
12. Transport equipment	7.5	5.1	5.4	6.8	5.6	4.8	6.9
13. Miscellaneous manufactures	0.6	1.0	2.3	3.5	3.4	3.1	3.5
14. Total	38.4	42.2	53.1	58.1	91.7	88.4	110.3
15. Ratio of line 14 to total imports of goods (per cent)	6.0	6.3	6.3	7.0	10.9	11.3	9.8
16. Ratio of line 14 to value of industrial product (per cent)	3.0	2.8	3.0	3.0	4.8	4.6	5.2
17. Annual increase in line 14 minus rate of increase of GNP (per cent)		−2.3	11.5	1.1	52.5	−5.0	13.6

SOURCE: Lines 1–13—Compiled from working papers of Imry Tov, based on *Monthly
Foreign Trade Statistics*, Central Bureau of Statistics.

Line 15—Total value of imported goods taken from Table A-10.

Line 16—Total imports (line 14) converted to pounds at formal rate of IL 3.00 per dollar
for 1962–67; IL 3.50 per dollar in 1968. Value of industrial production, from Table 3-2,
column 1, projected to 1968 on the basis of the increase in the index of industrial production
in 1967 and 1968.

Line 17—Data converted to 1950 dollar prices using index of import prices, Table 6-5.
Rates of change of GNP in 1955 IL prices are from Table A-2.

ports of the liberalized items, by industry,[11] and, in the bottom rows of the
table, the size of these imports in relation to other relevant economic aggregates. By the yardstick of the quantitative impact of the liberalization on the
size of imports it appears from the table that, although liberalized imports
were not very substantial even by the end of the process, in 1968, the act of

liberalization was probably not purely "nominal." The increase both in the absolute size of liberalized imports and in their relation to the total imports of goods, the value of industrial product, or the value of GNP took place mainly in 1966; and imports remained on the higher level of that year in the years following as well. It should be noted that, had the effective rate of exchange of these goods—almost twice the level of the formal rate, as will be seen shortly from the tariff data—been used in row 16, the size of liberalized imports in 1966 compared to 1968 would appear to be close to 10 per cent of the value of the local product against which these imports compete. This is not a high figure; it is considerably lower than equivalent figures which represent the weight of imports in the Israeli economy. But it does indicate that domestic production, at least in large sectors, became exposed to some competition from abroad.

iv. LIBERALIZATION AND THE DEGREE OF PROTECTION

The tariff accompanying the removal of administrative prohibition was intended to peg import prices at a level equal to local costs of production (or perhaps slightly lower, so as to force an "efficiency" effort). At these import prices—assuming the existence of equilibrium in the local market for each good before liberalization—imports would be forthcoming not at all or only in very small amounts, following the liberalization. To allow for the possibility of miscalculations, it was understood—although this was not formally part of the commission's decisions—that, should imports in a liberalized industry reach a level of 10 per cent of sales of the local product, this would provide an a-priori case for an appeal by the industry for revision of the commission's decision concerning either the principle of removal of restrictions or the tariff level fixed for the imported good.

Such a guiding principle would, of course, require the commission to determine *effective* rates of protection. In its decisions, the commission naturally imposed nominal tariffs on the final goods, rather than effective tariffs. It also seems that a precise estimate of the level of the effective tariff implied by any of the commission's decisions was not usually presented to the commission in its deliberations. From the minutes of the discussions of the commission it appears, however, that it did consider the level of effective protection. The material prepared by the subcommittees for the commission's deliberations always included an estimate of the ratio of value added in the total value of the final product. Most often, it could be assumed that the import component was free, or almost free, of import duties. In this way, an approximate idea of the level of the effective tariff implied by a given level of the nominal tariff could be gained with little effort. At the same time, it also seems clear that the commission did not, as a rule, attempt to tailor a precisely appropriate effective rate in each case. Rather, it worked within a few main broad categories of nominal tariffs, probably putting each good within that category which would bring the effective rate closest to what the commission considered to be appropriate.[12]

The rates of protection involved in the commission's decisions are presented in Table 3-4. A few of the findings may be highlighted:

First, the average level of the nominal tariff rates, which approached 80 per cent, is probably quite high in comparative terms. It is particularly high in comparison with the average level of import tariffs in Israel at the time of the introduction of liberalization. A simple calculation of averages would have shown an increase of the general level of tariffs resulting from the act of liberalization; but this, of course, would have little meaning, because tariffs replaced quantitative restrictions.

The average level of effective tariffs is, naturally, above the average level of the nominal rates—over 150 per cent. The reason is that imported inputs in production are by and large free of tariffs. Since an import component of 50 per cent is quite common in Israel—most averages of import components of large groups of commodities usually reach a figure of about this size—the ratio of the two averages in Table 3-4 seems indeed very plausible. It may be noted that for all individual goods, without exception, the effective tariff exceeds the nominal tariff,[13] again because of the general absence of tariffs on inputs. The highest ratio of effective to nominal tariffs presented in Table 3-4 is over 3.5 (in the clothing industry). Among individual goods, however, rather than groups, as in Table 3-4, ratios in the range of 5 to 6 are not uncommon.

The average level of effective protection indicated by these calculations is rather high even in comparison with the existing general system of protection in Israel, although the figure of 150 per cent is "gross" rather than "net" protection. Some of this protection serves to compensate for the low level of the formal exchange rate, which was IL 3.00 per U.S. dollar until November 1967. The effective rate of exchange on value added in import substitutes as derived from the average level of effective tariff rates was IL 7.6 per dollar. This was much higher than any figure mentioned, within or outside the government, as an equilibrium exchange rate during this period. The effective rate for exports, to cite an important example, reached only about IL 3.50 per dollar of value added toward the end of the period (that is, prior to the devaluation of November 1967). Likewise, the general level of protection of import substitutes was considerably lower, as will appear from the discussion in the next chapter.

The averages involved are derived from arrays of rates containing a

TABLE 3-4

Means (M) and Dispersions (σ/M) of Nominal Tariff, Effective Tariff, and Effective Exchange Rate, by Industry, 1967

| Industry | Nominal Tariff | | Effective Tariff | | Effective Exchange Rate[a] | | Ratio of Col. 1 to Pre-liberalization Nominal Tariff |
	M (per cent) (1)	σ/M (2)	M (per cent) (3)	σ/M (4)	M (IL per dol.) (5)	σ/M (6)	(7)
Meat, fish, oil, and milk products	72.8	1.107	103.8	1.469	6.1	0.750	1.10
Other food	105.7	0.361	140.4	0.809	7.2	0.535	1.00
Textiles	91.7	0.733	240.6	0.608	10.2	0.429	1.73
Clothing	110.2	1.630	396.7	1.382	14.9	1.103	1.11
Wood and wood products	63.9	0.197	76.5	0.637	5.3	0.275	1.04
Paper, cardboard, and their products	55.6	0.700	74.2	0.766	5.2	0.328	0.95
Leather and leather products	57.7	0.179	78.0	0.336	5.3	0.147	1.12
Rubber and plastic products	88.7	0.537	118.5	0.760	6.6	0.411	0.76
Chemicals	72.9	0.876	132.8	0.956	7.0	0.562	1.72
Nonmetallic mineral products	63.3	1.030	79.8	0.910	5.4	0.456	1.31
Basic metals	39.1	0.497	84.8	0.561	5.5	0.256	2.68
Metal products	57.0	0.503	104.3	0.525	6.1	0.274	1.21
Machinery	55.8	0.254	97.0	0.452	5.9	0.223	1.08
Electrical and electronic equipment	133.2	1.081	253.9	1.052	10.6	0.755	2.18
Transport equipment	115.0	0.568	179.5	0.739	8.4	0.474	2.90
Miscellaneous manufacturing	90.3	0.704	143.2	1.062	7.3	0.572	1.23
Total	78.1	1.018	153.3	1.385	7.6	0.842	n.a.

SOURCE: Tov, "Protection," various tables.

a. Expressed in relation to value added; formal rate = IL 3.00 per dollar.

sizable amount of dispersion. It may be more a matter of curiosity than of importance to observe the *maximum* tariff rates involved in the commission's decisions. These are presented, by main groups of commodities, in Table 3-5. It appears that the nominal tariff rate was on occasion as high as 900 per cent;

TABLE 3-5

Maximum Levels of Tariff Rates, by Industry, 1962–67

Industry	Nominal Tariff Rate (per cent)	Effective Tariff Rate (per cent)	Effective Exchange Rate[a] (IL per dol.)
Meat, fish, oil, and milk products	540	982	33
Other food	290	634	22
Textiles	900	1,664	53
Clothing	900	4,000	124
Wood and wood products	138	499	18
Paper, cardboard, and their products	190	353	14
Leather and leather products	100	198	9
Rubber and plastic products	175	304	12
Chemicals	330	710	24
Nonmetallic mineral products	345	283	12
Basic metals	100	300	12
Metal products	220	400	15
Machinery	83	178	8
Electrical and electronic equipment	550	1,150	38
Transport equipment	177	828	28
Miscellaneous manufacturing	400	1,025	34

SOURCE: Tov, "Protection," Table 4. Data refer to decisions of the Public Commission up to 1967.

a. Expressed in relation to value added; formal rate = IL 3.00 per dollar.

and the effective rate, as much as 4,000 per cent! More interesting, perhaps, is the distribution of nominal tariff rates by industry, which is presented in Table 3-6. There, it seems that nominal tariffs imposed by the commission were concentrated largely (close to 40 per cent of the decisions, and over 50 per cent when weighted by value added of the good) in the range of 60 to 89 per cent. But the very high ratios of over 150 per cent were applied to as much as 10 per cent of the goods. As might be expected, the distribution of effective protection rates (not shown in the table) was more dispersed than that of nominal rates.

The data in Table 3-4 also show a quite wide variation among averages of tariff rates of main industrial groups. Nominal rates varied from 39 per cent (for basic metal) to 133 per cent (for electrical equipment), whereas effective rates ranged from about 75 per cent (paper and wood) to close to 400 per cent (clothing). The average rates for industries would, of course, be of little significance if each of them consisted of a variety of widely dispersed individual rates. Dispersion within each group was indeed quite substantial. Yet, with

TABLE 3-6

**Frequency Distribution of Nominal Tariffs Imposed by Decision
of the Public Commission, by Industry, 1962–67**

(number of decisions)

Industry		Nominal Tariff Rate (per cent)						
	Exempt	1–29	30–59	60–89	90–119	120–149	150+	Total
Meat, fish, oil, and milk products	—	2	2	3	1	—	2	10
Other food	—	2	4	1	3	2	3	15
Textiles	—	9	10	12	6	2	11	50
Clothing	—	3	1	9	2	2	5	22
Wood and wood products	—	—	2	11	1	4	—	18
Paper, cardboard, and their products	—	5	—	9	3	—	3	20
Leather and leather products	1	1	11	5	2	—	—	20
Rubber and plastic products	—	—	7	20	3	2	3	35
Chemicals	2	4	36	15	2	—	3	62
Nonmetallic mineral products	—	6	7	8	2	1	2	26
Basic metals	1	7	14	5	1	—	—	28
Metal products	—	11	23	43	6	2	3	88
Machinery	—	7	28	33	—	—	—	68
Electrical and electronic equipment	—	—	7	21	2	—	7	37
Transport equipment	—	—	1	2	—	1	1	5
Miscellaneous manufacturing	1	3	10	20	3	5	11	53
Total	5	60	163	217	37	21	54	557
Percentage distribution of total	.9	10.8	29.3	39.0	6.6	3.4	10.0	100.0
Weighted by value added of industry	.2	7.5	22.2	51.1	6.7	2.1	10.2	100.0

SOURCE: Tov, "Protection," Table 5; and compilations of other data assembled by Tov.

a few exceptions, the dispersion of rates within groups was considerably lower than it was for all individual goods combined, as may be seen from columns 2 and 4 in Table 3-4. Two important exceptions are the clothing and electrical equipment industries, where dispersion is particularly high. That is, the high average tariff rates in these industries, which were mentioned before, reflect not uniformly high rates within these industries but the impact of a few subindustries with particularly high rates.

From column 7 of Table 3-4, it appears that the nominal tariffs determined by the commission were mostly higher—sometimes substantially so—than the preliberalization tariffs. This relation holds not just for averages of groups of commodities, which are presented in the table, but also for the overwhelming majority of individual goods. This phenomenon may be explained by the fact that preliberalization tariffs, which accompanied the administrative regulation (normally prohibition) of imports, were naturally not intended by and large to provide protection nor, for that matter, to affect the local consumer. They were imposed on a small amount of imports of each good, which were allowed to enter by special provisions, such as those applying to the transfer of capital by immigrants or by repatriating residents. These duties were thus not normally prohibitive by themselves. Hence, the commission usually found that a prohibitive tariff, in the absence of QRs, would have to be higher.

Had we comparisons of pre- and postliberalization *effective* protective rates which incorporated the implied tariffs in the QR system, they would be expected to show, if anything, the opposite difference. Effective rates could not be higher than those implied by the QR system, unless the commission miscalculated or left a wide safety margin for protection, in which case the explicit tariff would partly consist of an irrelevant portion ("water"). On the other hand, when liberalization is effective, the postliberalization effective rate would be lower than the implied preliberalization rate; this would not be true if an effectively liberalized good serves as an input in the production of another liberalized good, but these instances are of very little practical importance. The fact that the liberalization did lead to some increase in imports, as has been shown earlier, thus indicates a lowering, in many instances, of the level of effective protection.

Data about effective protective rates before liberalization do not exist. But the material presented before the Public Commission in its consideration of each good contained estimates not only of the proportion of value added in the good and its total size in the industry, but also of the price of the value added, i.e., an estimate of domestic resource costs (DRCs) in the industry. A comparison of this set with the figures for postliberalization effective protective rates derived from the very same source, that is, from the commission's decisions on nominal rates and the value-added ratios presented to the commission, shows that by and large postliberalization effective rates were higher, sometimes very much so, than the protection implied in the estimates of DRCs. On the average, effective exchange rates implied in the commission's decisions were about twice the estimated DRCs. This seems surprising, in view of the probable intention of the commission to afford each industry a level of protection just sufficient for it to operate at the existing costs in the industry. The discrepancy could have various explanations. One is simply that these are miscalculations, but this would not be consistent with the fact that both sets of calculations are derived from the same set of data as that which was available to the commission. Another is that there was a desire to allow wide safety margins; a corollary desire would be to provide margins not so much for the present as for future stages, when tariff rates were expected to be gradually lowered. Still another explanation is that the commission might have considered *marginal* DRCs to be higher than the estimates of *average* DRCs presented in the calculations, although this could certainly not account for the two-for-one ratio. While all these are plausible explanations, the main reason for the gap probably lies elsewhere, namely, in the unreliability of the estimates of DRCs. It should be recalled that one of the main criteria guiding the Public Commission's work was that of "efficiency": an industry "deserved" protection if it was "efficient." A low estimate of DRC was generally accepted as a proof of efficiency and of the profitability of an industry for the country's economy. In presenting its data, an industry (as well as, very often, government officials responsible for handling it) had a motive for showing a low estimate of DRC. At the same time, it was very common for an industry to demand an effective protective rate which far exceeded that low estimate. The inconsistency was sometimes reconciled by claiming that the estimated DRC reflected not actual costs, but a potentiality that would be realized shortly if the industry were allowed to bloom under continuing protection. In many other instances it was reconciled by the "good will" and "brand name" argument; that is, the DRC estimate was attributed to the "true" value of the local product which was the same as the value of the foreign product with which the local product was being compared, and it was argued that the local consumer unjustifiably discounted from this value in his own evaluation of the two competing goods. In many other instances the inconsistency in the claims was not explained at all, an oversight which was probably helped by the fact that what was explicitly discussed and decided upon was not the effective, but rather the nominal, tariff rate of the good.

v. THE PROGRESSIVE LOWERING OF PROTECTION SINCE 1968

By 1969, what was defined as the first stage of the liberalization process—the period of primarily nominal liberalization—was completed. Since that time, quantitative restrictions have been lifted on imports of several goods still subject to them in 1969. According to estimates of the Ministry of Commerce and Industry, imports competing with 92 per cent of industrial production were liberalized by the end of 1969, and the ratio climbed to 95 per cent by the end of 1972. These figures are probably biased upward; and agricultural produce, we recall, remained subject to quantitative restrictions to a greater extent than manufactures. Yet, it is quite safe to conclude that by 1969, quantitative restrictions were of only small over-all significance.

The stage of gradual lowering of the tariff protection afforded to the "liberalized" sector started at the end of 1968, although a reduction of the tariffs involved, by 10 per cent of the level of each tariff rate, had already commenced in November 1966. This stage had been assumed all along to follow the first stage of nominal liberalization. Its execution was apparently helped by two factors. One was a change, in 1965, in the personalities and approach in the Ministry of Commerce and Industry; the new ministers were more disposed to liberalization. A more important factor was probably the state of the economy. The recession years 1966 and 1967 were considered an inappropriate time to expose domestic production to further competition from abroad, whereas by the end of 1968, full employment had been restored.

In October 1968, a reduction of 15 per cent in the level of each tariff took place. A few months later, in January 1969, a further reduction was carried out, this time in a progressive manner. Tariff rates below 35 per cent were left intact; rates between 35 and 50 per cent were lowered by 10 per cent (of the tariff level); rates in the range from 51 to 75 per cent, by 15 per cent; rates in the range from 76 to 100 per cent, by 20 per cent; and rates exceeding 100 per cent, by 30 per cent.

In August 1969, the government adopted an explicit program of lowering of the protection afforded to liberalized industries, the main guideline of which was the gradual approach toward a uniform "target" rate of *effective* protection. The target effective rate of foreign exchange for value added in import substitution was set at IL 5.50 per dollar. Since the formal rate of exchange was then IL 3.50 per dollar, the implied target rate of effective protection was thus 57 per cent. The rate of IL 5.50 per dollar exceeded the effective rate of foreign exchange for value added in exports in 1969 by about 35 per cent, a figure quite close to the 25 per cent which was very often mentioned in government circles, throughout the years, as the extra premium which import substitution deserved. The target rate was scheduled to be reached by early 1975, through a tariff reduction in six equal installments in January of each of the years 1970 to 1975. The "equal" installments referred to the levels of *effective* protection, which meant, of course, unequal annual reductions of nominal tariffs. The levels of effective protection involved in the existing tariff system are calculated, in the machinery specified in the 1969 decision, by industry subcommittees of the Public Commission, although the full commission as such ceased to have a function in the process of liberalization. Prices of imports from Europe—but not necessarily from the potentially cheapest source if it was outside Europe—are to be taken as "international" prices for the calculations of effective protection rates. In addition, imports considered to be sold at "dumping" prices are expected to be discriminated against by special levies or by quantitative restrictions. Likewise, in cases where imports are considered to have a "snob appeal," the target effective exchange rate is raised by IL 0.5 per dollar of value added. All these provisions resemble, of course, the principles observed in the earlier deliberations of the Public Commission in carrying out the process of nominal liberalization.

The first round of tariff reductions within this declared program occurred in January 1970, when nominal tariffs were lowered by 5 to 15 per cent of the tariff levels. In January 1971 a similar reduction took place, although it applied only to a fraction of the imports concerned, since the act was intended on that occasion to take into account tariff concessions made during 1970 in connection with Israel's agreement with the European Economic Community. This was true also for the third reduction (delayed from January to April of 1972), in which tariff rates were lowered by 5 to 18 per cent of the nominal tariff level. Another tariff reduction, in the same degree, was undertaken two months later, in June 1972. Following the formal devaluation of August 1971, in which the exchange rate was raised from IL 3.50 to IL 4.20 per dollar, the target effective exchange rate was raised by about the same proportion—from IL 5.50 to IL 6.50 per dollar of value added; that is, the implied effective protection rate came close to 55 per cent—about the same level as before the devaluation.[14] In January 1973, tariffs were lowered so as to result in a reduction of the excess of the effective exchange rate for value added over the new target rate by 35 per cent. Finally, effective May 1973 but promulgated in February 1973, tariffs were further lowered across the board by 15 per cent of the nominal tariff levels (or 10 per cent of the specific tariffs).

Since the tariff reductions have been made on changing bases, it is impossible to compute the total reduction by simply adding up the whole sequence of individual reductions; an estimate of the total reduction would require careful research, which has not yet been carried out, because most of the tariff reductions are of very recent vintages. As a guess it may be assumed, on the basis of the quantitative description here, that since the end of 1966, and primarily since late 1968, effective protective rates have been lowered by over half of their excess in 1966 or 1968 over the implied target rate.[15] It may be assumed that some, perhaps many, tariff rates had "water" in them; so reductions of these tariffs within a given range had no impact. Yet, the tariff reductions undertaken thus far within this stage of the liberalization process seem impressive and significant in lowering the average level and the dispersion of rates of protection of industries formerly shielded by quantitative restrictions. Likewise, it appears that the declared policy of 1969 has been carried out approximately as scheduled; it may thus be expected that by 1975, the major fraction of the element of discrimination in the system of protection of liberalized industries will have disappeared.

An element which may be working in the opposite direction should, however, be noted at this point. Since 1968, military purchases of locally produced industrial goods have grown very substantially; although their size has not been disclosed, there is no doubt that they constitute a significant proportion of the country's industrial output. As will be pointed out in the next chapter, purchases of military imports have always been made at a low rate of exchange. Usually, this has meant the formal rate; that is, military imports have been free of duty; but since August 1971, they have been subject to the general import levy of 20 per cent which was imposed a year earlier. Details of the purchasing policy for military goods are not publicly known. It seems that purchasing agencies are generally instructed to buy from the cheapest source. If such a policy is carried out universally, it would mean that the relevant local industrial sector faces competition from imports at a low effective rate of exchange which includes no tariff duties beyond the general 20 per cent levy. It is believed, however, that the purchasing agencies are allowed to deviate from the "lowest-cost" principle when they see a reason for preferring to maintain local production of a specific military good, and that they have a wide discretion in interpreting this rule. It is thus possible that some military purchases of local goods are made at prices which imply high rates of effective protection—although, again, not much evidence is available on this point. To the extent that this phenomenon is widespread, the expansion of domestic military purchases serves to raise the level (and dispersion) of effective protection.

vi. GENERAL REMARKS ON THE PROCESS OF LIBERALIZATION

Severe quantitative restrictions on imports were imposed in Israel in the late 1940s and early 1950s, due to very intensive pressures on the balance of payments. The progressive devaluation of 1952–54, which was part of the shift to the use of the price mechanism, relieved most of these pressures. The absence of a general balance-of-payments motivation for quantitative restrictions since the mid-1950s led, indeed, to a rapid liberalization of most of the country's imports, including a large majority of the imports of raw materials and most imports of investment goods. These became effectively free of meaningful restrictions within a short span of years.

This did not apply, however, to imports which compete with actual or potential local production, mainly imports of finished or semifinished manufactures of consumer goods, none of which were liberalized during the 1950s or early 1960s. Only in 1962 was a policy of liberalization of such imports declared. And even then, it appears that the actual execution of this policy will have taken close to fifteen years. Of these, some seven years—from early 1962 to late 1968—were required for the first stage, which was primarily a nominal liberalization consisting of a switch from QRs to equal protection by tariffs; and seven or eight more years—from late 1968 to, as it seems now, 1975 or 1976—for the effective abolition of this protection or its drastic reduction. In general, if the rest of the liberalization process is carried out roughly on schedule, competitive imports will be effectively liberalized—not just in the sense of switching from one form of protection to another, but in the sense of removing entirely the protection originally afforded by the QRs —more than twenty years after the original balance-of-payments motivation for the QR system has disappeared.

The stage of nominal liberalization of competitive imports carried out between 1962 and 1968 was certainly much longer than was either necessary for technical reasons or anticipated at its inception. Indeed, when the liberalization policy was declared, in February 1962, such a stage was not contemplated. There is also no logical reason why an effective liberalization should necessarily consist of two stages—a nominal stage and a stage of tariff reduction. Yet it would be wrong to conclude that the period of nominal liberalization was a complete waste.

First, despite the general lack of effectiveness, in several instances liberalization was effective rather than purely nominal: it led to lower protection, an increase of imports, and probably some reallocation of domestic resources.

Much more important, however—and less easily measured—was the effect on new industrial ventures. Even though protection of established enterprises remained mostly intact, it was no longer the general practice to afford protection by total import prohibition to any investment in a new industrial enterprise. Since the introduction of liberalization, protection had to be afforded mainly by the imposition of tariff duties; and such protection very often could not be as high as that which would have been obtained by total import prohibition.

This points to another favorable aspect of the liberalization, one which, again, is not subject to measurement but is probably of considerable importance. Nominal liberalization, achieved by limiting imports by levying tariffs rather than by administrative regulation, makes explicit the *price* involved in the protection. This helps to strengthen public resistance to the granting of protection. It probably results in setting some ceilings to the protection afforded to new industries and contributes to stronger pressures for the lowering of existing protective rates.

Thus, while there is indeed no logical need for an effective liberalization to be implemented in this way, rather than by a single act, the gradual approach taken may prove to be a more feasible process, owing, partly to the benefits of making protective rates explicit. When these rates are known, it may be easier to estimate the effect on each industry of reducing or eventually eliminating tariffs. This also facilitates the *gradual* introduction of import competition; and it is hard to expect any import liberalization of goods whose local production has been sheltered all along to be implemented in any but a gradual fashion.

If any more general lesson can be learned from the Israeli experience, it is that once an economy has been subject to exchange control and import prohibitions for a long period, and its whole industrial structure has been determined accordingly, it is very difficult to introduce changes which open the economy to import competition. As long as liberalization *raises* effective protective rates, as liberalization of imports of raw materials most often does, it may be easy to implement. But an effective liberalization of finished or semi-finished manufactured goods, which generally lowers effective protection, faces strong objections from a sizable fraction of the economy's industries. Even if governments were entirely free to act, such liberalization would have to be introduced only gradually, owing to the quite high costs involved in the short run in the transition from one industrial structure to another.

NOTES

1. Often referred to in Israel as the "Second New Economic Policy," to distinguish it from the policy act of February 1952.

2. From the text of the policy declaration of the Minister of Finance on February 9, 1962.

3. The development of the system of export premiums will be described in the next chapter. It will be noted there that even before the 1962 devaluation, the variance of effective exchange rates was much smaller in exports than in imports. Substantial movements toward uniformity of the effective rates of exchange and rates of protection could thus emerge primarily from changes on the import side.

4. As will be mentioned, some lowering of tariffs also took place between 1966 and 1968, while the transformation of the "nominal" stage was still under way. These tariff changes are abstracted from in the following quantitative analysis.

5. The discussion in this section and the next two draws to some extent on Haim Barkai and Michael Michaely, "More on the New Economic Policy" (in Hebrew), *Rivon Le'Kalkala* [Economic quarterly] 39 (August 1963): 2–24; and more substantially, on Imry Tov, "Protection of Domestic Production in Israel, 1962–1967" (M.A. diss., Hebrew University, 1971; in Hebrew). Most of the dissertation was published in Nadav Halevi and Michael Michaely, eds., *Studies in Israel's Foreign Trade* (Jerusalem: Falk Institute and Hebrew University, 1972; in Hebrew), pp. 129–173. Part of the study appeared in Tov, "Import Liberalization Policy in Israel, 1962–1967" (in English), Bank of Israel *Economic Review* 37 (March 1971): 28–51.

6. A typical quotation: "To open trade in all goods at a uniform tariff would be the utmost absurdity. It must be realized that one industrial branch or industrial good is never like the other" [A. Dovrat (director of the Ministry of Commerce and Industry's Industrial Division), *Symposium on Problems of Domestic Protection* (Jerusalem: n.p., 1963; in Hebrew), p. 2].

7. A similar working rule, in the operation of the Indian tariff commissions in the 1950s, has been noted by Padma Desai, *Tariff Protection and Industrialization: A Study of the Indian Tariff Commission at Work, 1946–1965* (Delhi: Hindustan, 1970).

8. It will be recalled that by 1970, the share of manufacturing in the national product was about 26 per cent versus 6 per cent for agriculture; the corresponding shares of the two sectors in employment were 26 and 9 per cent.

9. As was mentioned earlier, some goods were liberalized during 1968, while Table 3-2 only covers the period up to the end of 1967; but these cases were very few.

10. Such promises very often also included the commitment to assure the investor a completely monopolistic position by preventing the local establishment of any competing plant during the specified period.

11. To be precise, these are annual imports of 1,029 items which had been liberalized by 1968; in each of the preceding years, some of these items were not yet liberalized. The table thus shows both the effect of additions to the list of goods liberalized in each year and the cumulative effect of liberalization in earlier years.

12. Since the mid-1950s, protection has generally been discussed by industry, government, or academic economists in Israel in terms of effective rather than nominal tariff rates.

13. This difference does not appear in Table 3-4, which is confined to categories rather than to individual goods.

14. After the 1971 devaluation the average effective exchange rate for value added in exports was about IL 5.20 per dollar. The target rate in imports thus exceeds the current export rate by 25 per cent, instead of the 35 per cent found in the comparison for 1969.

15. If we make the reasonable assumption that the target effective exchange rate of IL 6.50 per dollar of value added is roughly the same as the present equilibrium exchange rate, then the implied target "net" effective rate of protection would be zero. See the discussion in the next chapter.

Chapter 4

Protection Through the Price Mechanism

In the two preceding chapters, I surveyed and analyzed the system of quantitative restrictions, and pointed out the gradual transformation of Israel's trade policy from intervention through these restrictions to the use of the price mechanism. In the present chapter, the forms of discriminatory intervention through the price mechanism will be surveyed briefly, their quantitative significance will be estimated, and the major patterns of the system will be analyzed. I shall start with a description of the main instruments through which price intervention was exercised—whether or not such intervention was the function assigned to each instrument by the government.

i. METHODS OF PRICE INTERVENTION IN IMPORTS [1]

The major local determinant of the price of imported goods and services (i.e., of the effective exchange rate for imports) was generally the formal rate of exchange. As was mentioned earlier, a formal system of multiple exchange rates existed for about two and one-half years, from February 1952 to the summer of 1954. This involved—and was intended to involve—a considerable degree of discrimination among various uses of foreign exchange, as will be reflected later in the data.

The second most important element of price intervention was, naturally, the tariff system. It, too, as could be expected, involved a considerable degree of discrimination among various imported goods. As will be seen later, the formal rate together with the tariff always constituted, for the aggregate of imports, the overwhelming component of the effective exchange rate. Yet for various individual goods and services, some other forms were quite often of quantitative significance. Since these forms are somewhat less self-explanatory than the formal exchange rate or the tariff, they will be mentioned here at greater length.

Special Levies.

Unlike customs duties, special levies on imports are not enacted into law by the Knesset (the Parliament), but by administrative decree (although subject to approval by the Knesset's Financial Committee), and are presumed to be temporary. Such levies have been important mainly in two periods.

In the first, from the mid-1950s to the early 1960s, levies of two kinds were mostly intended to replace QRs. The episode of 1956, in which imports of a few major raw materials were liberalized, was accompanied by the imposition of special levies on these imports. Likewise, when the scrip system (discussed in Chapter 2, section iii) was abolished, the importation of "luxury" foods was allowed through the use of a so-called parallel market, in which imports were subject to high, special levies (as well as high tariff duties).

The second episode of significant use of import levies—on a much wider scale—began in August 1970 and is still under way. On that date, a general import levy of 20 per cent of the c.i.f. value of imports was imposed. This levy was clearly considered a partial substitute for devaluation, for it was imposed at a time when external reserves became critically low. As with other tax increases which preceded it by a few months, this levy also was intended to improve the country's balance-of-payments position by reducing the government's excess demand. Although a few important categories are exempt,[2] and it is applied in any case only to the importation of *goods,* not services, this is a widely uniform levy, thus differing materially in nature as well as in size from the special levies of earlier periods.

Equalization Funds and the Commercial Account.

These two instruments served to perform rather similar functions; but the former pertained to private transactions, whereas the latter involved the government's trading activity.

Equalization funds—for food, agriculture, and oil imports—were inherited from the British mandatory government. Originally, they were intended to ensure that the local price of an imported good would be stable, regardless of the foreign price actually paid in each import transaction, by paying compensation in cases of high foreign prices and appropriating the gain in instances of below-average foreign prices. Thus, the net income of the fund over a reasonable length of time was supposed to be approximately nil. With time, however, the funds became more an instrument of longer-term taxation or subsidization of the imports involved than a stabilizing device. This was particularly true of fuel imports, which were, in effect, taxed through the fuel equalization fund during the late 1950s and early 1960s, when a fall in foreign prices was not accompanied by a similar change in local prices, which remained stable. However, prices were also kept stable after the devaluation of February 1962 as well as after the devaluation of November 1967, thus converting the tax element in this arrangement to a subsidy. The 20 per cent levy of August 1970 again was not reflected in the local price of the product. Only in the spring of 1971 were local prices of fuel raised substantially, to an extent which still fell short of the total impact of the three devaluations, i.e., the formal devaluations of 1962 and 1967 and the general import levy of 1970.

The Commercial Account was a bookkeeping device through which the government's trading operations were reflected. As will be recalled, imports of major food materials (mainly wheat, sugar, edible oil materials, and milk products) have been handled exclusively by the government itself (through the Ministry of Commerce and Industry). Local prices of these goods are not necessarily equal to the foreign price multiplied by the formal rate of exchange and are, as a rule, kept stable for long stretches of time. Surpluses and deficits in the Commercial Account are thus created. A surplus amounts to a tax on imports; and a deficit, to a subsidy. While the aggregate surplus or deficit in the Commercial Account was not substantial in any given year, it reflected on occasion rather significant, albeit offsetting surpluses and deficits in the accounts for individual goods.

Other Subsidies.

Most import subsidies were handled through equalization funds and the Commercial Account. The most important exception was a subsidy for "rate differentials," which existed on a significant scale for about two years—from August 1954 to late 1956. In August 1954, it will be recalled, the higher formal rate of IL 1.80 per dollar was established for all imports. It was decided, however, that imposition of the higher rate would be only nominal for the imports of a few essential goods, which had been previously imported at one of the lower rates. This was done by granting these imports special subsidies, "rate differentials," which served to offset the higher formal rate. These subsidies gradually declined until by the end of 1956 they had practically disappeared.

ii. METHODS OF PRICE INTERVENTION IN EXPORTS

Although, as will be seen later, price intervention in exports had a lower impact on the economy than did the intervention in imports, in the former the devices were more varied and their explanation less obvious. They will therefore be described at somewhat greater length.

Besides the formal exchange rate, there were four categories of devices which affected export revenues: premiums on output, premiums on inputs, subsidies for exports through import entitlement programs, and "branch funds," which to an extent combine elements of the three other measures.[3]

Premiums on Output.

In one form or another, output premiums on exports have existed throughout almost the entire period with the exception, perhaps, of the years 1962–65, when they were confined to a few individual cases.

Until 1956, export premiums were given in a largely haphazard and varying manner. Starting in December 1949, premiums were granted on many export goods, mostly at a rate of 10 to 12 per cent of the total value of exports. In May 1950, this was changed so that premiums were granted on value added in exports, rather than on the total value. With the formal devaluation of February 1952, these premiums were discontinued; some special premiums granted from then until 1955 were usually intended to solve specific problems involved in the process of transition from lower to higher formal rates of exchange.[4]

In the period 1956–61 premium arrangements reached an apogee, and a nearly "classic" use of this device was demonstrated. This era started in February 1956, when a premium of IL 0.50 per dollar of value added in exports was introduced. The distinctive features of this arrangement were, first, its widespread application: it was presumably universal and uniform, although it excluded the two largest "traditional" export industries, citrus fruits and polished diamonds[5] (as well as exports of services); and second, its determination on the basis of *value added,* rather than total value. Under this plan, an exporter would be granted a rate of IL 1.80 per dollar (the formal rate) plus the premium (that is, a total of IL 2.30 per dollar when the plan was introduced) for the *net* value added in the economy, whether it was value added by his own production or in other local firms. The import component, on the other hand—again, whether it was inputs imported directly for his own production (the direct component) or imports involved in inputs bought from other local firms (the indirect import component)—would be granted only the formal rate of IL 1.80 per dollar. This was the rate at which the exporter also bought imported inputs, after taking into account the "drawback" plan, which freed imports for exports from import duties (although the indirect import component introduced a few complications on this score). While in principle the value added under this plan was supposedly calculated for each individual exporter, it was, in effect, calculated only for export industries as a whole, and was recalculated for each industry, if at all, only at long intervals.

Besides the general premium plan outlined above, a few other premium arrangements existed during the period 1956–61. Some of these were in effect confined to specific export industries and did not amount, in the aggregate, to any substantial sum. In addition, however, a general plan of specific premium rates for "marginal" exports went into effect in early 1959. The intent of the plan was to raise premiums without adding a rent element by paying higher premiums only for increases of exports. Generally, this meant an increase over the 1958 level of exports of a whole industry;[6] but the committee that determined premium rates for each industry interpreted this principle in a variety of other ways. Most often, the "marginal" premium rate was IL 1.20 per dollar of value added, instead of the general premium rate of IL 0.85 per dollar effective at that time, that is, there was an added premium of IL 0.35 per dollar above the general premium rate.

With the formal devaluation of February 1962, both the general premium arrangement and most of the specific ones were abolished. The most important exceptions were premiums for exports of the textile industry, a branch which had also enjoyed favorable treatment prior to the devaluation. In this industry, a substantial premium, partly carried out through a "branch fund," remained in effect. In a few other export industries, too, "branch funds"—which will be described later—provided subsidies, although on a smaller scale. But for the large majority of Israel's exports, premium elements after the devaluation became nil or insignificant. This remained true for over four years. Only in early 1966 was a premium plan reintroduced, in a manner which has remained in force ever since.

This plan, which was established in April 1966, has been disguised by the name "rebates of indirect taxes" but has nothing to do with those or any other taxes. Unlike in the premium plan of 1956–61, premiums in the current one are specified for the *total* rather than the *added* value of exports. The premium rate varies, however, according to the ratio of value added in the industry, with all industries grouped into particular classes according to average value-added ratios: the lower the value-added ratio of the class, the lower the premium rate granted to exports of industries in that class. It will be recalled that under the premium-for-value-added plan of 1956–61, ratios of value added were also ordinarily calculated for a whole industry, and usually not recalculated periodically. The difference between the two plans is thus not as radical as it may seem, and consists mainly in a reduction of the number of "classes" of industry from several hundred to just a few, thus discriminating in favor of the low-value-added industry and against the high-value-added industry within each class.

The premium rates involved in the plan were changed several times. Of the six changes until the end of 1971, four were upward; the two downward changes accompanied the episodes of formal devaluations in November 1967 and August 1971. The premium rates were lowered to offset part of the increase in export rewards emerging from the devaluation.

The premium rates under the plan of 1956–61 and under the one operating since 1966 are presented in Tables 4-1 and 4-2.

TABLE 4-1

Rates of Export Premiums, 1956–61
(Israeli pounds per dollar of value added)

Year	General Plan	Citrus Fruit[a]	Shipping	Aviation
1956[b]	.50–.70	—	—	—
1957		—	—	—
1958		.25	—	—
1959	.85	.36	.12	
1960		.50	.36	.85
1961		.70		

SOURCE: Michael Michaely, *Israel's Foreign Exchange Rate System* (Jerusalem: Falk Institute, 1971; in English), Table 2-5.

a. For the citrus industry, rates refer to agricultural years (October to September).

b. From February to July 1956, IL 0.50; from then on until January 1957, IL 0.70.

Premiums on Inputs.

Most premiums in this category were relatively unimportant. The only instance of a significant subsidy on a specific input was for fuel used in the cement industry, where it is an important cost element. Once in a while, transportation costs, either local (by train) or on international routes (by sea) were subsidized, usually through low rate quotations by government-owned shipping companies. Another instance of a transportation subsidy is the exemption of export shipments from the major part of port dues: these shipments are charged only one-fourth of 1 per cent of the value of the shipment, whereas import shipments are charged 2 per cent, the actual cost of producing

TABLE 4-2

Rates of Export Premiums, 1966–71

(Israeli pounds per dollar of total value)

	Export Class		
Value-added ratio of export class (per cent)[a]	26–45	46–65	65+
Apr. 1966–Oct. 1966	.05	.08	0.11
Nov. 1966–Feb. 1967	.11	.18	0.26
Mar. 1967–Oct. 1967	.18	.26	0.36–0.45
Nov. 1967[b]–Jan. 1970	.10	.20	0.35
Feb. 1970–July 1970	.20	.35	0.55
Aug. 1970–Dec. 1970[c]			
Gross	.80	.90	1.05
Net	.27–.41	.51–.65	0.80–1.05
Jan. 1971–July 1971[c]			
Gross	.83	.95	1.12
Net	.30–.44	.56–.61	0.87–1.12
Aug. 1971[d]–date[c]			
Gross	.85	.87	0.89
Net	.22–.39	.43–.58	0.60–0.89

SOURCE: Based on information from Ministry of Commerce and Industry.

a. Industries with value added of 25 per cent of total value of product or less were in principle not entitled to export premiums. Exceptions on an ad hoc basis may, however, be found.

b. Date of change in formal rate from IL 3.00 to IL 3.50 per dollar.

c. The net rate is exclusive of the import levy of 20 per cent imposed in August 1970, for which exports were not entitled to a rebate under the "drawback" arrangement.

d. Date of change in formal rate to IL 4.20 per dollar.

the services for which dues are levied lying probably somewhere between the two rates.

The only important widespread subsidy of an input was the plan for providing cheap short-term financing for exports; that is, providing a subsidy to help defray the cost of interest on short-term capital loans.[7] Facilities of one kind or another existed during the 1950s; but a general, almost universal, plan was established in 1962, and with only minor modifications has remained in effect to this day. In this setup, short-term financing for industrial exports is provided (from funds to which both the Bank of Israel and the commercial banks contribute) under three headings: for value added; for the import component; and for the time lag between shipment and receipt of money (that is, short-term credits provided by the Israeli exporter to his customers). Financing for value added is quoted in Israeli currency; whereas financing for the other two purposes is quoted in foreign currency. The rate of interest charged on this credit has been mostly 6 per cent. For credit quoted in foreign exchange, this amounted on the average to only a small subsidy, since the borrower (i.e., the exporter) has to carry the risk of a devaluation. Indeed, the extent to which exporters have availed themselves of this part of the credit scheme has fluctuated widely in accordance with the state of expectations of devaluation. Financing of value added, on the other hand, which is denominated in local currency, has amounted to a very substantial subsidy on the use of capital. The charge of 6 per cent being constant, the rate of this subsidization varies, of course, with changes in the market rate of interest, which is closely associated with changes in the rate of price increases. On the average, it may be assumed that the 6 per cent rate of interest represents a subsidy of about 10 per cent per annum of the credit used.[8]

The amount of credit from this source to which an exporter is entitled depends not only, of course, on the size of his exports but also on the length of the "production cycle," which is determined separately for each industry. It may well be the case that production cycles are generally longer in these calculations than is actually warranted by the production process. Moreover, financing is provided in a lump sum for the whole length of the cycle as calculated even though costs actually accumulate during the cycle rather than being all incurred at its inception. It may thus be assumed that short-term financing from the export fund covers more than the full extent of credit actually required and probably very often by a considerable margin; the excess credit is used, of course, in the exporter's other operations, namely, for production for the local market. The combination of the ample size of this credit and the highly favorable interest rate on it makes the subsidy element involved in this scheme a significant factor. From 1962 to 1966, when no general premium arrangement was in force, this was actually the main subsidization element granted to exports, although its size was obviously much lower than that which was provided by the direct premium schemes for output. It has been estimated—albeit, by the use of arbitrary assumptions about interest rate differentials—that subsidies provided through credit from export funds amounted in 1966, for instance, to roughly 8 per cent of the effective rate of exchange for value added (that is, about IL 0.3 per dollar) in exports of diamonds, and 3 per cent in other industrial exports. In later years, these rates have risen, since (with accelerated price rises in the economy) nonsubsidized interest rates increased. Such figures, it should be stressed, are only tentative illustrations; but they do point out that subsidization of exports through cheap credit facilities was of some importance during the 1960s and later as well.

Import Entitlement.

Subsidies through import entitlements were instituted in one form or another starting in the late 1940s. At first, however, they were sporadic, nonuniform, and relatively unimportant. This may be explained, perhaps, by the predominance of exports of citrus fruit and polished diamonds, Israel's two traditional export items in those earlier years. Since almost all the arrangements of this nature confined import entitlements to inputs which were "in the line of production" of the export industry, these two branches did not stand to gain by such arrangements. Since these were strictly export industries, their inputs were never restricted.

With the growing importance of exports of assorted manufacturing industries, the retention-quota plans grew in significance. In May 1953, the Pamaz[9] plan—the major form of the retention-quota system—was established in its full-fledged form. In this plan, all exporters (except those of citrus fruit and diamonds) were entitled to use *all* their export proceeds to buy imports of materials in their "line of production." Partly—in proportion to the import component in exports—these imports would be used for further production of another "cycle" of exports.[10] The other part, equivalent to the value added in exports, would thus be left for the purchase of imported inputs for production for the local market. Since at that time such imports were mostly restricted, whereas prices of the finished goods in the local market were already largely free, this import entitlement generated a quota profit. Since the imports of each exporter were confined to his "line of production" and Pamaz rights could not be transferred, the rates of extra profits differed, of course, from one industry to another.[11]

The Pamaz arrangement reached its peak around 1956 and then declined until it disappeared in 1959. This decline was partly by design and partly due to changing circumstances. The first factor which contributed to diminish the importance of the system was the introduction, in 1956, of general premiums. An exporter wishing to avail himself of the premium payment had to sell his foreign-exchange proceeds to the Treasury, thus forgoing his Pamaz rights. Given this alternative, many exporters opted for the premium rather than the Pamaz right.[12] Another important influence in the same direction was the process of gradual liberalization of imports of raw materials: obviously, Pamaz rights are of no significance when the needed inputs can be freely imported.[13] In addition, from 1956 on, the government took a number of measures limiting the extent of Pamaz rights.[14] At the end of 1959, the program was abolished altogether.

Besides the general Pamaz plan, a few other import-entitlement arrangements existed, mainly during the late 1950s. These "linkage" rights were sporadic and confined to a few specific industries. Exporters in those industries would be granted an import right in a specified ratio to the size of their exports (a ratio of one-to-one was quite common). Besides their sporadic nature, linkage arrangements differed from the Pamaz plan in two important aspects. First, it will be recalled that the owner of a Pamaz right had to use part of this right to purchase imported inputs for his exports; the excess profits from sales on the local market would be derived, therefore, only from the value added in exports. The owner of a linkage right, on the other hand, would finance his imported inputs by buying foreign exchange from the Treasury, at the official rate, thus deriving excess profits from the *total* value of his exports. Second, the user of a Pamaz right had to forgo the government's direct export premium, whereas exporters who entered into a linkage agreement could sell their export proceeds to the government at the premium rate, thus enjoying both the premium and the excess profits derived from imports.

Branch Funds.

Starting in 1959, and mainly since the early 1960s, a number of so-called branch funds were established in a form designed primarily to encourage exports. The number of such funds was limited to about seven or eight, but they related to quantitatively significant export industries (mainly in textiles). During the first half of the 1960s, before the reintroduction of general premiums, branch funds were the main source of export subsidies, although they were applied to only certain segments of exports. Each branch fund had its own unique structure and method of operation. In general the method of export subsidization through the funds was a combination of governmental premium and compensation through sales of restricted imports in the local market. But to some extent, the funds were merely cartel arrangements, backed by the government, which allocated sales among the local and foreign markets.

iii. EXCHANGE RATES AND PROTECTIVE RATES IN IMPORTS AND EXPORTS

For an analysis of the effect of intervention on the economy through the price mechanism, the various components of intervention have to be added and transformed into estimates of effective exchange rates and effective protective rates. The most comprehensive data available for the Israeli economy relate to effective exchange rates for imports and exports of goods. For the aggregates, as well as for large categories, data constructed by approximately consistent methods and definitions are available for the period from 1949 through 1971 (at this writing). Data by detailed commodity classification have been constructed for a large part of this period, namely, for the years 1949–62. The effective-exchange-rate data for exports relate to *value added* but for imports, they related to gross value, i.e., to final values of each imported good.[15] Thus, while for exports these data easily yield protective rates, this is not the case for imports. Estimates of protective rates for imports are thus much less abundant, as are also estimates of domestic resource costs (DRCs) in various industries.

Appendix B contains a discussion of the concepts and methods involved in the estimates of effective exchange rates and their relationship to effective protective rates. The data for the aggregates of imports and of value added in exports are presented in Table 4-3. As is explained in Appendix B, the transformation of export rates into effective protective rates for exports is straightforward, and will be presented shortly. On the other hand, estimates of protective rates for import substitution cannot be derived with the same ease. Likewise, estimates of DRCs in Israel are, unfortunately, sparse and often not very reliable. Although the concept of "the price of value added" (or, as it has been usually termed in Israel when applied to import substitution, "the value saved") has been in use as a policy guide in Israel as far back as the mid-1950s, consistent, universal estimates are lacking. Usually, such estimates were made for particular industries or firms, and most often, these were ex-ante estimates, designed to serve as a criterion for judging the advisability of undertaking a contemplated investment. The most complete set of data on DRCs is probably that which was prepared for the deliberations of the Public Commission in the process of the post-1962 liberalization; but, as was mentioned in the last chapter, these data are most probably gross underestimates, due to the purpose for which they were intended, and cannot be relied upon.

Direct estimates of rates of protection for import-substituting industries are also not generally available. But from the set of data of effective exchange rates for the final (total) value of each good, exchange rates for value added in import substitutes may be obtained by using the effective exchange rates for imported inputs for these industries. Such a set of data has been constructed. The calculations are based on detailed estimates of an 80 × 80 input-output matrix of imported inputs.[16] Such a matrix is available for the year 1958.[17] On the assumption that the production structure of each industry was close enough to that of 1958 in each of the two preceding and two following years, the 1958 coefficients were used to construct effective-rate estimates for the five years 1956–60. Effective exchange rates for value added in exports and import substitutes are presented by commodity group in Table 4-4, and their comparison is summarized in Table 4-5.[18]

In evaluating the meaning of the import rates, and in particular in comparing them with export rates, it should be realized that the former suffer— on the average, of course—from two deficiencies, both probably leading to gross underestimation.

First, in interpreting such data, it should be recalled that the estimates of effective exchange rates refer to *price* measures, but not to the QR system;

TABLE 4-3
Effective Exchange Rates for Imports and Exports of Goods, 1949–71
(Israeli pounds per dollar)

Year	Import Rate (1)	Export Rate (2)	Percentage Change of Col. 1 (3)	Percentage Change of Col. 2 (4)
1949	0.39	0.35		
1950	0.40	0.39	4.1	9.4
1951	0.39	0.41	−1.7	5.7
1952	0.81	0.81	103.8	98.3
1953	1.17	1.28	45.0	58.1
1954	1.80	1.73	54.2	35.3
1955	2.21	1.83	22.9	5.8
1956	2.26	2.05	2.3	12.1
1957	2.33	2.21	3.2	7.8
1958	2.35	2.37	0.7	7.2
1959	2.50	2.49	6.5	5.0
1960	2.57	2.58	2.5	3.6
1961	2.60	2.66	1.4	3.1
1962[a]	3.57	3.00	37.1	13.0
	3.47	3.02		
1963	3.49	3.04	0.6	0.7
1964	3.47	3.06	−0.6	0.7
1965	3.55	3.08	2.3	0.7
1966	3.59	3.27	1.1	6.1
1967	3.68	3.57	2.5	9.1
1968	4.13	4.04	11.6	13.1
1969	4.22	4.05	2.2	0.2
1970[b]	4.42	4.49	4.8	10.7
1971[b]	5.09	5.04	15.2	12.2

NOTE: Deviations of columns 3 and 4 from the corresponding percentage changes in columns 1 and 2 are due to rounding of the underlying data.

SOURCE: 1949–62—Michaely, *Foreign Exchange System*, Table 4-1; 1962–71—Valery D. Amiel, "Effective Rates of Exchange in Israel's Foreign Trade, 1962–70," Bank of Israel *Economic Review* 39 (August 1972; in English), pp. 28–53.

a. Due to the shift from one source of data to another in 1962 (see Source note, above), and slight differences between the two sources, two sets of data are presented for that year. The percentage change from 1961 to 1962 is based on the first set; from 1962 to 1963, on the second set.

b. Preliminary.

TABLE 4-4

Effective Exchange Rates for Value Added in Exports and in Import Substitutes, by Individual Industry, 1956–60
(Israeli pounds per dollar)

Code	Product Group	1956 Exports	1956 Import Substitutes	1957 Exports	1957 Import Substitutes	1958 Exports	1958 Import Substitutes	1959 Exports	1959 Import Substitutes	1960 Exports	1960 Import Substitutes
801	Cereals and pulses	—	1.94	—	1.97	2.68	2.44	2.92	2.21	2.65	2.28
802	Roughage	—	1.90	—	1.98	—	2.28	—	2.14	—	2.08
803	Cotton	—	1.79	2.66	1.78	2.64	2.22	2.64	1.78	2.71	2.18
804	Other field crops	2.35	1.65	2.73	1.86	2.81	2.19	3.12	2.28	3.01	2.23
805	Vegetables and melons	2.12	2.78	2.52	2.83	2.62	2.20	2.56	3.71	2.61	3.39
806	Cattle	—	1.93	—	4.03	—	2.01	—	2.33	—	3.40
807	Poultry	2.69	1.80	2.88	1.96	2.55	1.85	2.88	4.38	2.89	1.54
808	Other livestock	2.39	1.84	2.59	1.90	2.67	2.49	2.49	2.96	2.63	2.72
809	Citrus fruit	1.80	—	1.80	—	2.05	—	2.16	—	2.30	—
810	Fruit other than citrus	2.08	8.79	2.62	5.38	2.62	4.31	2.61	10.35	2.82	6.92
811	Other agricultural products	2.44	2.97	2.56	2.77	2.66	3.42	2.69	3.37	2.85	5.38
812	Gravel and scrap metal	2.35	1.83	2.70	1.88	2.68	1.85	2.84	1.88	2.88	2.24
814	Nonmetallic minerals	2.35	1.81	2.72	1.98	2.08	1.78	2.48	1.81	2.70	1.80
815	Meat and fish products	2.30	2.04	2.58	3.81	2.61	2.21	2.66	3.08	2.65	2.31
816	Dairy products	2.61	1.77	4.55	1.86	2.64	1.40	2.73	2.94	2.75	1.87
817	Edible oils and fats	2.35	—	2.70	—	2.68	—	2.65	—	2.65	—
818	Vegetable and fruit preserves, spices, and coffee	2.18	3.77	2.59	2.24	2.51	4.95	2.62	3.80	2.73	15.11
819	Flour-mill and bakery products	2.35	1.18	3.96	1.86	3.18	5.57	3.02	3.26	2.66	9.86
820	Sugar and confectionery	2.35	8.13	2.70	5.33	2.68	5.04	2.73	4.36	2.68	7.82
821	Beverages and ice	2.86	7.37	2.96	4.78	2.89	2.23	2.63	5.16	2.55	8.43

Code	Product										
822	Tobacco products	2.35	64.19	2.63	15.99	2.68	23.19	2.66	—	2.75	—
823	Cotton spinning	2.35	2.15	2.70	2.19	2.72	2.14	2.91	2.30	3.54	2.31
824	Wool spinning	2.35	1.78	2.70	1.78	2.29	1.73	3.08	1.66	2.80	1.84
825	Fabrics: weaving and finishing	2.26	2.63	2.63	2.52	2.63	2.62	3.05	3.27	2.66	3.48
826	Knitting, twine, and textiles n.e.s.	2.35	2.34	2.61	1.77	2.62	1.76	2.54	2.04	2.69	2.87
827	Clothing	2.44	2.08	2.65	2.02	2.65	2.44	2.76	2.51	2.77	2.36
828	Basic wood products	2.16	2.04	4.32	1.96	4.28	1.55	2.84	1.83	2.71	0.89
829	Carpentry and joinery	2.36	1.80	2.53	1.97	2.68	2.65	2.14	2.04	2.83	2.07
830	Paper and paper products	2.69	2.34	3.38	2.18	3.38	2.30	2.69	2.92	3.19	2.81
831	Printing and publishing	2.43	1.04	2.60	1.79	2.70	1.66	2.77	1.68	2.62	1.76
832	Leather and leather products	2.97	2.49	2.72	2.29	2.67	2.58	2.80	2.43	3.28	2.74
833	Rubber products	2.68	1.85	2.70	2.98	2.65	2.15	2.47	2.62	2.60	2.35
834	Manufacture and repair of tires	2.35	1.94	2.70	2.28	2.68	2.10	2.73	2.19	2.75	1.74
835	Plastic products	2.58	2.87	2.70	3.76	2.95	3.23	2.88	4.39	2.67	2.09
836	Basic chemicals	2.31	1.72	2.58	1.86	2.67	2.82	2.68	2.44	2.78	2.71
837	Oil, soap, and detergents	2.06	2.16	2.14	1.98	2.29	2.04	2.42	—	2.18	2.10
838	Paints	2.35	1.88	2.70	1.94	2.68	1.83	2.56	2.20	2.61	1.76
839	Oil refining	2.63	—	3.14	—	2.50	—	2.64	—	2.59	—
840	Pharmaceuticals, insecticides, and other chemicals	2.28	1.40	2.43	2.17	2.64	1.63	2.60	2.08	2.58	1.99
841	Glass and ceramics	2.30	2.31	2.22	2.38	2.26	2.59	2.67	3.21	2.63	2.86
842	Cement	2.61	35.36	2.40	37.16	3.08	—	2.74	—	2.72	24.85
843	Cement and lime products	2.37	1.86	2.70	2.00	2.68	1.81	2.73	2.11	2.66	1.97
844	Asbestos and nonmetallic mineral products n.e.s.	2.32	2.31	2.51	3.00	2.54	2.32	2.70	2.48	2.90	2.81
845	Diamonds	2.40	1.85	2.65	1.47	2.65	1.86	2.65	3.57	2.65	1.79
846	Basic iron and steel	3.33	1.93	2.70	1.79	2.47	2.12	2.36	1.81	2.50	2.43
847	Basic nonferrous metals	2.35	1.82	2.70	1.88	2.82	1.81	2.90	1.84	2.65	1.82
848	Metal pipes	2.49	2.14	2.73	1.77	2.61	2.01	2.54	1.92	2.54	1.85

(continued)

TABLE 4-4 (concluded)

Code	Product Group	1956 Exports	1956 Import Substitutes	1957 Exports	1957 Import Substitutes	1958 Exports	1958 Import Substitutes	1959 Exports	1959 Import Substitutes	1960 Exports	1960 Import Substitutes
849	Plumbing fixtures	2.35	1.81	2.79	1.98	2.32	1.78	2.72	1.87	2.57	2.87
850	Structural metal products	2.35	1.76	2.70	1.79	2.68	—	2.74	2.20	3.32	1.64
851	Tin products	2.35	1.92	2.70	1.79	2.92	1.90	2.67	2.03	2.78	1.72
852	Wire products	2.35	2.42	2.70	1.98	2.72	2.46	2.66	1.93	2.53	2.62
853	Kitchen utensils, tools, and galvanizing products	2.32	1.92	2.70	2.89	3.00	4.80	2.79	4.84	2.95	2.46
854	Other metal products	2.75	2.43	2.54	2.59	2.34	2.21	2.66	1.82	2.64	2.01
855	Industrial and agricultural machinery	2.48	1.81	2.63	1.84	2.62	1.96	2.69	1.95	2.70	1.82
856	Household equipment	2.45	2.65	3.26	2.63	2.68	3.28	2.67	6.22	2.66	1.79
857	Electric motors and transformers	2.44	1.75	2.70	1.80	2.65	1.96	2.80	1.81	2.58	1.63
858	Electric fixtures, batteries, and accumulators	2.35	2.61	2.70	2.15	2.68	2.56	2.50	2.57	2.53	3.27
859	Domestic electric appliances, radio, and communications equipment	2.45	2.46	2.75	2.49	2.74	2.49	2.78	4.00	2.77	3.75
860	Manufacture of motor vehicles	—	2.17	2.70	2.58	2.68	2.52	2.84	2.38	2.98	2.69
861	Repair of motor vehicles	—	1.87	—	1.78	—	1.75	—	1.86	—	1.76
862	Manufacture and repair of ships and aircraft	—	1.80	2.70	1.80	2.68	1.78	—	1.80	—	1.78
863	Precision instruments and manufactures n.e.s.	2.40	2.43	2.64	2.25	2.52	4.92	2.84	2.70	2.69	2.53
879	Miscellaneous, repairs, etc.	2.35	2.31	2.70	1.17	2.68	2.50	—	1.91	—	2.20
880	Fuel: extraction and refining	—	—	—	3.05	—	—	—	2.09	—	2.84

SOURCE: Michaely, *Foreign Exchange System*, Tables A-1 and A-5.

96

TABLE 4-5

Effective Exchange Rates for Value Added in Exports and in Import Substitutes, 1956–60: Summary Comparison

	1956	1957	1958	1959	1960
Number of product groups in which:					
$R_m > R_x$	11	10	11	15	12
$R_m < R_x$	28	35	28	26	30
$R_m = R_x$ ($\pm 10\%$)	11	9	14	9	10
Average export rate (IL per $)	2.05	2.21	2.37	2.49	2.58
Average import rate (IL per $)	3.26	2.91	2.63	3.16	3.47
Import rate as percentage of export rate	159	132	111	127	134

R_m = effective exchange rate for import substitutes.
R_x = effective exchange rate for exports.
SOURCE: Table 4-4.

that is, quota profits are not measured in the calculation of effective exchange rates. But this element exists, naturally, only with regard to protection of import substitutes, and not to exports, in which protection is afforded only by direct price elements. Thus, even were the estimates accurate and complete as far as they are supposed to go, they would not describe the full measure of protection afforded to imports. Hence, this measure is understated for imports in comparisons with estimates of protection for exports.

The second deficiency is due to the technique of the estimates. In deriving these by the use of input-output data, the effective exchange rate for each imported input was assumed—for lack of any alternative—to be the average exchange rate estimated for this import category. Were each such category a homogeneous product, this method would have been correct. But, in effect, every category includes a multitude of individual goods, each with its own effective exchange rate, with the rate for the category as a whole derived as an average weighted by the size of imports of each individual good.[19] This in itself would not be very damaging had the distribution of individual rates within each group of commodities been random. But, as will be seen later, and as is well known from the experience of many countries, this was not the case: exchange rates for raw materials or semimanufactured goods tend to be lower than the rates for final goods, and each category of goods usually consists of a mixture of goods at various stages of production. Thus, were the rates for goods within each category weighted by the size of imports actually used as inputs in domestic production, the average rate yielded would have been lower, as a rule, than the averages employed, in effect, in the calculations—

TABLE 4-6

Effective Rates of Protection for Exports and Import Substitutes, by Individual Industry, 1956–60
(per cent)

Code[a]	1956		1957		1958		1959		1960	
	Exports	Import Substitutes	Exports	Import Substitutes	Exports	Import Substitutes	Exports	Import Substitutes	Exports	Import Substitutes
801	—	−19	—	−26	1	8	10	−17	0	−14
802	—	−21	—	−25	—	−14	—	−19	—	−22
803	—	−25	0	−33	0	−16	0	−33	2	−18
804	−2	−31	3	−30	6	−17	18	−14	14	−16
805	−12	16	5	7	−1	−17	−3	40	−2	28
806	—	−20	—	52	—	−24	—	−12	—	28
807	12	−25	9	−26	−4	−30	9	65	9	42
808	−1	−23	−2	−28	1	−6	−6	12	−1	3
809	−1	—	−32	—	−23	—	−18	—	−13	—
810	−13	−266	1	103	−1	63	−2	291	6	161
811	2	24	−3	5	0	29	2	27	8	103
812	−2	−24	2	−29	1	−30	7	−29	9	−15
814	−2	−25	3	−25	−22	−33	−6	−32	2	−32
815	−4	−15	−3	44	−2	−17	0	16	0	−13
816	9	−26	72	−30	0	−47	3	11	4	−29
817	−2	—	2	—	1	—	0	—	3	—
818	−9	57	−2	−15	−5	−87	−1	45	3	470
819	−2	−51	49	−30	20	110	14	23	0	272
820	−2	239	2	101	1	90	3	65	1	195
821	19	207	12	80	9	−16	−1	95	−4	218

822	−2	2,575	−1	503	1	775	0	—	4	—
823	−2	−10	2	−17	3	−19	10	−13	34	−13
824	−2	−26	2	−33	−14	−35	16	−37	6	−31
825	6	10	−1	−5	−1	−1	15	23	0	31
826	−2	−3	−2	−33	−1	−34	−4	−23	2	8
827	2	−13	0	−24	0	−8	4	−5	5	−11
828	−10	−15	63	−26	62	−42	7	−31	2	−66
829	−2	−25	5	−26	1	0	−19	−23	7	−22
830	12	−3	28	−18	28	−13	0	10	20	6
831	1	−57	−2	−32	2	−37	5	−37	−1	−34
832	24	4	3	−14	1	−3	6	−8	24	3
833	12	−23	2	12	0	−19	−7	−1	−2	−11
834	−2	−19	2	−14	1	−21	3	−17	4	−34
835	8	20	2	42	11	22	8	66	1	−21
836	−4	−28	3	−30	1	6	1	−8	5	2
837	−14	−10	−19	−25	14	−23	−9	—	−18	−21
838	−2	−22	2	−27	1	−31	−3	−17	−2	−34
839	10	—	18	—	−6	—	0	—	2	—
840	−5	−42	8	−18	0	−38	−2	−22	−3	−25
841	−4	−4	−16	−10	−15	−2	1	21	−1	8
842	9	1,373	−9	1,302	16	—	3	—	3	838
843	−1	−23	2	−25	1	−32	3	−20	0	−26
844	−3	−4	−5	13	−4	−12	2	−6	9	6
845	—	−23	0	−45	0	−30	0	35	0	−32
846	39	−20	2	−32	−7	−20	−11	−32	−6	−8
847	−2	−24	2	−29	6	−32	9	−31	0	−31
848	4	−11	3	−33	−2	−24	4	−28	−4	−30

(continued)

TABLE 4-6 (concluded)

Code[a]	1956 Exports	1956 Import Substitutes	1957 Exports	1957 Import Substitutes	1958 Exports	1958 Import Substitutes	1959 Exports	1959 Import Substitutes	1960 Exports	1960 Import Substitutes
849	−2	−25	5	−25	−12	−33	3	−29	−3	8
850	−2	−27	2	−32	1	—	3	−17	25	−38
851	−2	−20	2	−32	10	−28	1	−23	5	−35
852	−2	1	2	−25	3	−7	0	−27	−5	−1
853	−3	−20	2	9	13	81	5	83	11	−7
854	15	1	−4	−2	−12	−17	0	−31	0	−24
855	3	−25	−1	−31	−1	−26	1	−26	2	−31
856	2	10	23	−1	1	24	1	135	0	−32
857	2	−27	2	−32	0	−26	6	−32	−3	−38
858	−2	9	2	−19	1	−3	−6	3	−5	23
859	2	3	4	−6	4	−6	5	51	5	41
860	—	−10	2	−3	1	5	7	−10	12	2
861	—	−22	—	−33	—	−34	—	−30	—	−34
862	—	−25	2	−32	1	−33	—	−32	—	−33
863	0	1	0	−15	−5	86	7	2	2	−5
879	−2	−4	2	−56	1	−6	—	−28	—	−17
880	—	—	—	15	—	—	—	−21	—	7

NOTE: A negative sign indicates negative protection.

SOURCE: Data for effective exchange rates for value added in exports and in import substitution are from Table 4-4. They were transformed into effective rates of protection as explained in Appendix B, with the following rates representing equilibrium levels ($\bar{R}$): 1956, IL 2.40 per dollar; 1957–60, IL 2.65 per dollar.

a. Product groups are identified by name in Table 4-4.

often, very probably, by a substantial margin. Using upwardly biased estimates for the rate of exchange for imported inputs leads, of course, to a
downwardly biased estimate of the effective exchange rate for value added.

A similar (although probably less important) bias in the same direction
is due to the method of estimating average rates of exchange for the final
good in each group: the rates of individual goods within the group are
weighted by the size of exports (for the export rate) or imports (for the import rate). As is well known, this procedure, as compared with a uniform-
rate one, increases the weights of exports with particularly *high* rates and of
imports with particularly *low* rates, thus raising the estimate of the value-
added rate for exports and lowering it for import substitutes.[20]

The estimates of effective exchange rates for value added in exports and
in import substitution may be transformed, in the manner described in Appendix B, into estimates of effective protective rates. These are presented in
Table 4-6. Since the ranking of rates is identical, due to the method of transformation used, whether effective exchange rates (for value added) are used
or effective protective rates (EPRs), the analysis of both sets of data will
yield identical conclusions. In the following discussion, the data on effective
exchange rates in Table 4-4 will be used, but the set of EPRs in Table 4-6
could be utilized just as well.

From Table 4-4, it seems that the variance of rates is much higher in
imports than in exports, both across groups and when changes within the five-
year period presented are considered. This is probably partly a result of the
crude and indirect way in which import rates were calculated. It is also probably partly due to the fact that while export rates were by and large known
to policymakers because of the subsidization methods, rates for value added
in import substitution, which contain elements of exchange rates on imported
inputs and reflect the size of the import component, were not known nearly
as well, and were not decided upon directly, thus leaving more room for
chance to play a role. At least to some extent, though, the large variance
shown in rates of exchange for value added in import substitutes must also
reflect the actual dispersion of final-value rates, as will be seen in the next
section.

From the summary presented in Table 4-5, it appears that in most groups
import (value-added) rates were *lower,* in all five years considered, than export rates. In view of the probably gross underestimation of import rates, it is
doubtful whether any conclusion could be based on this finding. When *average*
rates for total exports and imports are considered, on the other hand, the data
in the table show that the import rate always exceeds the export rate.[21] In
this instance, awareness of the biases involved should, of course, serve to increase confidence in the conclusion, namely, that for production in the
economy as a whole, the protective rate in import substitution exceeded the
protective rate for exports.

This inference is strongly supported by preliminary findings of a study relating to a later year, 1965, in which protective rates were estimated by a somewhat more refined procedure.[22] Input-output coefficients were still the main basis of the estimates; but important inputs were examined more carefully, to enable discretionary decisions to be made about the proper inputs and input rates to be included. These findings are summarized in Table 4-7.

TABLE 4-7

Effective Rates of Protection, by Major Industrial Sector, 1965
(per cent)

Sector	Domestic Sales	Export Sales
Agriculture	46	8
Food, tobacco, etc.	153	−1
Textiles and leather	116	121
Other light industries	16	7
Chemicals and minerals	78	−9
Metal industries	64	−16
Total	66	10

SOURCE: Preliminary data provided by Joseph Baruch, "The Structure of Protection in Israel, 1965 and 1968" (Ph.D. diss. in progress, Hebrew University).

It can be seen in the table that in two of the six major sectors—textiles and leather and other light industries—protective rates were about equal in import substitution and in exports. In the other four, effective protection in import substitution was clearly and substantially higher than in exports; effective protective rates in exports even appear to be negative in two of these four sectors, and positive only in one (in the fourth it is practically nil). For the aggregates, the effective protection rate seems to be substantial (66 per cent) in import substitution, and rather low (10 per cent) in exports. Excluding the textile industry, aggregate exports would appear to be subject to negative protection, although not to a high degree. This is due to the previously noted scarcity of export premiums and other subsidies, except in the textile industry, from the devaluation of 1962 to the end of 1966; at the same time, the "drawback" scheme, which in principle frees exporters from import duties on inputs for exports, does not operate perfectly; in particular, it does not provide for refunds of duties paid on the indirect component of imports in exports.

The textile industry has been investigated in some detail, in a study in which both effective protective rates and domestic resource costs have been determined for a sample of goods drawn from the various subbranches of the industry, where the individual goods are defined in great detail.[23] Rates have been calculated separately for import substitution and for exports. The findings are summarized in Table 4-8.

In comparing effective protective rates in import substitutes (column 3) and in exports (column 6), no general rule seems to emerge.[24] On the basis of these findings, it would not be warranted to assert that import substitution has enjoyed more protection than exports. It should be recalled, however, that effective exchange rates and effective protective rates have persistently been higher, by a substantial margin, for exports of the textile industry than for exports of most other industries, but no such general discrimination in favor of the textile industry has been apparent in import substitution. Thus, even equality of protective rates for exports and imports in the textile industry would have suggested a generally higher rate of protection in import substitution than in exports in other industries.[25]

The findings of Table 4-8 may be more illuminating, however, for another issue: this is apparently the only available set of data which provides reliable estimates for both EERs (and EPRs) and DRCs for the same precisely defined, specific goods. In perfect markets and under equilibrium conditions, the effective exchange rate for value added and the domestic resource cost at the margin should be equal for each good. The existence of monopolies, the imperfect mobility of factors, factor price rigidities, "water in the tariff" (i.e., lack of effective competition from imports at the existing price), and similar phenomena would lead to divergences between the two.[26] Likewise, the estimates of EERs do not take into account the operation of QRs or of various other forms of governmental interference (such as subsidization of long-term capital charges, tax concessions, and the like). Thus, in practice the two measures could be found to diverge widely for any given good. It would thus be interesting to compare the two in the case at hand. The estimates of DRCs in Table 4-8 do not include an adjustment for possible differences between market prices (in the production of each good) and shadow prices of factors.[27] But other reasons for divergence between EERs and DRCs should be reflected in this comparison.

Comparison of columns 1 and 2 in Table 4-8 shows that in import substitution EERs almost always exceed DRCs, often by a substantial margin.[28] The unweighted average difference between the two is 52 per cent of the DRC. On the average, however, the EERs in column 2 exceed the formal rate of exchange by 140 per cent, compared to which the 52 per cent excess of EERs over DRCs does not seem overwhelming. In exports, moreover, the excess of EERs (column 5) over DRCs (column 4) is on average only 13 per cent, whereas the excess of EERs over the formal rate of exchange is 106 per cent. Perhaps not less important is the comparison of *rankings* of the EERs and DRCs. The rank correlation coefficient between columns 1 and 2 (import substitution) is .79; between columns 4 and 5 (exports), it is .69. The coefficients of determination (r^2) of the series in original units are .72

TABLE 4-8

Domestic Resource Costs and Effective Protection in the Textile Industry, 1968[a]

Product	Import Substitutes			Exports		
	DRC (IL per $ of value added) (1)	EER (IL per $ of value added) (2)	EPR (per cent) (3)	DRC (IL per $ of value added) (4)	EER (IL per $ of value added) (5)	EPR (per cent) (6)
Cotton yarn						
Corded, 81/1	7.4	9.9	182	13.5	10.3	194
Combed, 40/1	12.3	16.0	357	20.9	16.2	363
Cotton fabric						
Semiprocessed drill	5.8	9.7	177	10.8	12.9	274
Poplin polyester	6.2	13.8	294	8.9	8.5	143
(Blended) cotton fabric						
Semiprocessed drill	6.9	9.9	182			
Poplin polyester	6.5	11.6	231			
Combed woollen-type yarn						
Pure knitting wool, 32/2	4.3	6.1	74	6.6	6.0	71
Acrylic, 37/2	2.8	3.9	11	3.8	5.2	49
Acrylic, 60/2	3.8	4.4	26	5.0	5.2	49
Woollen-type fabric						
Polyester	3.4	6.7	91	4.7	5.6	60
Polyester (solid)	4.3	3.3	−6	6.9	6.6	89
Blended polyester	3.8	7.5	114	4.6	6.8	94
Blended polyester (solid)	4.4	6.1	74	5.4	7.3	109
Woollen trousers						
Of imported fabric				5.6	5.6	60
Of domestic fabric				5.1	4.7	34
Poplin polyester shirt						
Of imported fabric				3.9	4.6	31
Of domestic fabric				5.0	6.9	97
Knitted						
Lambswool shirt				5.0	6.8	94
Jersey dress				4.5	4.7	34
Girl's dress				4.6	6.1	74

Notes to Table 4-8.

DRC = domestic resource costs.
EER = effective exchange rates.
EPR = effective protective rates.
SOURCE: Data for domestic resource costs (DRC) and effective exchange rates (EER) from Aharon Ornstein, Haim Ben-Shahar, and Yoram Weinberger, "The Textile Industry in Israel: Profitability, Productivity, and Policy" (in Hebrew), *Rivon Le'Kalkala* [Economic quarterly], June 1970, pp. 118–130, and September 1970, pp. 220–230, Tables 19 and 20. EERs converted to effective protective rates (EPR) by the formula $(R_i - R)/R$, where R_i is the rate for the individual product and $R =$ IL 3.50 per dollar.

a. Exact year is not specified in the source, but may be implied from accompanying text.

---

for import substitution and .86 for exports. The outcome of all these measures suggests a rather close resemblance between the series of EERs and DRCs.

The resemblance of the two sets of estimates suggests, first, that the estimates of EPRs could not be wide of the mark as indicators of the degree of protection afforded to an industry, despite the elements missing from the estimates. Beyond that, the association of the two sets could be explained in two alternative ways. It may be assumed, first, that effective exchange rates for each activity are determined in an independent way (that is, by considerations other than costs). The size of production in each activity then expands or contracts to the point at which the cost of value added (the DRC) becomes roughly equal to the effective exchange rate (for value added); that is, market forces work without much hindrance. In the alternative explanation an opposite adjustment would be assumed: At each point in time, the government may be assumed to take the costs of production in each activity as given, and grant the activity an effective exchange rate which would result in an approximate coverage of the costs of this activity. There is no feasible way of deciding which one of these hypotheses should be accepted. Circumstantial evidence suggests that both explanations are plausible: the similarity of the two sets of estimates is probably the combined outcome of both processes. It may also be assumed that the "tailoring" of effective exchange rates to cover costs is more prevalent in the textile industry, particularly for exports, than in most other industries.

iv. FORMAL DEVALUATION AND THE USE OF OTHER PRICE COMPONENTS

Except in the years 1952–54, the formal rate of exchange was uniform for almost all foreign-exchange transactions. Government intervention in trade via the price mechanism was mainly through premiums and other subsidies on exports and tariffs and levies on imports; these constitute the nonformal components of the effective exchange rate. In order to judge the significance of this intervention, three interrelated questions must be answered: How large was it in terms of its average size? Was it actually a specific intervention in the working of the mechanism or merely a substitute for the use of the formal exchange rate, i.e., for devaluation? And was it discriminatory or applied uniformly? The first two questions are dealt with here; the third, in the section following.

It may be seen, from Table 4-9, that the nonformal component amounted, at its peak in the early 1960s, to somewhat over 30 per cent of the effective rate (that is, close to half of the formal rate), for both exports and imports. The averages for the period as a whole were, of course, lower, but very often quite close to this peak level. It may thus be seen, by way of a general impression, that these forms of price intervention were not trivial, but rather of considerable quantitative significance.

The data in Table 4-9, together with those of Table 4-3, may very tentatively provide a clue to the extent to which nonformal components were used as a substitute for formal devaluation. In this respect, some difference appears between exports and imports. Table 4-3 shows that annual changes in the effective exchange rate over time were as a rule more uniform for exports than for imports. Since changes in the formal rate were mostly identical for exports and imports, this difference must, of course, be due to the behavior of the nonformal components. It appears indeed, from Table 4-3, that in exports this component was used, over the long run, to smooth out the process of devaluation, at least until the latter half of the 1960s. Formal devaluations were substantial, but between devaluations the nonformal component of the rate kept rising. Upon formal devaluation, however, the nonformal component would be drastically reduced, to mitigate considerably the effect of the formal change on the effective rate of exchange. The devaluation of 1962, entailing an increase of 67 per cent in the formal exchange rate, thus led to an increase of only about 13 per cent in the effective exchange rate for exports. In principle, this tendency was true also for the two later episodes of formal devaluation (November 1967 and August 1971), but to a much smaller extent, probably because these devaluations were themselves mild (17 per cent in the former and 20 per cent in the latter). By and large, it may therefore be assumed that the nonformal component of the export rate was used as a substitute for formal devaluation: it was gradually raised between devaluations, and reduced (or even eliminated) at times of formal devaluation. The guiding principle for such a policy might have been the prevention of short-term rent payments to exporters, a principle which, as will be pointed out later, served also to a large extent to determine the pattern of differential rates among export industries.

In imports, the level of the nonformal component, as well as its fraction

TABLE 4-9

**Formal and Nonformal Components of Effective Exchange Rates
in Exports and Imports, 1949–71**

(Israeli pounds per dollar)

Year	Formal (Official) Rates		Nonformal Components[a]		Nonformal Component as Percentage of Effective Rate	
	Exports (1)	Imports (2)	Exports (3)	Imports (4)	Exports[b] (5)	Imports[c] (6)
1949		0.340	0.012	0.046	3.4	11.9
1950		0.357	0.028	0.045	7.3	11.2
1951		0.357	0.050	0.038	12.3	9.6
1952	0.702	0.694	0.105	0.111	13.0	13.8
1953	1.163	0.830	0.113	0.337	8.9	28.9
1954	1.663	1.506	0.063	0.293	3.6	16.3
1955		1.800	0.027	0.411	1.5	18.6
1956		1.800	0.249	0.461	12.1	20.4
1957		1.800	0.409	0.534	18.5	22.9
1958		1.800	0.569	0.550	24.0	23.4
1959		1.80	0.69	0.70	27.6	28.1
1960		1.80	0.78	0.77	30.1	29.9
1961		1.80	0.86	0.80	32.2	30.9
1962						
(Feb.–Dec.)		3.00	0	0.57	0	16.0
1963		3.00	0.04	0.49	1.3	14.0
1964		3.00	0.06	0.47	2.0	13.3
1965		3.00	0.08	0.55	2.7	15.5
1966		3.00	0.27	0.59	8.6	16.4
1967						
(Jan.–Nov.)		3.00	0.57	0.68	16.0	18.5
1968		3.50	0.54	0.63	13.4	15.3
1969		3.50	0.55	0.72	13.6	17.1
1970		3.50	0.99	0.92	22.2	20.8
1971						
(Jan.–Aug.)		3.50	1.29	1.24	26.9	26.0
(Sept.–Dec.)		4.20	1.03	1.38	19.8	24.7

SOURCE: For 1949–62, Michaely, *Foreign Exchange System*, Table 4-2; 1963–71, calculated from data in Amiel, "Effective Exchange Rate."

    a. Includes premiums and other subsidies on exports and tariffs and levies on imports.

    b. Column 3 divided by the sum of columns 1 and 3.

    c. Column 4 divided by the sum of columns 2 and 4.

of the total size of the effective rate of exchange, fluctuated much less than in exports. Only in the episode of the devaluation of 1962 does it appear clearly that part of the formal change of the rate was used to replace the nonformal component—and even on this occasion the replacement is much smaller than in the case of exports. Excluding the first few years, it appears that even at its low points, just after formal devaluations, the nonformal component constituted about 15 per cent of the effective exchange rate for imports, whereas in exports this component was very often nil or amounted to just a few percentage points. It may thus be inferred—necessarily, in a very tentative way—that in imports the nonformal component of the rate was much less extensively used than in exports as a substitute for formal changes in the rate of exchange. If this is true, then this component must be related to the conventional functions of tariffs and duties on imports, namely, raising revenue for the government and protecting specific industries. This interpretation, in turn, would lead one to suppose that the nonformal component was used in a more discriminatory fashion in imports than in exports; that is, the degree of dispersion in the effective-exchange-rate system would be higher in imports than in exports. This is indeed the case, as I explain in the following section.

v. DISCRIMINATION IN THE EXCHANGE-RATE SYSTEM

The data used for determining whether the exchange-rate system for exports is discriminatory are somewhat deficient. Although the direct premium elements have been estimated with reasonable accuracy, other subsidy elements, realized through compensation in the local market and through branch funds, are mostly missing from the estimates. Quantitatively, the most important estimate missing is for the subsidy element in the Pamaz system of the mid- and late 1950s.[29] This deficiency is not serious so far as estimates for exports as a whole, or major export categories, are concerned: Such average rates would be only little affected by the missing magnitudes, since their total size was not substantial. For a few individual goods, however, these elements were important, and probably led to very high effective exchange rates. But, although in this way extreme values were eliminated from the estimates, available fragmentary information about the extent of use of these subsidization forms suggests that conclusions about the attributes of the rate system for exports as a whole would not be altered significantly by this deficiency of the data.

Bearing this reservation in mind, it appears from the data on rates for individual goods (not presented here) that the rate system was largely uniform: deviations of individual rates from each other, or from the average, were quite small, seldom exceeding a range of, say, 10 to 20 per cent of the average. This may be gathered from the fact that the main subsidization forms —the premium programs of 1956–61 and from 1966 on—were applied in a rather uniform way. So far as major export groupings are concerned, deviations from the average—again, not very substantial—may be seen mainly in the two traditional export categories, citrus fruit and polished diamonds, and in textiles. Effective exchange rates for value added for these major groups are presented in Table 4-10.

Until the mid-1950s, apparently, none of the three major export categories covered in the table was systematically discriminated against or treated with special favor. From that time until the 1962 devaluation, diamonds received the prevailing rate for industrial exports (IL 2.65 per dollar), exports of citrus fruits received a lower rate, and textiles, a higher one. From the time of the 1962 devaluation until 1965, when export premiums were as a rule nonexistent, exports of textiles received favorable treatment. From 1966 on, with the reintroduction of general export premiums, the favorable treatment of textiles was reinforced, but both diamonds and citrus fruits were discriminated against relative to other exports—the former more than the latter. These two traditional exports, it may be recalled, did not (and could not, by their nature) enjoy the benefits of the Pamaz (retention-quota) plan of the 1950s or other forms of compensation through the local market. It may thus be assumed that in comparison with other exports, these two have been discriminated against during most of the period since the mid-1950s.

The special favorable rate for textiles has been part of an over-all effort to encourage the growth of that industry, which was judged by the government to be most suitable for the newly established towns in Israel, in the framework of a general policy meant to encourage the dispersion of population. The discrimination against citrus fruits and diamond exports was due, most probably, to both demand and supply considerations. In these two industries (and only in these two, among export categories) Israel has a significant share of the world market. Consequently, foreign demand for Israel's exports of goods in these two categories is probably less elastic than in others. In the citrus industry, but not in diamonds, supply factors are also involved: since local consumption absorbs only a minor share of the country's production (some 20 to 25 per cent), and the gestation period of investment in plantations is quite long, the short-term supply of exports is rather inelastic. In the short run, then, high export premiums for citrus products would largely constitute a rent, while their impact on the government's budget—due to the size of these exports—would be significant. Short-term supply considerations —and it may be suspected that the government's considerations in this area

TABLE 4-10

Selected Effective Exchange Rates for Exports, 1949–70

(Israeli pounds per dollar of value added)

Year	Citrus Fruit	Polished Diamonds	Textiles	Total Exports of Goods
1949	0.34	0.39	0.35	0.35
1950	0.38	0.39	0.37	0.39
1951	0.41	0.42	0.37	0.41
1952	0.76	0.95	0.82	0.81
1953	1.22	1.20	1.26	1.28
1954	1.80	1.47	1.80	1.73
1955	1.80	1.87	1.80	1.83
1956	1.80	2.40	2.33	2.05
1957	1.80	2.65	2.65	2.21
1958	2.05	2.65	2.66	2.37
1959	2.16	2.65	2.83	2.49
1960	2.30	2.65	2.75	2.58
1961	2.49	2.65	2.92	2.66
1962[a]	3.00	3.00	3.18	3.05
1963[a]	3.00	3.00	3.18	3.05
1964[a]	3.00	3.00	3.18	3.05
1965[a]	3.00	3.00	3.18	3.05
1966	3.11	3.00	4.44	3.27
1967	3.23	3.08	5.76	3.57
1968	3.94	3.50	5.79	4.04
1969	3.95	3.50	5.84	4.05
1970	4.27	3.79	6.18	4.49

SOURCE: For 1949–61, Michaely, *Foreign Exchange System*; the textile rate is calculated as a weighted average of five industry subgroups, using total size of exports of each subgroup for the whole period as weights. For 1962–70, Amiel, "Effective Exchange Rate."

a. The rates for 1962–65 are averages for that period.

were primarily of a short-run nature—thus were an added argument against granting high exchange rates to the citrus industry. It may well be that the lack of discrimination against this industry until the mid-1950s was at least partly due to a higher supply elasticity in those years. During World War II and again during the War of Independence, a very large fraction of the citrus plantations was badly damaged. Some plantations could not be restored; but in others, yields could be increased fast by investment in restoration of the trees as well as by introduction of modern techniques. Profits could, therefore, at that time have a substantial impact even on short-term supply.

On the import side, the degree of dispersion of the exchange-rate system seems to be much greater. This has already been noted earlier in the discussion of effective rates for value added in import substitutes. Effective rates for final import goods, too, varied widely from each other. Detailed data on effective rates for individual imported goods (whose number changed from a few hundred at the beginning to over a thousand in later years), which are available for the years 1949–62, show a high degree of dispersion. This may be verified by a few alternative measures, one of which is presented in Table 4-11.

TABLE 4-11

Coefficients of Variation of Import Exchange Rates, 1949–62

Year	Coefficient	Year	Coefficient
1949	.383	1956	.452
1950	.161	1957	.261
1951	.142	1958	.345
1952	.315	1959	.240
1953	.468	1960	.395
1954	.285	1961	.435
1955	.306	1962	.268

SOURCE: Michaely, *Foreign Exchange System*, Table 4-7.

It appears from Table 4-11 that the coefficient of variation in the rate system[30] during most of the period was substantial, in some years reaching 0.4 or above.[31] Other measures (such as frequency distributions or Lorenz curves), also yield the same impression.

What gives this dispersion special significance is that the ranking of each product in the system remained quite consistent over the years, that is, the rates were consistently discriminatory against some goods and consistently favorable toward others.[32] It is thus reasonable to ask what were the discriminatory aspects of the rate system for imports.

Chart 4-1 presents frequency distributions of the *rankings* (from lowest to highest exchange rates) of 138 commodity items classified into three categories: raw materials, machinery and equipment, and finished consumer goods. The rankings shown are averages for each item for 1955–61.[33] It seems

CHART 4-1

**Ranking of Importers' Exchange Rates by Principal Commodity Groups,[a]
Averages for 1955–61**

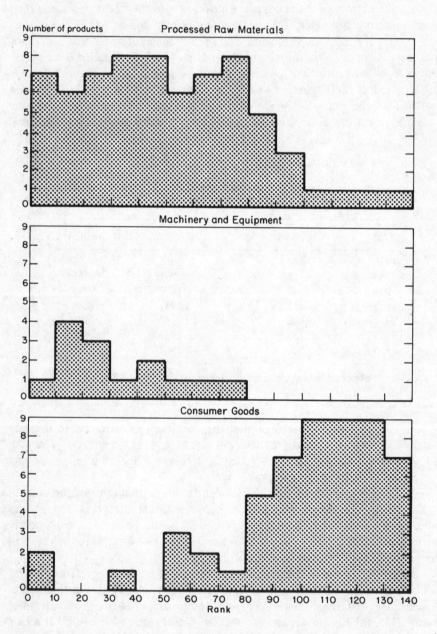

Notes to Chart 4-1.

SOURCE: Michael Michaely, *Israel's Foreign Exchange Rate System* (Jerusalem: Falk Institute, 1971; in English), Fig. VIII.

a. The ranking, proceeding from the lowest to the highest exchange rates paid by importers, includes 138 commodities, of which 69 are classified as processed raw materials; 14, as machinery and equipment; and 55, as consumer goods.

---

very clear that machinery and equipment goods were concentrated at the top of the ranking order; that is, their exchange rates were lowest. Final consumer goods, on the other hand, were just as consistently concentrated at the tail end of the ordering, that is, their exchange rates were highest. The third category, raw materials, seems also to tend toward the top of the ordering (lower exchange rates), but to be much less concentrated than the other two, that is, the degree of variation of rates *within* the category is higher. Despite this variance of raw materials, there seems to be a clear ordering of the categories: machinery and equipment goods are imported at the lowest effective exchange rates; raw materials follow; and final consumer goods are imported at the highest rate.

Similar frequency distributions are not available for other years.[34] However, estimates of average rates for large categories of imports classified by economic destination are available for the whole period from 1955 to 1971. These are shown in Table 4-12 and confirm the impression gained earlier. The highest exchange rates are found, as a rule, for final consumer goods, with rates for durable goods and processed foods usually occupying the top places. Lowest rates are found for investment goods and, in recent years, fuel: the level of rates in this category is usually close to the formal rate of exchange (including, since August 1970, the general 20 per cent levy on imports). The main exception is imports of transportation equipment, trucks being subject to high duties. Raw materials for the most part occupy a place in between, with construction materials having considerably higher rates than other raw materials.

To sum up: Import exchange rates showed wide variations throughout the years. Consistently, the lowest exchange rates were accorded to investment goods, and the highest, to final consumer goods, with raw materials in between. This pattern largely agrees with the observations made, in earlier chapters, about quantitative restrictions. It will be recalled that the first goods to be liberalized, whether formally or de facto, were raw materials and machinery and equipment. Only much later did the process of liberalization of final consumer goods get under way, and imposition of high tariff duties accompanied the move, tariffs which, of course, influenced the effective exchange rate of imports.

TABLE 4-12

Effective Exchange Rates for Imports, by Category, 1955–71
(Israeli pounds per dollar of gross value)

	1955	1956	1957	1958	1959	1960	1961	1962	1963	1964	1965	1966	1967	1968	1969	1970	1971
Final consumer goods																	
Nondurable consumption	2.01	2.08	2.20	2.46	3.22	3.44	3.50							5.84	5.56	5.77	7.20
Food	2.03	2.31	2.30	2.54	3.79	4.23	4.47							6.32	5.79	5.99	7.39
Durables[a]	2.26	2.30	2.28	2.42	2.48	2.58	2.71							5.90	6.60	6.83	8.29
Total[a]	2.05	2.13	2.22	2.45	3.00	3.16	3.19	4.81	4.73	4.58	4.83	5.35	5.26	5.86	5.98	6.20	7.60
Raw materials																	
For industry	1.87	1.95	2.00	2.06	2.14	2.18	2.20							3.88	3.89	4.11	5.22
For agriculture	1.69	1.74	2.21	2.57	2.43	2.64	2.73							3.68	3.75	3.98	5.19
For construction	2.61	2.61	2.62	2.63	2.77	3.20	3.17							5.47	5.30	5.53	7.10
Fuel	2.91	2.89	2.98	3.30	3.72	3.77	3.75							3.55	3.55	3.55	4.26
Total	2.06	2.15	2.24	2.36	2.41	2.48	2.50	3.38	3.37	3.35	3.36	3.33	3.40	3.90	3.94	4.14	5.29
Investment goods																	
For industry and construction	1.84	1.84	1.85	1.86	1.95	1.92	2.17							3.81	3.85	4.08	5.39
For agriculture	1.85	1.87	1.83	1.84	1.84	1.91	2.07							3.62	3.53	4.08	5.08
For transportation	2.03	2.00	1.94	2.03	2.06	2.34	2.03							3.95	4.45	4.59	5.81
For other services	1.84	1.91	2.07	2.27	2.34	2.09	2.50							3.87	3.94	4.17	5.55
Total	1.92	1.90	1.91	1.94	2.00	2.02	2.10	3.37	3.36	3.37	3.45	3.47	3.55	3.86	4.03	4.23	5.54
All import goods	2.03	2.09	2.16	2.28	2.38	2.43	2.45	3.47	3.49	3.47	3.55	3.59	3.68	3.99	4.01	4.33	5.58

SOURCE: For 1955–61, Joseph Baruch, "Import Taxes and Export Subsidies in Israel, 1955–61," Bank of Israel *Bulletin* 18 (March 1963), Table 1. For 1962–71, Amiel, "Effective Exchange Rate," Tables 2, 6, and 24.

Since Baruch and Amiel used different methods of estimation, the data shown do not constitute entirely consistent time series. For the same reason, the 1955–62 estimates for total imports shown here are not identical to the estimates shown in other tables in this chapter.

a. The estimates of the rate for durable goods for 1955–61 seem questionable. Amiel's estimate for the rate in 1961 is 3.72, rather than 2.71. It is likely, therefore, that estimates of the rates for total consumption for 1955–61 are biased downward.

NOTES

1. In this section and the next, descriptions of forms and mechanisms for the period until 1962 are heavily drawn from Michael Michaely, *Israel's Foreign Exchange Rate System* (Jerusalem: Falk Institute, 1971; in English).

2. The most important exemptions were as follows: (a) military imports were first exempted on the assumption that levies on these would be just a "transfer from one pocket to another" of the government. But a year later, with the formal devaluation of August 1971, military imports, too, became subject to the 20 per cent levy. This was done to obtain a more accurate estimate of the size of these imports and the magnitude of defense expenditures and to encourage the substitution of locally made items for foreign ones by increasing the cost of the latter. The defense budget was exempt from the income effect of the levy because an amount equal to it was allocated to the budget. (b) Most imports of investment goods have been exempted from the levy, since they were imported for the use of "approved" investments. The rationale of this procedure is that these investments are carried out by foreign investors, whose capital imports are transferred at the formal rate of exchange, and who should therefore pay no more than this rate for their imports of investment goods. (c) Imports of major food products have also been mostly exempted from the levy. Since the majority of such imports are handled by the government itself, this procedure is reflected, as will be explained later in the text, not through the loss of revenue from the levy, but through a loss (or absence of profit) in the government's commercial account (that is, by setting lower prices on local sales of these goods). Here, too, many prices were raised (to include, in effect, the August 1970 levy) with the formal devaluation of August 1971.

It may be mentioned that imports for exports have *not* been exempted from the levy, although, as a rule, the "drawback" system (i.e., the rebate of tariff duties on the import component in exports) applies to them. The reason is that simultaneously with the imposition of the import levy, export premiums were raised so as to compensate for the levy on the import component in exports.

3. "Premiums" is the term conventionally used in Israel for export subsidies.

4. For instance, the season for exports of citrus fruits runs from October to May. Most exporters were benefited by the shift of the rate from IL 1.00 to IL 1.80 per dollar in May 1953. To compensate citrus exporters for the subsidy forgone after May, they were granted a special premium of IL 0.136 per dollar during the 1953–54 season.

5. Diamonds were, in fact, subject to the universal premium arrangement. But mainly because of the possibility of negative reactions of other countries involved in this industry, the premium was disguised by other schemes. Exports of citrus fruits were also granted a premium for value added, but at a much lower rate. Gradually this rate approached the general premium rate, until the two coincided on the eve of the 1962 devaluation.

6. In all the cases involved in the actual application of the plan, no concern was expressed about distinctions between an industry and the individual firms included in it. This was because individual industries consisted either of a single firm—a fairly common phenomenon at that time—or were organized under some cartel agreement.

7. Almost since its beginnings, Israel has also had a widespread arrangement for providing *long-term* capital for investment at below market (or below equilibrium) interest rates as well as various other subsidy devices (such as special income-tax facilities) for aiding investment. Despite their undoubted importance, these provisions are not discussed here because they cannot be considered export subsidies. Although export inten-

tion and capacity were among the major criteria used in judging the applicability of these provisions for a contemplated investment, the facilities granted were not in effect dependent on export performance; and they were not even intended to vary with the amount or fraction of exports of the plant involved.

8. A fully free market for short-term (or long-term, for that matter) credit has never existed in Israel. During most of the 1960s, the rate of interest was subject to a legal ceiling of 11 per cent per annum and of 10 per cent for lending to industry and agriculture; earlier it had been 9 per cent. A semilegal and largely free market ("third-side lending" or "I.O.U. arbitrage") developed, however, which amounted to a very sizable fraction of total short-term lending. Interest rates in this market were much higher than the legal ceiling. Varying with market conditions and, of course, with the quality of the borrower, they were mostly in the range of 15 to 25 per cent per annum.

In early 1970, the maximum-interest law was abolished, and something approximating a free credit market has existed since (excluding credit such as that from export funds discussed here, and other subsidized lending to local industries, which still form a substantial part of total short-term credit). Interest rates on short-term credit from the banking system, in the three years since then, have usually ranged from 15 to 18 per cent.

9. The term "Pamaz" is derived from the Hebrew initials for "foreign-currency deposits." This points to the origin of the arrangement, which at first (before 1953) was intended merely to provide the exporter with deposits of foreign exchange which were built up from his export proceeds and were meant to free him from the bureaucratic costs involved in requesting foreign-exchange allocations to finance his imported inputs.

10. When exports were not stable but increasing, the exporter would get "credits" (in a bookkeeping sense) of foreign exchange, enabling him to finance the increased requirements for imported inputs.

11. In fact, the exporter was not forced to buy materials according to their proportions in his export production, but could concentrate his purchases as he saw fit. He could thus buy inputs and resell them to other industries in which he could obtain high prices for them. For instance, exporters of chocolate and sweets at one time used most of their Pamaz rights to buy cellophane packaging paper, which was in large demand in the local market. If each industry uses many inputs, even in very small amounts, it is likely that each such input can be bought by many industries. This would, in turn, tend to lower the profit differentials among industries from what they would have been if inputs were bought by each industry according to the weight of the inputs in production.

12. As the available data show, exporters rarely made an all-or-none decision between the alternatives. Presumably, in each industry, exporters used their Pamaz rights to the point where, *at the margin,* extra profits fell to the level of premium payments, selling all the remainder to the Treasury at the premium rate. Since the number of exporting firms in each industry was usually small, thus giving some monopolistic position to each, a considerable gap might have often existed between the *marginal* profit rate (equal to the premium) and the (higher) *average* rate.

13. It will be recalled that very often, the process of liberalization of imports of raw materials was accompanied by the imposition of special import levies. On a few occasions, exporters using their Pamaz rights were exempted from the duty; in effect, this exemption amounted to a subsidy for such exports.

14. For instance, exporters were required to sell part of their foreign-exchange proceeds to the Treasury, at the formal rate, as a counterpart to the value of the indirect import component used in the production process (which otherwise could be used to

provide extra profits through Pamaz purchases). Pamaz rights were also often lowered beyond this.

15. The import exchange rates presented here are for imports *subject to duty*. Duty-free imports of goods that are generally subject to duty are excluded. The latter category consists of two groups: imported inputs for exports, which are generally duty free under the drawback system; and imports (referred to in Israel as subject to "conditional exemption") that are duty free when imported by and for the use of an organization such as, say, a hospital or nonprofit institution, which is exempted from payment of these duties.

16. That is, for each of the 80 industrial groups, 80 separate import coefficients were used. These refer to *total* (i.e., both direct and indirect) inputs.

17. Tables for 1965 and 1968 have also been completed recently. They could not be utilized for the purpose on hand, however, because detailed estimates of effective exchange rates for imports of individual commodities are not available beyond 1962.

18. Table 4-4 contains fewer than 80 commodity groups, since in about 20 groups, there are no exports or imports.

19. The 80 groups included over a thousand individual goods.

20. Data on domestic production classified by individual commodities, which could have served instead for weighting, are not available.

21. The weights used for these averages were identical for exports and imports: 1958 value added in each group of commodities.

22. Joseph Baruch, "The Structure of Protection in Israel, 1965 and 1968" (Ph.D. diss. in progress, Hebrew University).

23. This study has been prepared by the Israeli Institute for Financial Research. The main findings are contained in Aharon Ornstein, Haim Ben-Shahar, and Yoram Weinberger, "The Textile Industry in Israel: Profitability, Productivity, and Policy" (in Hebrew), *Rivon Le'Kalkala* [Economic quarterly], June 1970, pp. 118–130, and September 1970, pp. 220–230.

24. As noted in Table 4-8, the transformation of effective exchange rates into effective protection rates has been carried out by the use of the *formal* exchange rate, rather than the equilibrium rate advocated in Appendix B. The reason is that the method for approximating an equilibrium rate suggested in the appendix and employed in the construction of Table 4-6 is not appropriate for 1968. In that year, effective exchange rates for exports only slightly exceeded the formal rate except for the export of textiles, for which the high rate may be explained by reasons other than balance-of-payments considerations. In any case, for the purpose in hand, the comparison of protection for exports and import substitution, it is immaterial which exchange rate is used.

25. Domestic resource costs in the textile industry appear to be universally higher in exports than in import substitution. This, however, is an almost inevitable result. Each of the goods listed is assumed to be homogeneous; so costs of production are assumed to be equal whether a unit of the good is exported or used for home consumption. Value added in exports, on the other hand, is universally lower for exports than for home consumption (import substitution), since transportation costs of the final good must be added to the former.

26. See, for instance, Anne O. Krueger, "Evaluating Restrictionist Trade Regimes: Theory and Measurement," *Journal of Political Economy* 80 (January–February 1972): 48–62.

27. The lack of such adjustment is helpful in the present context because the purpose of the comparison is not selection among alternative investment projects but deter-

mination of the relevance of EERs (and EPRs) for market developments, as the latter are reflected in the level of costs.

28. At least some consistency in this margin should be expected on a-priori grounds: under conditions of perfect markets, EERs should be equal to *marginal* DRCs, whereas the estimates are concerned with average DRCs, which presumably are lower.

29. As is explained in Appendix B, the subsidy generated by this system was assumed, in the estimates, to be equal to the level of the general export premium.

30. The coefficient is $\sqrt{[\Sigma(R_i - \bar{R})/\bar{R}^2 \Sigma M_i]}$, where R_i is the effective rate for imports of commodity i; M_i is the weight ($=$ annual value) for imports of i; and $\bar{R} = \Sigma R_i M_i / \Sigma M_i =$ average effective rate for imports.

31. To illustrate: the coefficient of variation would be around 0.33 in a system of two rates (equally weighted) in which one rate is twice the other; it would be 0.5 when one rate is three times the other.

32. This is demonstrated by a number of measures in Michaely, *Foreign Exchange System,* pp. 109–112.

33. This averaging procedure is legitimate, of course, only because ranks in each year were quite similar to those of other years, as was just noted: had the rank of each good fluctuated widely from one year to another, the average rank for the seven years would not be of much significance.

The 138 goods shown are taken from a list of 277 items which appeared in the arrays of all seven years. The goods selected were ones which could be clearly classified into one of the three categories. The nature of the other goods either could not be judged from their definitions or they could be assumed to belong to more than one category.

34. Detailed estimates of exchange rates for individual commodities have not been carried out beyond 1962. For years prior to 1955, the number of goods for which estimates of exchange rates exist for all (or most of) the period is rather small; so consistency of ranking could not be examined.

Chapter 5

The Process of
Devaluation

In the last chapter I dealt with the protective, discriminatory aspects of the Israeli exchange-rate system; in this chapter, I will analyze the macroeconomic aspects of changes in the foreign-exchange rate. I begin with a brief recapitulation of the main changes in the foreign-exchange rate during the period under review. This will be followed by an examination of the nature of the demand policies associated with each episode of devaluation. In connection with this, the relationship of the devaluation to local prices will be discussed and the extent to which nominal devaluations have also been "real" in the sense of changing the ratio of prices of tradables to local prices. Finally, the effectiveness of devaluation, in its impact on exports and imports, will be analyzed.

i. MAIN EPISODES OF DEVALUATION

Changes in the exchange rate, which have been mentioned often in earlier chapters, will be surveyed here in chronological order. It will be recalled, from the discussion of the last chapter, that for large aggregates the major part of the effective rate has always been the formal component. Likewise, major changes in effective rates have taken place through changes in the formal rate.

When the state of Israel was established, the Israeli pound (introduced in August 1948) was on a par with the pound sterling. A broken cross-rate system, however, was in existence, inherited from the last few years of the British mandatory regime: while the rate of exchange between the dollar and the pound sterling implied a cross rate of about IL 0.250 to the dollar (some-

119

what above $4 per pound), the direct rate of exchange between the Israeli pound and the dollar (and the implied rates with a few other hard currencies) was about IL 0.333 to the dollar ($3 per pound). With the British devaluation of September 1949, the Israeli pound remained on a par with sterling, and the rate of exchange with the dollar was made equal to that of sterling—IL 0.357 per dollar ($2.80 per pound). Thus, the changes in September 1949 left the rate of exchange of the Israeli pound against some currencies (mainly sterling) unchanged, but against some other currencies (primarily the U.S. dollar) the pound was devalued by about 7 per cent.

The next formal change in the rate of exchange took place in 1952. On February 14, 1952, the New Economic Policy was announced, the most important component of which was a progressive and rapid increase of the foreign-exchange rate, which was started on that same date. A multiple formal exchange-rate system was introduced: the rate of IL 0.357 per dollar (referred to from then on as rate A) was maintained as the official rate, but was made applicable to only a small category of transactions. Most transactions were to be conducted at two higher rates, one (rate B) twice the lower rate (i.e., IL 0.714 per dollar) and the other (rate C) IL 1.000 per dollar. Throughout 1952, transactions were gradually shifted from lower to higher rates (i.e., from rate A to rate B, and from the latter to rate C), until in early 1953 the large majority of transactions were conducted at rate C. In April 1953 a still higher rate, IL 1.800 per dollar, was added. The rate was formally established by adding IL 0.800 per dollar to rate C as a premium for exports and a levy on imports. Again, transactions were progressively and rapidly shifted to this higher rate until, by the end of 1953, this rate applied to most transactions. In December 1953 the two lowest rates, A and B, were formally abolished; rate C, IL 1.000 per dollar, was declared the new official rate, although by that time only a minority of transactions were conducted at this rate. In August 1954 rate C was also abolished, and only the higher rate of IL 1.800 per dollar remained, although it was not formally established as the official rate until July 1955.[1] From then on, a single-rate system again prevailed, with the next formal devaluation coming only in 1962.[2] By and large, the process of devaluation was complete within about two and a half years—from early 1952 to mid-1954. To recapitulate, during that period the formal rate was raised from IL 0.357 per dollar to IL 1.800 per dollar, a devaluation of just over 400 per cent; that is, the rate increased fivefold.

In February 1962 came the next episode of formal devaluation: the rate of exchange was raised from IL 1.80 to IL 3.00 per dollar,[3] an increase of two-thirds. As was mentioned in Chapter 3, much of the change introduced by this devaluation resulted in a unification of the effective-rate system—the lowering of the degree of dispersion introduced into the system by its non-formal components—rather than an increase in the aggregate level of the exchange rate. The net devaluation amounted to about 37 per cent in imports, and a mere 13 per cent in exports, compared with the gross (formal) devaluation of 67 per cent. To the extent that a net devaluation did take place, it was apparently motivated not so much, if at all, by any current pressure on the balance of payments, as by anticipations of adverse developments in the future. A large fraction of the country's capital imports was expected to disappear soon, since reparations payments from Germany were to be completed in 1963, and personal restitution payments were also expected to decline (an assumption that has proved to be wrong); at the same time, the economy's excess demand for imports (over exports) was expected to increase with the economy's growth. The devaluation was thus considered a preventive measure, in contrast to the devaluation of 1952–54, which was made under urgent and severe pressure. This difference in motivation may at least partly explain the difference in the policies accompanying the two episodes (see section 2, below).

Following the 1962 devaluation, the formal rate was maintained for close to six years, until November 1967, when the Israeli pound was devalued in the same proportion as the devaluation of the pound sterling: the rate of exchange was raised from IL 3.00 to IL 3.50 per dollar. This was, then, a devaluation of close to 17 per cent against the dollar (and most other currencies), but the previous rate was maintained against the pound sterling (and the few other currencies which followed it). The next and last formal devaluation, at this writing, came in August 1971, following by a few days the Nixon announcement of severance of the formal connection between the dollar and gold. The rate was raised then from IL 3.50 to IL 4.20 per dollar, an increase of 20 per cent. Since the dollar itself was devalued against most other currencies, during the few months which culminated in the Smithsonian Agreement of December 1971, this meant a somewhat higher devaluation of the Israeli pound against major currencies other than the dollar.[4]

As has been pointed out in the last chapter, the main quantitative importance of the nonformal component of the effective exchange rate in its aggregate effect was apparent during the long period of close to eight years, from 1954 to February 1962, during which the formal rate remained constant. During those years, the effective rates, particularly in exports, increased gradually through changes in the nonformal component. Likewise, it should be recalled, the net devaluation in February 1962 was substantially smaller than the gross devaluation—again, particularly in exports—owing to the reduction in the informal components of the rate of exchange (export subsidies and import duties) which accompanied the formal devaluation. To some extent, a similar process can be observed between the devaluation of 1962 and that of 1967, and again between the latter and the devaluation of 1971. Since 1954, thus, the process of net devaluation was more gradual (and also, as a trend,

TABLE 5-1

Formal and Effective Exchange Rates, 1949–71

(annual averages)

| | Israeli Pounds per Dollar | | | | | | | |
| | Formal Rate | | Effective Rate | | Annual Percentage Increase of: | | | |
Year	Exports (1)	Imports (2)	Exports (3)	Imports (4)	Col. 1	Col. 2	Col. 3	Col. 4
1949	0.34		0.35	0.39				
1950	0.36		0.39	0.40	5.0		9.4	4.1
1951	0.36		0.41	0.40	0		5.7	−1.7
1952	0.70	0.69	0.81	0.81	96.6	94.4	98.3	103.8
1953	1.16	0.83	1.28	1.17	65.7	19.6	58.1	45.0
1954	1.66	1.51	1.73	1.80	43.0	81.4	35.3	52.4
1955	1.80		1.83	2.21	8.2	19.5	5.8	22.9
1956	1.80		2.05	2.26	0		12.1	2.3
1957	1.80		2.21	2.33	0		7.8	9.2
1958	1.80		2.37	2.35	0		7.2	0.7
1959	1.80		2.49	2.50	0		5.0	6.5
1960	1.80		2.58	2.57	0		3.6	2.5
1961	1.80		2.66	2.60	0		3.1	1.4
1962	3.00[a]		3.02	3.47	67.0		13.0[b]	37.1[b]
1963	3.00		3.04	3.49	0		0.7	0.6
1964	3.00		3.06	3.47	0		0.7	−0.6
1965	3.00		3.08	3.55	0		0.7	2.3
1966	3.00		3.27	3.59	0		6.1	1.1
1967	3.00[c]		3.57	3.68	0		9.1	2.5
1968	3.50		4.04	4.13	16.7		13.1	11.6
1969	3.50		4.05	4.22	0		0.2	2.2
1970	3.50		4.49	4.42	0		10.7	4.8
1971	3.75[d]		5.04	5.09	12.9		12.2	15.2

SOURCE: See Table 4-9.

a. Effective in February; until then, the rate was IL 1.80 per dollar.

b. Since the sources for the effective rate in columns 3 and 4 change after 1962, the rates of change are based on the 1962 data from the earlier source: IL 3.00 per dollar for exports and IL 3.57 per dollar for imports.

c. Effective through November 19, after which the rate became IL 3.50 per dollar.

d. The rate was IL 3.50 per dollar until August 21; it has been IL 4.20 per dollar since then.

somewhat more substantial) than the process of gross (formal) devaluation. The formal and the effective rates for the whole period 1949–71 are presented as annual averages in Table 5-1.

ii. DEMAND POLICIES ACCOMPANYING DEVALUATION

Under conditions of full employment—or at least when unemployment is structural, and the national product is at its short-term ceiling—the impact of devaluation on exports and imports and on the import surplus is dependent on the degree of restrictiveness or expansiveness of the demand policy which accompanies the devaluation. By and large, conditions of full employment have indeed prevailed in the Israeli economy. To examine the likelihood of success of the devaluation process in Israel, the demand policy accompanying it must therefore be investigated. I shall focus on a few main variables of monetary policy, primarily on the money supply,[5] and on the public sector's excess demand for goods and services as an indicator of the direction of fiscal policy.[6] Attention will be paid mostly to the two episodes of substantial formal devaluation: the progressive devaluation of 1952–54 and the devaluation of February 1962. The rest of the process of devaluation will be mostly ignored, for two reasons. First, in Israel, no substantial devaluation has ever been performed over a short period through changes in the nonformal component of the rate. Thus, the examination of demand policy would be fruitful only for periods of formal devaluation. Second, the two later episodes of formal devaluation are less interesting than the earlier ones. The devaluation of November 1967 was not only minor (close to 17 per cent for the formal rate, and only some 12–13 per cent for the effective rates for exports and imports), but it was undertaken while the economy was still in recession (and following the impact of substantial budgetary expansion due to the Six-Day War). Therefore, it was both atypical of the Israeli economy and difficult to analyze. The latest devaluation episode, that of August 1971, is probably still too recent to analyze. Besides, it was again of much smaller proportions than the devaluations of 1952–54 or even that of 1962: it amounted to an increase of only some 12–14 per cent in the effective rates.

Table 5-2 contains data for the major monetary-fiscal variables during 1949–56, that is, the devaluation years 1952–54 as well as a few years preceding and following them. In column 3, the increase in the government's combined domestic and external debt stands as a proxy for the government's excess demand for goods and services, of which no direct estimate is available.[7] Column 4, which shows this magnitude as a percentage of the GNP, is probably a better indication of the expansive or restrictive impact of the gov-

TABLE 5-2
Major Monetary-Fiscal Variables, 1949–56

Year[a]	Increase in Government Debt (IL millions)			Column 3 as Percentage of GNP (4)	Increase During the Year (per cent)	
	Internal Debt (1)	External Debt (2)	Total of (1) + (2) (3)		Money Supply (5)	Credit to Public (6)
1949	50.1	19.2	69.3	20[b]	39.1	37.8
1950	65.4	22.6	88.0	19.2	35.4	42.3
1951	33.0	43.1	76.1	10.9	27.2	28.9
1952	8.8	62.1	70.8	6.8	6.5	23.5
1953	19.6	128.5	148.1	11.3	24.5	38.0
1954	44.8	234.1	278.9	16.2	20.1	13.1
1955	49.5	224.9	274.4	12.9	20.4	10.8
1956	154.7	220.5	375.2	14.7	23.2	18.7

SOURCE:

Col. 1—From *Statistical Abstract of Israel*, 1961, pp. 424–425 (excluding compulsory loan).

Col. 2—From *Statistical Abstract of Israel*, 1953–54, pp. 188–189, and ibid., 1956–57, p. 213, including, among others, unilateral receipts from the U.S. government and from German reparations.

Col. 4—GNP data (current prices) from Nadav Halevi and Ruth Klinov-Malul, *The Economic Development of Israel* (New York: Praeger, 1968), App. Table 1.

Cols. 5 and 6—From Don Patinkin, *The Israel Economy: The First Decade* (Jerusalem: Falk Project for Economic Research, 1959; in English), App. B, pp. 142–143.

a. Data on government debt (columns 1, 2, and 3) are for fiscal years (April to March); GNP (denominator for column 4) and monetary data (columns 5 and 6) are for calendar years.

b. Rough approximation.

ernment's excess demand in a fast-growing economy such as Israel's—particularly at that time. It appears from column 4 that excess demand declined by about half from 1949 and 1950 to 1951, from a level of some 20 per cent to about 11 per cent of the national product. In 1952, it declined considerably further—to less than 7 per cent. In 1953, it increased to the level of 1951; but it was lower than in 1954–56, when it increased further to close to 15 per cent. It may be inferred, then, that fiscal policy turned contractionary in 1951, proceeded more intensively in that direction in 1952, and continued to be somewhat contractionary in 1953, compared to policy subsequently or before 1951. Since the fiscal data are for budgetary years, which run from April to March, April 1951 would appear to be the turning point toward a restrictive policy. In the absence of quarterly fiscal data, the actual turning point cannot be established, just as the turn upward toward expansion cannot be dated precisely. But in rough terms, it may be said that fiscal policy became restrictive about half or three-quarters of a year before the start of the devaluation process (in February 1952), and remained so for about three years, turning upward by about mid-1954, a year before the end of the period of progressive devaluation.

Data on the money supply, in column 5, show roughly similar movements. The expansion of the money supply, which was very substantial in 1949–50, subsided somewhat in 1951, and declined sharply in 1952. In this case, quarterly data (not shown) permit a more precise dating of events. A radical slowdown—almost a halt—of the expansion of the money supply, occurred abruptly in the third quarter of 1951. The near-freezing of the money supply lasted through 1952. In early 1953, the money supply started again to expand at a substantial rate—not quite as rapidly as before mid-1951, but at about the same rate as through the following years, 1954–56. Thus, the contraction in the rate of expansion of the money supply began about four or five months before the start of the process of devaluation, and lasted for about a year and a half.

Monetary change in this period was due primarily to two factors. One was the reduction in the government's borrowing from the banking system, which was associated with a reduction of the government's excess demand. This reduction may be seen in the data on the government's internal debt (column 1), the overwhelming component of which was debt to the banking system. This borrowing declined in 1951, was negligible in 1952, and remained low in 1953. An important step in this direction was taken in June 1952, on the occasion of a currency conversion: a 10 per cent tax was imposed on almost all money (cash and demand deposits) held by the public. The other important source of change was the development of bank credit to the public (total credit of the commercial banking system other than to the government). As may be seen from column 6, the rate of expansion of credit to the public declined from a level of about 40 per cent per year during 1949–50 to about 25 per cent during 1951–52 (the change in pace occurring, again, in about September 1952 and the reverse change in the spring of 1953). The amount of credit was supposedly controlled by reserve ratio requirements, which were extremely high (90 per cent at the margin, i.e., on deposits added after a given base date); but banks could lend "beyond the reserve requirements" [8] by governmental authorization, and credit was extended mostly by this means. The new expansion of credit that began in early 1953 was the main factor in the increase in the rate of expansion of the money supply at that time, whereas the accumulation of foreign-exchange reserves explains the expansion of money supply in 1954, when expansion of bank credit to the public as well as to the government was again modest. [9]

It appears then that for about a year and a half or two years, from the summer or fall of 1951 to the spring or summer of 1953, fiscal and monetary policies were restrictive—even highly so, in comparison with preceding years. Such policies were, indeed, specifically included in the New Economic Policy declared in February 1952, along with the first step of the devaluation process undertaken then. As may be seen, the restrictive demand policy even preceded the devaluation by about half a year and was thus announced when it was already in force.[10] This restrictive policy lasted for about a year or a year and a half after the start of the devaluation process, and was reversed—although without its returning to the expansionary proportions it had assumed prior to mid-1951—before the final stages of the devaluation process were completed.

In Table 5-3, the monetary-fiscal variables are presented for the two years, 1960 and 1961, preceding the devaluation of February 1962, as well

TABLE 5-3
Major Monetary-Fiscal Variables, 1960–66

Year	Increase During Year (per cent)			Excess Demand of Public Sector	
	Money Supply (1)	Foreign Assets[a] (2)	Credit to Public (3)	IL Millions (4)	Percentage of GNP (5)
1960	21.3	63.7	21.9	193	4.4
1961	10.1	34.1	18.3	175	3.3
1962	29.7	138.8[b]	27.4[b]	430	6.8
1963	28.1	18.0[c]	19.7	381	5.1
1964	6.1	2.8	15.7	356	4.1
1965	11.2	14.3	12.5	452	4.4
1966	5.7	−4.0	23.7	688	6.0

SOURCE:
Cols. 1–3—From Bank of Israel, *Annual Report*, 1965, 1966, Table XV-1.
Col. 4—From ibid., 1963, 1965, 1966, Table VII-1.
Col. 5—GNP data in current prices from Halevi and Klinov-Malul, *Economic Development of Israel*.
a. Underlying data valued in Israeli pounds.
b. These rates of change reflect, among other things, the increase in the value of foreign assets and foreign-exchange-rate-linked public credit resulting from the February 1962 devaluation. Excluding this effect, the rates of change for 1962 would be 76.4 per cent (column 2) and 16.2 per cent (column 3).
c. In part, this reflects the effect of an extensive prepayment of government external debts, financed by a special borrowing from the Bank of Israel of IL 148.7 million. Were this magnitude to be added to external assets, the increase in column 2 in 1963 would have been 29.8 per cent.

as the five years, 1962–66, following it. The impression gained from these data stands in striking contrast to that which has emerged from the analysis of the earlier devaluation episode: the devaluation of 1962 seems to have been accompanied by *expansive* (or increasingly expansive) demand policies, rather than by contractionary (or decreasingly expansive) policies. The annual rate of expansion of the money supply (column 1) approached 30 per cent during 1962 and 1963, the two years following the devaluation, far exceeding the rates of expansion in either the preceding or the following years; indeed, one has to go as far back as 1950–51 or as far forward as 1971–72 to find similar rates of increase of the money supply. The excess demand of the government for goods and services (column 4) as a percentage of GNP (column 5) was twice as high in 1962 as in 1961. In 1962 and 1963, this magnitude was considerably higher than in the two preceding or two following years. Judged by this measure, fiscal policy, too, became expansive in the period following devaluation.

As has been mentioned earlier, the basic difference between the two episodes of devaluation probably lies in the motivation for each. In 1952–54, the government felt the urgent need for contractionary demand policies both because foreign-exchange reserves were totally exhausted, and because inflation had led to the feeling of a complete breakdown of the system of management of the economy: it was obvious that a concerted effort was required to deal with these two problems. In 1962, no similar stresses were apparent: foreign-exchange reserves were high and still rising, and the rate of inflation in preceding years, although somewhat higher than in the late 1950s, was not felt to be a serious threat to the orderly running of the economy.

On that score, moreover, it is very likely that the expansionary fiscal policy in 1962–63 was at least partly due to the fear of price increases and to a misconception about the source of such increases and the manner of combating them. From the circumstantial evidence available for the period, it appears that the government saw the process of price increases as originating not from excess demand in the economy, but from cost increases. Budgetary policy was thus directed toward the goal of creating offsetting pressures from the cost side. This was done by lowering (or refraining from raising) taxes on various expenditures and by granting subsidies. These steps contributed, in turn, to the increase in the government's excess demand.

The expansionary monetary policy which followed the devaluation of 1962 may be explained primarily by the dominance of foreign assets in the determination of monetary developments, a dominance which was almost entirely absent in the first half of the 1950s. As may be seen from Table 5-3, columns 2 and 3, the rate of expansion of bank credit to the public was much more stable, over the years covered in the table, than the rate of expansion of the banking system's foreign assets, and the variation in the rate of expansion of the money supply seems to be closely related to fluctuations in the size of foreign assets.

In Chart 5-1 the relationship just described may be observed over the whole period, 1949–72. No association between external reserves and the money supply may be traced before 1957. Indeed, reserves during the first half of the 1950s were so low that even large fluctuations in their rate of change would not have been very significant. Beginning in 1957 or 1958, however, the rates of change of the two move together: practically without exception, the rate of change of the money supply rises and falls with the rate of change of the country's external reserves (the latter being itself negative as well as positive).[11] In this sense, monetary policy in Israel appears to adhere closely to the classical gold-standard "rules of the game." This adherence may be explained by a number of factors. One would be an active compliance with the rationale of the rules, namely, a recognition that monetary policy should be expansive when the country's foreign assets grow, and contractionary when foreign assets fall. While such a recognition may have played a role once in a while, it has not presumably been the main factor in the explanation of the phenomenon at hand. More probably, the explanations lie in the technique and manner of conduct of monetary policy in Israel. The Bank of Israel has not usually attempted—either because it did not wish to do so or because it assumed it was not able—to change the rate of expansion of credit to the public enough to offset the effect of fluctuations in the country's external assets; to do so would sometimes have meant actually contracting the supply of this credit.[12] Rather, the policy of the Bank of Israel was most often aimed at achieving a roughly stable rate of expansion of bank credit, thus avoiding only the secondary effect of fluctuations of external assets through their impact on the liquid assets of the banking system. Of at least the same importance, however, has been the large measure of inflexibility in the conduct of monetary policy due to the techniques used. Open-market operations, or their equivalent, are only a recent phenomenon in Israel; and even now, in the early 1970s, they are still conducted on a modest scale. From the late 1950s to the late 1960s (and to a large extent also in the 1970s), the major instrument of monetary policy was minimum reserve requirements. Due to the complexity of the decision-making machinery, moreover, this instrument was not used very frequently: the frequency could be stated in years, or half-years, rather than in weeks. As a result, any discretionary change by the Bank of Israel was time-consuming and involved a long lag. Automatic factors, chiefly fluctuations of foreign-exchange reserves, thus played a major role.

To all of these elements should be added the fact that most aspects of foreign-exchange policy are not handled by, or coordinated with, the monetary authority. The large accumulation of foreign-exchange reserves in 1962 resulted partly from the initiative of individuals (including firms and banks),

CHART 5-1
Money Supply and External Reserves, 1949–72

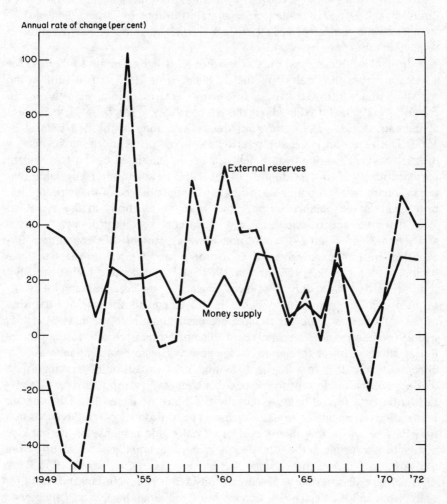

Annual rate of change (per cent)

SOURCE:
External reserves—Table 2-2. Note that "foreign assets" in Table 5-3 refer to the Bank of Israel only, and are valued there in Israeli pounds.
Money supply—From Don Patinkin, *The Israel Economy: The First Decade* (Jerusalem: Falk Project for Economic Research, 1959; in English); Bank of Israel, *Annual Report*, various years.

many of whom had anticipated the devaluation and delayed capital transfers to the country until afterward. But at the same time, the Treasury was actively engaged in encouraging, securing, promoting, and guaranteeing a variety of forms of short- and medium-term capital transfers to Israel, disregarding completely the impact of such transfers on monetary developments and on demand in the economy.

In light of the association discussed here, it is interesting to digress, for a moment, from the analysis of the devaluation of 1962 and to turn to the recession which followed it by a few years. This recession, the only one in Israel since 1953, started at about the fall of 1965 and reached its lowest point at the end of 1966, the upturn apparently beginning in the first quarter of 1967. The recession is usually referred to—most of all by the policymakers themselves—as resulting from a deliberate policy initiated by the government partly in response to the "failure" of the 1962 devaluation: recognizing that expansionary demand policy was to blame for the absence of the expected improvement in the balance of payments after devaluation, so the argument goes, the government decided to revert to a contractionary policy. A glance at Table 5-3 and Chart 5-1 would not, however, support this contention. Excess demand of the government, as a proportion of GNP, appears to have been slightly higher in 1965 than in 1964, and considerably higher in 1966; thus, at least so far as this measure is concerned, the recession cannot be attributed to a change in fiscal policy. On the other hand, the rate of expansion of the money supply appears to have been substantially lower in 1964, 1965, and 1966 than in earlier years;[13] and this corresponds closely to the change during those years in foreign-exchange reserves, whose rate of increase declined radically. It is true that in 1964 and 1965 expansion of banking credit to the public also slowed down; but this cannot be attributed to the implementation of a discretionary policy by the Bank of Israel, since it took no contractionary measures in these years. The slowdown of credit expansion may thus be reasonably interpreted as an automatic response of the banking system to the decline in the rate of expansion of its liquid assets resulting from the slowdown in foreign-exchange accumulation. Only in 1966 did the Bank of Israel take discretionary measures (considerably reducing reserve ratio requirements and increasing the amount of its rediscounting), which succeeded in overcoming this secondary impact, leading to a substantial expansion of credit despite the decline of foreign-exchange reserves in that year. If this interpretation of the data is correct, the recession would appear to have been an automatic response of the economy to the slowdown—virtually, in fact, a complete cessation—in the accumulation of foreign assets, rather than the result of discretionary government policy. Even so, it might of course still be argued, perhaps correctly, that the government could have counteracted this automatic development by a more expansionary policy than it actually undertook, or by a more rapid one, and that the failure to do so indicates that the contractionary development seemed desirable to the government.

Turning back to monetary developments following the devaluation of 1962, another important element, also related to foreign assets, should be pointed out. It will be recalled that, starting in 1957, recipients of personal restitution payments from Germany have been entitled to retain a portion of their receipts in two forms of foreign-exchange deposits—either deposits out of which foreign exchange may actually be withdrawn or deposits denominated in foreign exchange, the value of which in Israeli pounds is thus linked to the rate of exchange (see Chapter 4). At first, these accounts were of minor importance. But with time, as the size of restitution payments expanded and past accumulations of these deposits kept growing, foreign-exchange deposits assumed significant proportions. This may be seen in Table 5-4, in which these deposits are presented both in absolute values in terms of the Israeli pound (column 1) and in relation to the size of the money supply

TABLE 5-4

Foreign-Exchange Deposits of Local Residents, 1957–71

Year	End-of-Year Value (IL mill.) (1)	Ratio to Money Supply (per cent) (2)	Ratio to Annual GNP (per cent) (3)
1957	23	3.9	0.8
1958	38	5.8	1.1
1959	85	11.7	2.2
1960	174	19.8	4.0
1961	247	25.5	4.7
1962	547	43.5	8.7
1963	633	39.3	8.4
1964	780	45.7	8.9
1965	965	50.8	9.2
1966	1,124	56.0	9.8
1967	1,601	63.1	13.4
1968	1,924	66.4	13.7
1969	2,498	84.1	15.7
1970	3,000	88.7	16.3
1971	4,783	110.2	21.0

SOURCE:

Col. 1—Derived from balance sheets of Bank of Israel, in Bank of Israel *Bulletin*, various years.

Cols. 2 and 3—See Source note to Table 5-3 for columns 1 and 5. GNP data for 1967 and after from Bank of Israel, *Annual Report*, various years.

(column 2) and annual GNP (column 3). In the late 1950s, the foreign-exchange deposits were still of minor importance. But throughout the 1960s they grew very rapidly. By the end of 1971, they were larger than the money supply and equal to more than 20 percent of the national product in that year.

A formal devaluation automatically increases the local-currency value of the foreign-exchange deposits by the proportion of the devaluation. This has an expansionary effect in three interrelated ways. First, this part of the wealth of holders of foreign-exchange deposits increases by the given proportion,[14] thus leading presumably to increased consumption expenditures. Second, it is the liquid part of wealth that increases; those with no desire to raise the proportion of their liquid assets would shift their holdings to real assets, thus adding another expansionary factor. And third, since these expenditures entail the conversion of foreign-exchange deposits into local-currency deposits, they raise the liquidity of the banking system, thus increasing its capacity to expand credit to the public.[15] These factors would be strengthened when the devaluation had been long anticipated, and when no further devaluation was expected in the near future.

At the time of the February 1962 devaluation, this element was already of considerable importance. As may be gathered from the data in Table 5-4 for the end of 1961, the formal devaluation of some 67 per cent (from IL 1.80 to IL 3.00 per dollar) raised the size of the inventory of foreign-exchange deposits by a value equivalent to about 15 per cent of the money supply, or 3 per cent of the 1961 national product. It is probably not feasible to give a quantitative estimate of the direct impact of this increase on demand in the economy. However, an estimate is available of the probable effect of this element on conversion of foreign-currency deposits into local-currency deposits.[16] This conversion is assumed to be a function of the inventory of existing foreign-exchange deposits and of current receipts of restitution payments. When a multiple regression function was fitted using predevaluation data, the rate of conversion into local currency in 1962, the first year following the devaluation, was found to be only slightly higher than "normal." In 1963, on the other hand, it was substantially higher and became a major factor contributing to the expansion of the money supply. Apparently, the effect of devaluation on the rate of conversion was delayed, partly (as would seem from other indications) because at first some expectations of a further devaluation were entertained.

It should also be noted that when foreign-exchange reserves rise—as they did in 1962 and 1963—the formal devaluation increases the local-currency value of the addition to reserves. This is another expansionary monetary factor, contributing again to the automatic expansionary effect of the devaluation on monetary developments.

An understanding of the role of foreign assets and foreign-exchange-denominated assets thus helps to explain the contrast between monetary policy and performance following the 1952–54 and 1962 devaluations. In the earlier episode, foreign assets had been nil before the devaluation, and remained so for the two years following it. At the time of the later devaluation, on the other hand, foreign-exchange-linked assets were substantial; and the country's external reserves kept growing rapidly after the devaluation. The automatic expansionary effect on the economy's liquidity was thus substantial in the devaluation of 1962. The growing importance of foreign and foreign-exchange-linked assets has been an added constraint on the use of monetary policy since the late 1950s. The knowledge that, owing to the strong automatic expansionary effect of these assets, a devaluation would require a more strongly contractionary fiscal and credit policy than otherwise has probably served as an additional source of resistance to the use of changes in the foreign-exchange rate as a policy instrument.

iii. THE FOREIGN-EXCHANGE RATE AND DOMESTIC PRICES

To affect decisions by economic units, changes in the foreign-exchange rate must be *relative* to the price level maintained in the local market: to reduce imports and raise exports, the foreign-exchange rate must rise more (or fall less) than prices of home products in sales to the local market. This, indeed, is the other side of the demand policy discussed in the preceding section. Under circumstances of full employment, local prices will tend to rise more after devaluation, the more expansive demand policy is. These prices are then more likely to rise by as much as (or even more than) the increase in the rate of exchange resulting from devaluation, thus tending to cancel the tendency toward an increase in the relative price of exports and imports versus prices in the home market.

One difficulty encountered in examining price changes following devaluations in Israel is that during at least part of the period of most intensive devaluation, 1952–54, available price indexes are only a poor guide to actual price changes. It will be recalled that controls, rationing, the use of the black market, and the level of black-market prices all reached their peaks at the time of the devaluation of 1952. Official price indexes, on the other hand— the only ones available—reflected only legal ceiling prices. These indexes show a combined increase of the consumer's price index of only about 10 per cent from the end of 1948 to the end of 1951, a figure which evidently bears only little resemblance to actual price increases in the domestic market (including its nonsanctioned sector). Some indication of what prices might have been in a free market may be obtained from monetary data. From the end of

1948 to the end of 1951, the money supply increased by about 140 per cent. Income and product data are available only from 1950 on. From 1950 to 1951, GNP in constant prices increased by about 25 per cent.[17] It is usually assumed that the national product increased at a slower rate in earlier years. Therefore, over the period from late 1948 to late 1951, GNP may have increased by about 70 to 75 per cent. Consequently, assuming equilibrium prices in 1948, a strict quantity theory applied to income data would thus have yielded a figure for the increase in the general price level over those three years of about 40 per cent, that is, roughly 30 per cent more than the 10 per cent shown in the cost-of-living index. With the devaluation of 1952, it will be recalled, a process of gradual liberalization and removal of controls and rationing was begun. In 1954, at the end of the period of progressive devaluation, the scope of the black market had greatly declined, and differences between its prices and the prices recorded in constructing the official indexes were not radical. Thus, the increases for 1952–54, and perhaps shortly after, shown by such price indexes (primarily the cost-of-living index, which served to measure consumption prices) are *overstatements* of actual price increases, since black-market prices rose much less than official prices and sometimes even declined. In other words, the recorded price increases of 1952–54 actually reflect also the unrecorded price rises (estimated, in the rough exercise above, at 30 per cent) of the preceding years.[18] This should be borne in mind in analyses involving price data for those years.

Table 5-5 and Chart 5-2 present the time path of movements of the foreign-exchange rate and of local prices. In Chart 5-2, annual averages of the effective rate of exchange, the index of consumer prices, and the index of the GNP price deflator are shown. The effective rate is calculated as an average of export and import rates weighted by the annual amounts of imports and of value added in exports. Table 5-5, on the other hand, contains quarterly[19] data on the rate of foreign exchange and on the index of consumer prices for three selected periods in which the main devaluation episodes took place: 1952–56, 1962–65, and 1967–71.

The contrast between the period of progressive devaluation, 1952–54, and the period following the devaluation of February 1962 is striking. During 1952–54 the domestic price increase, although substantial, was far below the increase in the rate of exchange. In fact, only by the end of 1970 did local prices rise above their 1951 level to the same extent as had the rate of exchange by the end of 1954. At the latter date the increase in domestic prices over the 1951 level was only about one-fourth as much as the increase in the rate of exchange. This lag of movement of local prices behind the exchange rate is all the more remarkable in view of the preceding comment on the strong upward bias involved in the use of official price indexes for the years 1952–54.

TABLE 5-5

Effective Exchange Rates and Consumer Prices,
Quarterly Data for Selected Periods, 1952–71

1952–56 (end 1951 = 100)			1962–65 (end 1961 = 100)			1968–71 (end 1967 = 100)		
Year and Quarter	Effec- tive Rate	Con- sumer Prices	Year and Quarter	Effec- tive Rate	Con- sumer Prices	Year and Quarter	Effec- tive Rate	Con- sumer Prices
1952 I	129	116	1962 I	130	103	1968 I	113	102
II	195	143	II	130	105	II	113	103
III	232	157	III	130	106	III	113	102
IV	246	168	IV	130	111	IV	114	102
1953 I	215	174	1963 I	130	112	1969 I	114	103
II	276	183	II	130	112	II	115	105
III	311	193	III	130	113	III	115	104
IV	324	199	IV	130	116	IV	115	106
1954 I	370	206	1964 I	130	118	1970 I	119	106
II	433	206	II	130	118	II	119	110
III	504	211	III	131	119	III	134	111
IV	537	217	IV	131	121	IV	134	118
1955 I	548	217	1965 I	131	125	1971 I	134	121
II	560	220	II	132	129	II	134	124
III	563	223	III	132	128	III	153	125
IV	566	227	IV	132	131	IV	153	133
1956 I	570	229						
II	572	236						
III	577	238						
IV	582	240						

SOURCE: Consumer prices—*Statistical Abstract of Israel*, various years; "end of year" for 1951, 1961, and 1967 is average for last quarter of the year.

Effective rates—For 1952–54, import rate from Michael Michaely, *Israel's Foreign Exchange Rate System*, vol. II, *Tables* (Jerusalem: Falk Institute, 1968; in Hebrew); for 1955–56, import rate interpolated from annual data; for 1957–61, Tables 4-2 and 4-3, above; for 1962–65, weighted average of import and export rates (change in 1962 reflects the February 1962 devaluation; other data are annual); for 1968–71, weighted average of import and export rates. The base of the index for 1968–71 is the rate in 1967 through November 19. Changes took place in November 1967 (1968I), February 1970 (1970I), August 1970 (1970III), and August 1971 (1971III). Minor changes shown during 1968–69 are interpolations from annual data.

CHART 5-2

Effective Exchange Rate, Consumer Prices, and Implied GNP Price Deflator, 1950–71

(annual averages)

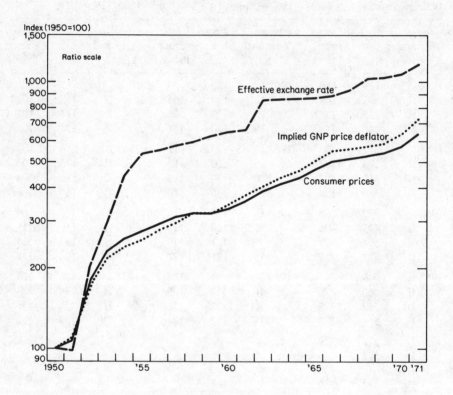

SOURCE:
Effective exchange rate—Weighted average of cols. 3 and 4 of Table 5-1, above.
Consumer prices and implied GNP price deflator—Table A-17.

In the period following the February 1962 devaluation, on the other hand, the lag of domestic prices was much briefer. By early 1964, domestic prices increased by about three-fifths of the degree of devaluation; and by mid-1965, they had increased in almost the same proportion. Since the time sequence does not indicate the functional relationship between the two variables—that is, the contribution of devaluation to the rate of increase of domestic prices—it cannot be inferred that the devaluation did not lead to a relative increase of the price of foreign exchange beyond this period of about three years: some domestic price increase would have most probably occurred without the devaluation. In other words: the return of the relative price of foreign exchange to its predevaluation level within some three years does *not* necessarily mean that this policy act was meaningless beyond this period.

As may be judged from Chart 5-2, domestic prices and the rate of exchange showed similar increases during the long period extending from late 1954 until just before the formal devaluation of February 1962. Since changes in the effective rate were minor in those years, it would seem unreasonable to assume that they were the factor which determined the rate of increase of domestic prices. Insofar as a causal relationship existed here, it must have been in the opposite direction: the exchange-rate policy of the government during that period may have been intended to result in periodic changes of the effective rate in the same proportion as increases in domestic prices. On the other hand, in the sequence of changes in the rate from 1967 on, causal relationships probably ran in both directions: from price rises to changes in the rate of exchange and then in the opposite way. The devaluation of November 1967, coming when recession was still felt, left domestic prices almost intact. However, the effective devaluation of August 1970, the result of imposing the 20 per cent import duty, and the formal devaluation of August 1971, were followed within a short time by similar increases in local prices. This development would be clearly evident if preliminary data for 1972 were added. Here, too, it would be mistaken to conclude that these price rises—in whole or in part—would not have taken place without the devaluations. But like the episode of the 1962 devaluation, the behavior of local prices is consistent with the demand policy adopted, which was expansionary throughout most of this period.[20]

iv. THE EFFECTIVENESS OF CHANGES IN THE EXCHANGE RATE

In the preceding section the movement of domestic prices following devaluation and the relationship of devaluation to accompanying demand policies have been discussed. I now analyze the effect of *relative* changes in the foreign-exchange rate, that is, changes in the price-level-deflated effective exchange rate (PLD-EER), on the main balance-of-payments magnitudes of exports and imports.

Annual rates of change of EERs adjusted for purchasing power parity are shown in Table 5-6 for exports (column 2) and imports (column 4). The purchasing power parity (PPP) is the rate which would leave unchanged the price ratio of exports or imports to local sales of home-produced goods.[21] An increase in the PPP-adjusted exchange rate would thus mean a rise in the price of exports or imports in relation to the price of domestic goods; and a

TABLE 5-6

Relative Prices and Quantities of Exports and Imports, 1951–71

(annual percentage changes)

		Exports		Imports for Civilian Use	
Year	Purchasing Power Parity (1)	PPP-adj. Effective Exchange Rate (2)	Quantity (net of change in GNP) (3)	PPP-adj. Effective Exchange Rate (4)	Quantity (net of change in GNP) (5)
1951	3.0	3.0	−8.1	−5.0	−18.6
1952	49.5	32.0	28.0	36.8	−19.9
1953	35.1	16.9	24.9	6.9	1.5
1954	6.7	27.0	15.4	44.6	−13.8
1955	0.5	5.0	−14.8	22.9	−7.1
1956	4.9	7.1	5.7	−2.8	−2.0
1957	0.9	7.0	10.9	2.5	0.6
1958	11.0	−3.3	1.9	−9.3	1.4
1959	6.5	−1.7	17.8	0	−3.7
1960	2.2	1.7	17.9	0.4	8.7
1961	10.2	−6.4	5.2	−8.0	12.8
1962	9.6	2.7	7.7	25.2	−0.1
1963	6.1	−4.9	6.0	−5.0	−5.5
1964	4.1	−3.3	−2.9	−4.5	11.4
1965	6.6	−5.8	2.0	−4.3	−10.0
1966	5.2	1.0	10.0	−4.0	−3.8
1967	2.8	6.1	7.8	0	−1.6
1968	3.2	9.5	12.1	8.8	21.2
1969	−1.5	2.2	−6.1	3.4	−0.6
1970	8.3	2.2	2.2	−3.4	3.3
1971	10.6	1.7	19.4	4.3	10.2

SOURCE:

Col. 1—See text note 21. P_H, domestic price level (implied GNP price deflator) is derived from GNP data at current and constant prices in *Statistical Abstract of Israel*, various years, and is shown in Chart 5-2. P_T, average price level of exports and imports, is computed from Table 6-6, column 2.

Cols. 2 and 4—From Table 5-1, columns 3 and 4, and changes in PPP estimates in column 1 above.

Cols. 3 and 5—Export and import data in dollars from *Statistical Abstract of Israel*, various years, deflated by corresponding price indexes in Table 6-5. GNP in constant prices, 1950–69, from Don Patinkin, "The Economic Development of Israel" (unpublished, 1970; in English), App. Table 7; 1970–71, from Bank of Israel, *Annual Reports*. See also accompanying text.

decrease in the adjusted rate would mean the opposite. Table 5-6 also contains annual rates of change of exports (column 3) and imports (column 5) *net* of the rate of change of the national product. In the case of exports, for instance, the change presented is the proportional increase in exports over (if the net change is positive) or below (if it is negative) the proportional change in GNP. It is implicitly assumed in such a presentation that in the absence of changes in relative prices, exports and imports would remain a fixed proportion of the national product, and deviations from these proportional changes may thus be associated with changes in relative prices. The export and import data refer to goods and services. However, imports exclude the purchases of defense material and equipment. These are roughly identified by the import item "government, n.e.s." in the services account of the balance of payments. Imports of military goods have been substantial and very volatile, and presumably depend little on price movements—at least in the short run and within a wide range of price changes. The inclusion of such goods in import data would thus be likely to yield misleading results when the impact of changes in relative prices on imports is analyzed.

In data such as those presented in Table 5-6, apparent associations of year-to-year movements of the variables cannot be expected to be very high even when the actual impact of one variable on the other is strong. This is due to the time lag which must exist in the response of quantity to prices and to the effect of using annual averages in the observations. It may be presumed that a full response requires much more than a single year for its manifestation, whereas comparisons of annual averages may not reflect even a large part of the impact that does take place within a single year (or may even, in extreme cases, point in a misleading direction). In addition, it should be noted from Table 5-6 that during most of the period the changes in the (adjusted) rates of exchange were quite mild. With minor changes in relative prices— just a few percentage points—random changes in exports and imports, as well as errors in measurement, become important relative to the impact of changes in relative prices, and the associations sought for inevitably appear weaker.

It is not surprising, therefore, that the data in Table 5-6 do not, for most of the period covered, suggest any clear association of price and quantity changes.[22] The outstanding exception is the period of the first half of the 1950s, in which the quantities of exports and imports seem clearly to respond to the price movements, which in this period were both large and consistent. During the three years 1952–54, the PPP-adjusted exchange rate increased at an average annual rate of 25.3 per cent, in comparison with an average increase of 1.3 per cent for all other years presented in Table 5-6. The average annual increase of exports (net of the change in GNP) was 22.8 per cent in the years 1952–54, versus 5.3 per cent for all other years. In 1952–55, the average annual change in the exchange rate for imports rose 22.8 per cent;

the quantity index fell 9.8 per cent. For the other years covered in the table, the exchange rate was unchanged and the quantity index rose 1.4 per cent.

This comparison yields the rough impression that relative-price changes of exports and imports do have an impact in the "right" direction on both exports and imports. Elasticities of supply of exports and demand for imports for Israel, developed on the basis of two recent studies, make it possible to carry the analysis somewhat further.[23]

Halevi's study[24] is concerned with both aggregate exports of goods, and, more particularly, with industrial exports (excluding diamonds), which since the late 1950s constitute the major category of exports, and are presumably more sensitive to price changes than any of the other export categories of goods.[25] Value added in exports, at constant prices, is shown in this study as a function of the relative price of exports (that is, the adjusted effective exchange rate for value added in exports) and the size of capital, which is taken as an indicator of productive capacity. For total exports of goods, the PPP-adjusted exchange rate, like the earlier figures shown, is based on domestic prices of GNP; and the capital variable used is aggregate capital stock in the economy. For the period 1955–69, the relative-price elasticity of the supply of exports as obtained from the function is 0.50 (with an R^2 of .989); for the years 1960–69 only, it is 0.65 (with an R^2 of .970). For industrial exports alone, the capital variable used is the capital stock in industry; and in the PPP adjustment, two alternative domestic price levels are employed: GNP prices and the level of industrial prices. The former alternative yields a higher elasticity of supply than the latter, and both values are higher than the elasticity found for total exports of goods. When the price variable is the PPP-adjusted effective exchange rate for industrial exports, in which GNP prices are utilized, the elasticity of supply of industrial exports is found to be 1.19 (R^2 is .987) and when local industrial prices are used, the supply elasticity is 0.87 (R^2 is .980). Halevi also attempts a distributed-lag model, to introduce the possibility of responsiveness to relative price changes which stretches beyond a single year. In the regression fitted, about two-thirds of the total adjustment is found to take place over the first year following the price change. The supply elasticity thus obtained using the industrial-prices variant in the PPP adjustment, is 1.34—considerably higher than the figure of 0.87 reached in the simple, nonlagged regression.

From Halevi's estimates, it appears that the supply elasticity of exports is substantial, and probably even high. This impression is strengthened by the realization that these estimates must, for a number of reasons, be biased downward. It should be noted, first, that the estimates exclude the first half of the 1950s, when the exchange-rate changes were not only at their strongest but appear from my data to have had relatively the strongest impact: as has been argued before, slight variations in the exchange rate would result in lower estimates of elasticities (of supply or demand) than major price changes, because of errors in measurement. It has also been pointed out that the use of annual averages, which inherently incorporate errors in measurement, tends to lower the estimates of the elasticities. No less important is the time lag involved in the response of quantity to price. The use of a distributed-lag model partly solves this difficulty, but does not eliminate it altogether. Thus, Halevi finds a very high elasticity of supply (roughly, 2) of industrial exports in relation to the change in capital stock. It may be assumed that the bias toward exports in the process of growth of capital stock, which is indicated by this elasticity, is itself at least partly a reaction to earlier changes in relative prices in favor of exports. If this is true, part of the quantity reaction to relative price changes would be disguised, even in a distributed-lag model, as a response to changes in capital stock.

Import elasticities of demand are investigated in Weinblat's study,[26] where three main import categories (as well as major subcategories) are examined separately: final consumer goods, investment goods, and intermediate inputs.[27] Imports of each category are assumed to be a function of total domestic use of the category (i.e., respectively, total private consumption, total investment in fixed assets, and total product of industries using intermediate inputs) and of relative prices, that is, prices of imports of the category relative to local prices of the respective local use of the category.[28] Annual averages for 1952–67 are used as observations. As might be expected, the highest (in absolute size) relative price elasticity of demand for imports is for final consumer goods: -3.07 (R^2 of the function $= .720$). The elasticity of demand for investment goods is somewhat lower, but still rather high: -2.27 ($R^2 = .966$). On the other hand, for intermediate inputs, which form the bulk of Israel's imports, the elasticity is rather low: -0.39 ($R^2 = .986$). Given the composition of imports in recent years—when intermediate inputs formed close to two-thirds of the total; investment goods, roughly one-fourth; and final consumer goods, about one-tenth—a weighted average of the three elasticities would yield an elasticity of demand for total imports of close to unity. Weinblat's direct estimate of this elasticity, on the basis of observations for 1952–67, is -1.358 ($R^2 = .976$). This size is not inconsistent with the average of the three groups, since the share of imports of final consumer goods was much higher in the earlier part of this period than later.[29]

These findings indicate a substantial relative price elasticity of demand for imports of about unity. The difference in demand elasticities of these various categories in itself contributes to a decline with time of the elasticity of demand for imports: owing to the strong responsiveness of imports of final consumer goods, the major increases in the relative prices of all imports during the first half of the 1950s helped to engender a particularly large reduction (relative to the size of the economy) of the former and thus, to a decline of their weight in total imports. In other words, imports consist of more of a "hard core" in later than in earlier years. Yet, the degree of such "hardness" is probably exaggerated by the findings: it seems very likely that the estimate of the elasticity of demand for imports of intermediate goods is biased downward, probably to a substantial degree, by the use of annual observations. The response to price changes of imports of final goods may be expected to be rather fast, although even there it could hardly be expected to be exhausted within a year. On the other hand, changes in imports of intermediate goods may be assumed to be rather slow. An increase in the relative price of imported inputs may be expected to lead to a lowering of imports in three ways: a change in the production techniques of individual industries, leading to the substitution of inputs available locally (whether primary or produced) for imported inputs; the expansion of local production of inputs; and a change in the composition of output (due to the impact on prices of final goods), from industries that are relatively large users of imported inputs to industries that are not. All these are production responses, which require a long period of adjustment. Moreover, it may be assumed that these responses will not be forthcoming unless the relative price changes are themselves durable and consistent, rather than mild and reversible, fluctuations. It will be recalled that price changes of the latter sort have, by and large, characterized the period since 1955. It may thus be argued that, first, the estimate of price elasticity of demand for imported inputs is biased downward because it does not take into account the responses beyond the first year following a price change—presumably the period of main response; and, second, that a different pattern of price changes—one in which the latter would be substantial and persistent—would have led to higher "true" demand elasticities. In view of these biases, the elasticity of demand revealed by the available estimates would indicate a rather high degree of responsiveness of demand for imports to changes in their relative prices.[30]

v. CONCLUSION: DETERMINANTS OF SUCCESSFUL DEVALUATION

The Israeli experience has been quite short. Effective changes in the rate of exchange—"net" rather than "gross" devaluations—have been substantial mainly during a single episode, the devaluation of 1952–54; and significant changes in the *relative* level of the exchange rate, that is, in the purchasing-power-adjusted effective exchange rate, have been even less frequent. Conclusions about the process of devaluation can therefore be only tentative and to some extent speculative.

It seems, first, that substantial changes in the exchange rate have more impact than small changes, in relation to their size, on trade flows. Since quantities respond to changes in relative prices only with a lag, small changes could not be expected to have much impact: they cannot be relied upon to endure, and thus offer little motivation for changes in the behavior of producing enterprises. This would not follow if such small changes occurred continuously over a long period, because they might then have a cumulative effect, and lead economic units to expect the process to continue; but this has not been tried in the case of Israel.

In the Israeli experience, the importance of the time lag of response seems to be evident more in exports than in imports: the performance of exports could be explained more often than that of imports as resulting from an earlier episode of devaluation. Taking the lagged response into consideration, the supply elasticity of exports appears to be considerable—certainly above unity. The elasticity of demand for imports appears to have been approximately unity, but with considerable differences among import categories: while elasticities of demand for finished consumer goods and for investment goods were high—particularly the former—the demand for intermediate inputs was relatively inelastic. This difference in elasticity may account for the more substantial effects of the major devaluation of 1952–54 compared to the rather limited achievements of later devaluations. Since the effect of relative price changes varies among the different import categories, changes occur in the composition of imports following a devaluation: imports of intermediate goods decline relatively less, and their share in total imports increases. This process clearly appears in the Israeli experience of the 1950s, when it was helped by the structure of QRs, which favored imports of intermediate goods. The increased weight of imports for which the demand is relatively inelastic leads, in turn, to a lower elasticity of demand for imports as a whole. Thus, the more devaluation proceeds and the more the relative price of imports rises, the smaller will be the impact of further devaluations on imports.

The major process of devaluation in Israel has been carried out through formal, statutory changes in the rate of exchange: over the period as a whole, the rates of change of the formal and the effective rates of exchange have been quite similar. The nonformal components of the effective rate—import duties and export subsidies—have served, apart from their discriminatory, protective functions, as devices for smoothing out the process. Between episodes of formal devaluation, the nonformal components were increased gradually, to about the same extent as domestic prices, so as to keep the PLD-EERs on an approximately stable level. When formal devaluations were undertaken, the nonformal components were usually reduced, so that the effective net devaluation was lower than the gross devaluation. This was particularly true for the supposedly major devaluation of February 1962: a gross devaluation of 67 per cent (from IL 1.80 to IL 3.00 per dollar) was reduced, by the lowering of tariffs and export subsidies, to a net devaluation of about 30 per cent on average (37 per cent for imports and 13 per cent for exports). Combined with monetary-fiscal developments which followed the devaluation, this much lower rate of net change helped to confine the effectiveness of this devaluation to a very short period.

As would be expected, a major factor in determining the degree of success and duration of effectiveness of a devaluation is the demand policy accompanying it. The 1952–54 devaluation was not only of very substantial proportions but was also accompanied, for about two years, by restrictive monetary and fiscal policies. On the other hand, the 1962 devaluation was accompanied by the opposite demand policy. As one of the results, domestic prices increased by only a fraction of the increase in the price of foreign exchange even many years after the 1952–54 devaluation. By contrast the relative increase in the price of foreign exchange was almost completely dissipated within about three years following the 1962 devaluation, thus rendering the devaluation ineffective within a relatively short time. A similar process has also taken place, apparently, during the last few years. The formal devaluation of August 1971, together with the de facto devaluation introduced by the 1970 special levy on imports and some increases in export subsidies during these years, resulted in an increase in the effective exchange rate of about 30 per cent from the beginning of 1970 to the end of 1971. But an expansionary monetary and fiscal policy instituted in late 1970 or early 1971 had by early 1973 restored the PLD-EER to its predevaluation level.[31]

The accompanying of devaluation by restrictive monetary policies has gradually become a more difficult task due to the increasing role of foreign assets and their automatic monetary impact. The devaluation of 1952–54 was aided by the fact that foreign-exchange reserves were nil and automatic forces were absent. At the time of the devaluations of 1962 and of 1971, foreign assets were substantial and rising. The devaluation, by increasing the local-currency value of both the stock and current accumulation of such assets, thus had a strong automatic expansionary impact on money and liquidity in the economy. In principle, this impact could be countered and neutralized—to a greater extent than would be required in the absence of automatic expansion —by a restrictive credit policy, as well as a contractionary fiscal policy. In the Israeli experience, however, the government has normally been unable to conduct such a neutralizing policy. The lesson which may be drawn is that the existence of automatic expansionary forces may be expected to reduce severely the likelihood of success of the process of devaluation.

These automatic forces have been further strengthened by the availability in Israel, since the early 1960s, of large and increasing holdings by the public of foreign-exchange-denominated assets. The linkage of assets to the foreign-exchange rate was meant to induce savings and reduce liquidity.

But this has led to a drastic reduction of the efficacy of the foreign-exchange rate in fulfilling its major function, namely, the changing of relative prices of tradables, and has strengthened the reluctance of the government to use of this instrument.

The automatic expansion of money and liquidity is not realized when devaluation is carried out by manipulating the nonformal component of the exchange rate, that is, by increasing import duties and export subsidies rather than the formal rate of exchange. With such a de facto devaluation, the local-currency value of the stocks and accumulation of foreign assets and foreign-exchange-denominated assets is not increased. A further advantage of this form of devaluation is that it leads to a budgetary surplus, because of the excess of imports over the combined size of exports and government capital imports (assuming that import tariffs and export subsidies increase at the same rate). The imposition of the 20 per cent import levy in 1970—which was *not* lifted with the formal devaluation of 1971—may be an indication that the government has decided to pursue de facto devaluation; but being a single instance, the episode of 1971 is as yet of little significance. It may also be assumed that the taxation of private capital transfers and the circumvention of the foreign-exchange linkage of local assets implied in this procedure cannot proceed very far before the protests of the injured parties prevent its further extension.

In interpreting the short historical experience of Israel's foreign-exchange-rate policy, it probably would be fair to conclude that, by and large, the government responded in the "right" way to the economy's needs, although often with a substantial time lag. As will be argued in the next chapter, the need to devalue arose out of the decline in the relative size of capital imports. Another aspect of this "right" response was, however, the crucial role of emergency situations: by and large, the dating of main points in the process of devaluation may be explained by such emergencies, as expressed in the position of the country's external reserves. Only twice may a devaluation be said to have taken place in anticipation of future needs. One of these occasions was in November 1967, when the British devaluation was seized upon to introduce an Israeli devaluation not otherwise planned. Coming at a time of recession, this devaluation was successful without the addition of any supporting measures. The other occasion was the devaluation of 1962, which over-all should probably be judged a failure. This points to another lesson which could probably be drawn from the Israeli experience: when the government is not acting in an emergency situation, it is less likely to accompany a devaluation by a restrictive monetary-fiscal policy. The contrast between the 1952–54 and the 1962 devaluations provides a glaring example of this rule. A more recent example is given by developments during 1970 and 1971. In early 1970 external reserves were at a very low level and still falling rapidly, and a clear sense of emergency prevailed. Monetary development was then restrictive primarily because of the automatic impact of the decline of external assets; but fiscal policy also took a restrictive turn as a result of deliberate measures. Later in the year, external reserves started to rise, mainly due to a major U.S. loan for military purchases. Almost immediately, fiscal policy reversed its course and became expansionary, and so did monetary development, largely owing to the automatic impact of the external reserves.

The ability of the government to accompany devaluations by a restrictive demand policy only in an emergency situation is apparently due to two factors. First, restrictive fiscal policy (and to a lesser extent monetary policy) is painful, in that it raises taxes and lowers expenditures. It is thus politically expedient when a general recognition of emergency prevails, and much more difficult to implement otherwise. The other explanation takes us back to the role of external assets. Since a condition of "emergency" is recognized (as it usually is in Israel) by low and falling reserves, the automatic expansionary impact of devaluation on money and liquidity is absent during an emergency; whereas when reserves are high and rising, an automatic expansion follows.

NOTES

1. Israel joined the International Monetary Fund in late 1954. The rate of IL 1.800 per dollar was established as the currency's initial par value; but this was done only in 1957.

2. This applies to current transactions. To some transfers on capital account, lower formal rates were applied for some time. In April 1958, these special low rates were abolished, making the system uniform all around.

3. The shift in the designation of the rate of exchange from three to two decimal places follows the abolition in 1959 of the smallest currency unit, the "prutah," which was one-thousandth of an Israeli pound. Since then, the smallest unit is the "agorah," which equals one-hundredth of a pound; and the general practice is, accordingly, to specify no more than two decimal places.

4. The fluctuations in the prices of foreign currencies in terms of each other, which have become gradually more important, make the meaning of the "change in the rate of exchange" of the Israeli pound (or of any other currency) somewhat ambiguous. I follow here the Israeli convention of citing the rate of exchange as the price in pounds of the U.S. dollar. It is also the practice in Israel to leave the rate of exchange thus defined unchanged unless a decision to devalue is undertaken. Thus, throughout the period of changes in the international monetary system which started in February 1973, the rate of exchange remained IL 4.20 per dollar. This has meant, of course, a devaluation of varying proportions of the Israeli pound against most other currencies. Since March 1973, the Israeli pound has been fluctuating with the U.S. dollar against all other major currencies.

5. Another major monetary variable, the interest rate, is of no significance in analyzing this area of the Israeli economy. Until 1970, interest rates were subject to a

ceiling, and remained unchanged over very long periods. Consequently, no free-market interest rate could be found that would serve as a meaningful indicator of the level of interest rates. Likewise, the Bank of Israel discount rate—again, very low and unchanged for many years—did not fulfill the normal function of a central-bank discount rate.

6. The public sector in Israel includes, besides the central government and municipalities, the rather substantial Jewish Agency. For earlier years, however, data are confined to the central government alone. In any case, changes in excess demand of the government are the overwhelming component of changes in excess demand of the public sector as a whole.

7. This is because defense expenditures were not disclosed. The defense budget has been almost fully and accurately presented in the government's publicly disclosed budget only since the late 1960s; for at least the preceding decade, however, the defense budget reported in the government's public budget did show the major part of total defense expenditures. In the early 1950s, on the other hand, only a fraction of defense expenditures were publicly disclosed, the rest (probably the major part) being conducted through a special secret budget. Data on the latter have never been made public. But it has become known that the major source of finance of this special budget was the sale of short-term Treasury bills to the Issue Department. The amount of the sale was not disclosed at the time, but published a few years later. Thus, the data on the government's debt, which do include these Treasury bills, reflect the true size of the government's budget, although it is possible that some minor sources of finance and indebtedness, both domestic and external, are still missing from the data.

8. Loans authorized in this way were considered part of the bank's reserves.

9. From mid-1951 to the end of 1953, foreign-exchange reserves had almost no impact on the money supply because they were practically nil and fluctuations in them were insignificant.

10. This is emphasized in Don Patinkin, "Monetary and Price Developments in Israel," *Scripta Hierosolymitana* (Jerusalem: Hebrew University, 1956; in English). Patinkin argues that the New Economic Policy actually started in mid-1951, and was merely given official recognition in February 1952.

11. Available data for the period since 1962 show that rates of change of the economy's *net* reserves (but not, of course, absolute amounts) were by and large similar; so the same conclusions would follow if net rather than gross reserves were used.

12. Credit from the Bank of Israel to the government—the third important element in the determination of the money supply—is primarily a function of budgetary policy-making, and its control has been almost entirely out of the hands of the bank.

13. The turning point—the slowdown in the rate of expansion of the money supply—occurred at about the middle of 1964. Available studies show there is in Israel a time lag of some 10 to 12 months between a change in the money supply and its impact on demand in the economy.

14. This statement should be qualified somewhat. It will be recalled that the part of foreign-exchange deposits that could actually be withdrawn in foreign exchange (which is roughly a third to two-fifths of the total) could also, since 1958, be sold to other Israeli residents at a freely determined price. In devaluation, the value of this part would rise, therefore, by the extent of the change in the free-market price. In the periods immediately following all three relevant formal devaluations (1962, 1967, and 1971) the latter price increased by less than the proportion of the formal devaluation.

15. Foreign-currency deposits are not part of bank reserves. The public's deposits

of foreign exchange are redeposited by the commercial banks at the Bank of Israel in a similar way, creating a separate system of foreign-exchange deposits in which an approximately 100 per cent reserve ratio is maintained by the banks.

16. See Miriam Beham, *Monetary Aspects of the 1962 Devaluation* (Jerusalem: Falk Institute, 1968; in English), particularly pp. 46–54.

17. Owing to the aforementioned deficiencies of the official price indexes, this estimate itself most probably suffers from a substantial upward bias; it is derived by use of a price deflator which is biased downward because it is heavily weighted by official prices.

18. In the course of an attempt to adjust the consumer price index for the existence of black-market prices, Yoram Weiss estimated that the adjusted index increased during 1949–51 by about 50 per cent more than the official index, and that the relationship of the two indices was reversed by approximately the same factor during the period 1952–53. See Yoram Weiss, "Price Control in Israel, 1949–58" (in English), Bank of Israel *Economic Review* 37 (March 1971): Table 2, p. 82.

19. Strictly speaking, the exchange-rate data are quarterly only for 1952–54; for all other years, they are a hybrid of annual data and of data for particular dates when changes took place. For details, see notes to Table 5-5.

20. At the time of writing, the latest devaluation was too recent to permit a more precise analysis of accompanying monetary-fiscal policy.

21. Starting with an exchange rate R_0 for the base period, the purchasing power parity for period 1, R_1, is computed as:

$$\frac{R_1}{R_0} = \frac{P_{H1}/P_{H0}}{P_{T1}/P_{T0}},$$

where P_H is the domestic price level and P_T is the level of foreign-currency prices of the country's tradable goods. In the calculations, P_H is represented by an estimate of the implied GNP price deflator. In principle, exports should have been excluded, so that only prices of sales in the local market would be covered; but in the case of Israel, the inclusion of exports does not lead to significant distortions, because the share of exports is small. P_T is estimated as the weighted average price level (in foreign exchange) of Israel's exports and imports, with last year's values serving as weights.

22. The coefficient of determination (r^2) is .305 for the simple regression of column 3 on column 2; it is .123 for the regression of column 5 on column 4.

23. The following discussion is based on the studies of Nadav Halevi, "Devaluation, Relative Prices, and Exports in Israel" and Jimmi Weinblat, "The Effect of the Effective Exchange Rate on Imports: 1950–1967," both in Nadav Halevi and Michael Michaely, eds., *Studies in Israel's Foreign Trade* (Jerusalem: Falk Institute and Hebrew University, 1972; in Hebrew).

24. Ibid., pp. 26–39.

25. The two other major categories are agricultural exports and polished diamonds. The production cycle of diamond polishing is quite short (probably not longer than five or six weeks), and the size of production could change quite rapidly, both because of technical facilities and because the proportion of permanent workers in the labor force is particularly low in this industry. The responsiveness of exports (which in this industry in Israel are practically identical with production) to price changes may therefore be expected to be relatively strong. But, unlike most of Israel's other industrial exports, its exports of polished diamonds constitute a large share of the world market; and demand in this market is very volatile. Export of diamonds is thus heavily affected by fluctuations of foreign demand, only part of which is presumably reflected in changes in the foreign

price of exports. Likewise, monopolistic restrictions in the market for raw diamonds are important in the determination of Israel's production of polished diamonds at any given time. If such factors could be accounted for, the price elasticity of supply of this export category would probably have been found to be high; but this is only a presumption, whose verification would require an elaborate study.

A somewhat similar problem is found in agricultural products: the random factor introduced by weather conditions complicates the identification of responses to price changes. But more important in this case is the effect of the long time lag involved in such response. Citrus fruits constitute the largest share of exports in this category; and the gestation period (from planting to first marketable yield) of investment in citrus fruit is at least six years. Thus, it would be unwarranted to expect that a change in the exchange rate in one year would be sufficient to induce a significantly large new planting. Even if it were, the result would not show up in the export figures until many years later. Also, price changes could only slightly affect the allocation of a current crop between the local and the foreign markets since almost all the fruit which is technically exportable (being free of deficiencies) is exported. Hence, annual observations of price and quantity of exports of citrus fruit could hardly be expected to reveal any positive supply elasticity.

26. "Effect of Effective Exchange Rate," pp. 67–128.

27. This follows the conventional classification in Israel's trade statistics. A fourth category, excluded from Weinblat's study, is fuel. Also, ships constitute a separate category, and are not included in this study among investment goods. Since the time between ordering and delivery of ships is extremely long, their inclusion in an investigation based on annual observations is likely to be misleading.

28. Weinblat also tried alternative functions in which the two price levels appear as separate variables.

29. The use of 1952 weights, for instance, would have yielded an average elasticity of aggregate demand for imports of about −1.45.

30. In fact, in view of these a-priori considerations the estimate of elasticity of demand for imports of intermediate inputs—close to −0.4—appears to be surprisingly high. It may be assumed that the estimate is heavily influenced by speculative changes: when a devaluation is anticipated (as it may be assumed to have been on a number of occasions), inventories of intermediate inputs are built up, to be run down after the devaluation (whether formal or through changes in import duties) takes place.

It may be mentioned also that the elasticity of demand for imports of fuel, which are excluded from the estimates, is probably quite low. This, if true, would contribute to a lowering of the aggregate elasticity of demand for imports. But this impact could not be very significant, since fuel imports amounted most of the time to some 6 to 8 per cent of total imports of goods.

31. Dating of fiscal policy is difficult. Quarterly data are poor, and circumstantial evidence must therefore be used.

Chapter 6

The Exchange System and the Growth of the Economy

Sources of economic growth include changes in both the amounts and productivity of the factors of production. The possible effects of the exchange system on the rate of growth will be discussed here in those terms.

It may be safely assumed that the effect of the exchange system on the size of the labor force is negligible: it is unlikely that this system could have any considerable impact—at least in the circumstances of Israel—on either the rate of natural increase of population, the amount of immigration (or emigration), or the rate of participation in the labor force. The present discussion will, therefore, be confined to the possible effects of the system on capital formation. The two sources of capital accumulation are domestic savings and the inflow of capital from abroad. Capital inflow is discussed in section i, below; domestic savings, in section ii. In the discussion of the probable effect of the exchange system on productivity, the focus will be on the impact of the severe quantitative restrictions of Phase I. The role of the exchange rate in the growth process will then be analyzed and, finally, the degree of openness in the development of the economy, that is, the growth of exports versus import substitution.

i. THE SIZE OF CAPITAL: FOREIGN INVESTMENT

The greater part of capital inflow into Israel has been derived from sources which may be said to depend very little, if at all, on normal profit motiva-

150

tions. This is true even of a source such as Government of Israel Development (formerly Independence) bonds sold abroad and, of course, other major sources such as contributions to the United Jewish Appeal, loans and grants from the U.S. government, and payments by the German government for reparations or personal restitutions. All these may be motivated, some strongly, by factors such as the rate of immigration to the country or the country's security situation, but not by expectations of private profit. To some extent, the size of capital inflow from these sources is conceivably also dependent on the domestic economic situation in Israel—the worse it is, the larger the inflow. In that sense, it may be said that the exchange system, through its effect on general economic conditions, might have an impact on capital inflow from these sources. But this is very indirect, and the degree of causal connection of this nature must in any event be very small. The investigation here is confined, therefore, to that part of capital inflow which may be assumed to respond to profit motivations, namely, to private foreign investment.

Exchange control and quantitative restrictions may be expected to affect private foreign investment mainly in two ways working in opposite directions. First, foreign capital may be attracted to specific industries if they are granted protection and their profitability is consequently raised. If import-replacing industries that are encouraged by grants of QRs attract foreign investment more than do export industries or industries that produce solely for the domestic market, the result would be a net increase in foreign investment. A case might be made for the claim that this was the situation in Israel, at least in the earlier years of its existence.

On the other hand, exchange control is likely to lead to a large measure of bureaucratic intervention in capital inflows from abroad and in investment decisions; it may also result in a high degree of uncertainty about the course of future events concerning such issues as capital repatriation or the stability of the degree of protection granted to each industry. These factors would tend to hinder capital inflow into the country. During the first half of the 1950s, this was indeed one of the main arguments voiced in Israel against the economic policy of that time.

Table 6-1 contains data on private foreign investment in Israel. It must be pointed out that the quality of these data is probably the poorest of all among the balance-of-payments estimates, although their accuracy has improved over the years. Estimates of reinvestment of profits are the worst component of the data on capital inflow from this source and are often no more than rough guesses; estimates for the period prior to 1955 are available, but are not presented here because they are believed to be completely unreliable and misleading, grossly overestimating the correct levels. There is almost no

TABLE 6-1

Private Foreign Investment, 1955–72

Year	In Millions of Dollars (1)	As Percentage of Total Investment in Israeli Economy (2)
1955	15.8	5.4
1956	17.6	6.0
1957	19.0	5.2
1958	13.8	3.4
1959	25.4	5.7
1960	53.4	10.9
1961	59.6	9.5
1962	92.7	18.6
1963	168.7	32.3
1964	169.4	24.9
1965	114.9	18.5
1966	104.3	20.9
1967	51.6	18.2
1968	41.9	7.8
1969	56.2	7.2
1970	44.4	4.4
1971	92.5	7.0
1972	183.3	11.7

SOURCE:

Col. 1—Balance-of-payments data for 1955–60 from Bank of Israel, *Annual Report*, various years; for 1961–67, ibid., 1970, Table III/26; for 1968–72, from ibid., 1972, Table 14/26.

Col. 2—Data in column 1 converted to Israeli pounds at current formal rate and divided by value of net investment in current prices. Formal rate from Table 5-1; net investment from Bank of Israel, *Annual Report*, various years.

doubt that, in these years, recorded private "foreign" capital was to a large extent domestically owned repatriated capital disguised as foreign capital because the latter was accorded special privileges.[1]

The argument that QRs attract foreign capital to the protected industries could not be tested directly, for lack of data about the allocation of foreign investment by industries. From Table 6-1 it may be seen, however, that in the mid-1950s (and presumably in earlier years as well), the total size of foreign private investment was very small—about $10 million–$20 million annually or roughly 5 per cent of total investment in the economy. It may be concluded that even if the grant of QR protection attracted foreign investment, the amount could not have been large enough to have had a significant impact on growth.

Foreign investment started rising, and assumed substantial proportions, only in the late 1950s. As may be seen from Table 6-1, in both absolute size and as a ratio to total investment, it was many times larger in the 1960s than in the 1950s. This could conceivably be explained by the process of liberalization, in line with the argument mentioned above: the effect of the largely liberalized exchange system of the 1960s was to reduce the obstacles to private capital inflow presented by the exchange-control system of the earlier period. Unfortunately, however, various other explanations could be given for the phenomenon, and it is hard to devise a method of refuting any of them, or to assign to each of them a measure of importance.

First, in Israel, the size of private foreign investment is without any doubt correlated with the country's security position. In the early and mid-1950s Israel's position on this score was considered to be problematical; only beginning in late 1957 or early 1958 did expectations of roughly a decade of relative peace start to prevail.[2] Another set of factors which might have attracted foreign investment was the greater heterogeneity of the economy as time progressed, the higher income level, larger and more varied supply of skills, etc., all of which may be assumed to facilitate foreign investment. It should also be noted that worldwide total private foreign investment has been rising rapidly.

To sum up, it may be deduced from available data that (a) during the era of stringent exchange controls and QRs, private foreign investment was negligible; and (b) in later years, private capital inflow increased very substantially, an event which may be explained by several economic factors and circumstances, one of which is the policy of liberalization.

ii. THE SIZE OF CAPITAL: DOMESTIC SAVINGS

Savings of Households.

Personal savings may be affected by the exchange system primarily in two ways. One is through the possible impact of the system on interest rates, which in turn may affect household savings. However, for the reasons noted below, it may be assumed that the size and structure of interest rates in Israel were very little influenced directly by the exchange system, although the rates were undoubtedly affected to a large extent by the economy's relationship with the outside world. The other channel of influence of the exchange system on personal savings patterns could conceivably be through the mechanism of repressed inflation. If QRs, low prices, and rationing of imports are part of a general program of price control and rationing, they may conceivably lead to some forced saving. In Israel, this could apply to the early half of the 1950s, and particularly to the years 1950–51.

Data on savings in Israel are rather poor. As a rule, savings are derived as a residual (that is, as the surplus of domestic investment over the import surplus) and incorporate all the net errors of the national accounting estimates.[3] Moreover, it follows that the separate components of savings are not estimated; household savings are, therefore, not known. Some estimates of magnitudes could have been constructed on the basis of consumer surveys, but even these are not available for the earlier part of the period. In Table 6-2, therefore, only savings as a whole (estimated as a residual) are presented.

TABLE 6-2
Ratio of Savings to GNP, 1950–65

Year	Ratio (per cent)	Year	Ratio (per cent)
1950	1.5	1958	−0.9
1951	8.2	1959	2.1
1952	−1.2	1960	1.7
1953	−5.3	1961	2.5
1954	−3.9	1962	−0.8
1955	−2.2	1963	−0.4
1956	−8.1	1964	−0.2
1957	−2.4	1965	−1.4

SOURCE: Nadav Halevi and Ruth Klinov-Malul, *The Economic Development of Israel* (New York: Praeger, 1968), Table 32. For further explanation, see accompanying text and note 3.

It appears that the economy's savings rate was indeed unusually high in 1950 and particularly in 1951. In view of the crude nature of the data, not much could be inferred from it; but it does appear likely that controls and rationing, which reached their peak in 1951, did indeed contribute to the "forced" creation of considerable personal savings.

Savings of Firms.

Hypotheses about the way in which savings of firms might be affected by the exchange system are not readily apparent, aside from the possible impact through interest rates. Furthermore, empirical verification is, in the case of Israel, not really feasible, since there are practically no comprehensive, aggregate data on business saving. From various surveys and case studies, the general impression gained is that business saving in Israel is probably nil, or at least extremely low in comparison with normal patterns elsewhere.[4] This pattern could not be attributed directly to the exchange system. It is most probably due to the structure of the long-term capital market in Israel, in which capital imports have played a dominant role, particularly in earlier years. Capital imports received by the government (or the Jewish Agency, which for the present purpose is rather similar to the government) at first constituted the major source of revenue in the government's development budget, which in turn was the major source of financing of domestic investments. Firms availing themselves of this financing enjoyed two advantages: first, they received it at a very low interest rate compared to what it would have been in a free market. And, second, they were not required to maintain a minimum level of net worth relative to the size of investment, as a firm seeking free-market financing would have had to do. The two normal motivations of business saving—namely, the high level of interest on borrowed capital, and the dependence of such borrowing on capital accumulation in the firm itself— were thus absent in the greater part of the Israeli economy. This financing mechanism has been in use since the establishment of the state of Israel, except that in recent years it has been less dependent on capital imports: a larger part of the government's resources for financing has been raised in the local market from pension funds, other institutions, and through some voluntary purchases of government bonds by the public. However, the manner in which funds have been lent to firms has remained basically unchanged, leaving them with little motivation to save and increase their net worth.

Government Savings.

Decisions about savings are part of the general scheme of government policies, and it would not be feasible to construct an even approximately reliable model of government behavior and the role of the exchange system in this scheme. In the case of Israel, however, one specific factor may be pointed out and even quantified, albeit in a most tentative way. As already noted several times in this study, the government of Israel is a major recipient of capital imports, mainly in the forms of sales abroad of Independence and Development bonds, the reparations payments from Germany (during 1953–63), and grants and loans from foreign governments (mainly the United States). To this should be added the income of the Jewish Agency from the United Jewish Appeal, which for the present purpose is almost equivalent to a government income. A rule of behavior to which the government has normally adhered is that government receipts from abroad are allocated to the development budget.[5] Since capital imports are recorded in the government's accounts at the formal rate of exchange, maintaining a rate below the equilibrium level leads to a *reduction* in the size of these receipts as expressed in local currency. This would be so even if the *effective* rate for foreign trade purposes were not below its equilibrium level: maintaining a rate higher than the formal rate by means of duties on imports and subsidies to exports implies, in effect, a net result in which part of the potential revenue in the development budget (from capital imports) is diverted, as revenue from tariff duties, to the current budget.[6]

In Table 6-3, column 1 contains one possible, and arbitrary, estimate of this revenue loss. The estimate is initially based on the assumption that the *average* effective exchange rate (EER) for value added in exports is the equilibrium exchange rate. This assumption facilitates the computations involved, but there is almost no doubt that it *under*estimates the level of the equilibrium rate and thus also the results in column 1.[7] The figures shown in this column are derived by multiplying the excess of the EER for exports over the formal rate by the amount (in foreign exchange) of the capital inflow recorded as revenue in the development budget. The results are then put in perspective by comparing them with GNP (column 2) and net domestic investment (column 3). Although the size varies markedly in different years (naturally, it is smallest immediately after a formal devaluation and then rises gradually), it is as a rule rather significant. This impression is strengthened if the downward bias just pointed out is borne in mind and if it is noted that the estimate in column 1 is based only on the budget of the government proper, and not on the accounts of the Jewish Agency, in which a similar element is contained.[8]

It thus seems that maintenance of a below-equilibrium formal exchange rate was of some consequence in reducing governmental saving. It must again be emphasized that a calculation such as that presented in Table 6-3—based as it is on arbitrary assumptions—could not yield more than a general impression. Moreover, even such a tentative conclusion must be hedged by recalling that it is based on a mechanistic assumption regarding the government's method of operation, namely, that changes in the government's receipts from abroad are fully reflected in the development budget without any offsetting, discretionary changes by the government. To what extent such a mechanistic view of the government's decision-making process in this matter is correct would not be easy to determine.[9]

Importation of Investment Goods.

It will be recalled that, throughout the period of study and with only few exceptions, investment goods have been consistently imported at the

TABLE 6-3

Effect of Exchange Rate on the Development Budget, 1951–68

Year[a]	Loss of Revenue in Development Budget (mill. IL) (1)	Column 1 as Per Cent of	
		GNP (2)	Net Domestic Investment (3)
1951	5	0.8	3.3
1952	7	0.7	2.6
1953	36	2.6	12.2
1954	70	3.9	19.0
1955	3	0.1	0.5
1956	32	1.3	6.2
1957	59	2.0	8.9
1958	85	2.5	11.8
1959	104	2.6	13.1
1960	111	2.5	13.0
1961	156	2.9	13.8
1962	0	0	0
1963	8	0.1	0.5
1964	13	0.1	0.6
1965	18	0.2	0.9
1966	51	0.4	3.4
1967	87	0.7	10.3
1968	133	1.0	7.2

SOURCE:
Col. 1—Derived from the government's budgetary accounts, by the method explained in the accompanying text.

Cols. 2 and 3—Underlying data on GNP and domestic investment are in current market prices. GNP is from Table A-2; net investment, from Bank of Israel, *Annual Report*, various years.

a. Budgetary data, on which column 1 is based, are originally for fiscal years (April–March) and are applied here arbitrarily to calendar years.

lowest exchange rates, and most investment goods were usually free of tariff duties. Likewise, the process of liberalization from QRs was much faster and more comprehensive for machinery and equipment than for most other goods. The main argument submitted in Israel for this policy has been that it encourages investment and thus increases the stock of capital and accelerates the process of economic growth.

There is no doubt that cheap imports of investment goods raise the yield of investment projects, and thus increase the *demand* for investment. For this actually to lead to an increase of investment and capital, however, it must also induce an increase either of domestic saving or of capital inflow from abroad.

One possibility of such an effect occurring is that the increased demand will lead to a higher income and, with a positive (marginal) propensity to save, to higher savings. This would be the case, of course, where, without the added demand, the economy is below the full-employment equilibrium level. In Israel, however, full employment, usually with some inflation, has been the normal situation. And it is hard to believe, although the point cannot be easily verified, that without the extra push given to investment by the exchange system, aggregate demand would be low enough to lead to unemployment. Given relatively full employment, it may thus be assumed that the policy under consideration could lead to increased savings only at the expense of consumption.

It might be argued that the increased yield of investment projects leads to higher interest rates in the market, and that this may, in turn, lead to a reduction of consumption by households. The last link in such a reasoning is conceptually doubtful; but even if it were not, this argument would not be relevant for the case of Israel. Interest rates in Israel almost throughout its history have been little affected by market forces; and there has been almost no connection between long-term rates on business borrowing and most of the rates significant to households—either as borrowers or as lenders. It might be more plausible to expect business firms to increase their savings in response to the higher profitability of investment projects. It will be recalled, however, that this component of saving in Israel is believed to have been nil most of the time, although data to substantiate this impression are scarce. This by itself is not a proof that the effect of the profitability factor on business saving was also nil, since conceivably these savings might otherwise have even been negative. And without any feasible way of testing this hypothesis, I must rest the argument at that.

The low rate of exchange for imports of investment goods does clearly increase only one element of saving, namely, saving by the government. It works to offset part of the loss, just discussed, to the development budget because the importation of investment goods at low prices tends to increase the real value of allocations (grants or loans) from the development budget. Put differently: had tariff duties been imposed on imports of investment goods, part of the expenditure on these goods would have been used not to buy real assets but to pay the duties; and this part would have augmented the government's current budget, that is, public consumption rather than investment. Thus, this absence of duties has to be offset against the aforementioned loss in the development budget; that is, from estimates such as those in col-

umn 1 of Table 6-3, there must be subtracted the (assumed) difference between the equilibrium and formal rates of exchange multiplied by the (foreign-exchange) value of imports of investment goods.

Finally, it is necessary to ask whether the increased profitability of investment projects may not lead to the encouragement of private foreign investment, and thus increase the productive capacity of the economy. In principle, foreign capital inflow should respond favorably to increased profitability. But it should be pointed out that another important attribute of the exchange system was that private foreign investors were usually granted only
the formal rate of exchange.[10] Had a higher (say, the equilibrium) exchange
rate been fixed for both capital transfers and imports of investment goods (for
the projects contemplated by foreign investors), the net result should have
been an *increase,* rather than a decline, in the profitability of projects undertaken by foreign investors.[11]

iii. PRODUCTIVITY OF THE ECONOMY: EFFECT
OF QUANTITATIVE RESTRICTIONS

There are several reasons for expecting the productivity of an economy to be
low in a period of controls in general and of quantitative restrictions of imports in particular. The reasons are too well known to be discussed here at
any length and will be surveyed only briefly.

First, of course, is the allocative inefficiency involved in a process in
which prices and profits are largely disregarded as indicators for the use of
resources and the channeling of investment, and are replaced by administrative decisions. This inefficiency may be assumed to be particularly great in a
situation such as that of Israel in the early 1950s, where large-scale controls
were imposed within a short period, without being preceded by a long learning period during which the administrative machinery might have gradually
developed decision-making processes and rules to help reduce the misallocation involved in the arbitrary nature of the system.

The allocative inefficiency alluded to here is primarily a longer-term
phenomenon that is concerned with the patterns of investment in the economy.
We may, however, note also other factors, resulting from the frictions of a
bureaucratic mechanism, which contribute more to shorter-term losses of
productivity (although they, too, may eventually have long-term consequences).

One important source of such inefficiency is an inappropriate level of
inventories. Since inventories of raw materials and other purchased inputs are
not determined under a QR system solely by firms themselves, the latter often
find themselves too short on inventories. In a developed (currently), or semi-

developed, economy such as Israel's, production in many industries is de-pendent on the availability of a large variety of purchased items, the exhaus-tion of any one of which may easily frustrate or even halt altogether the pro-cess of production. On the other hand, and for precisely the same reason, firms may be expected in such situations to try to maintain unusually large inven-tories. Since they cannot be certain, under a QR system, about the availability of current supplies of imported inputs, they tend to hold a higher stock of ma-terials than they would under a price-regulated economy; and presumably some firms, not necessarily always the same ones, succeed in securing the higher level of inventories they desire. Thus, there are two opposite ways by which QRs can lead to losses of production due to the holding of nonoptimal levels of inventories: irregularities in production created by insufficient in-ventories; and waste of capital (as well as the cost of physical maintenance and protection of the materials) involved in keeping excessively high in-ventories.

Quite similar phenomena may be expected to be found in the case of fixed capital assets. On the one hand, plants stand idle, their construction uncompleted, because some of the necessary pieces of machinery and equip-ment or construction materials could not be secured, at least not on time. On the other hand, knowing the difficulties which must be met in trying to buy the required machinery, firms try to anticipate their needs far into the future, and to order machinery when the need for it is neither immediate nor quite certain. They may also buy machinery and equipment which are at least partly inadequate, either because they are so directed by the controlling au-thority or because these are available at a certain moment, and the firm does not see a reasonable chance of securing better equipment in the future. Thus, for two opposite reasons—inaccessibility of some capital assets and anticipa-tory stockpiling of others—part of the capital may lie idle.

For all these reasons, it may be expected that inefficiency and waste would be widespread when QRs are extensive; and that a shift to price deter-mination of imports would lead, at the time of the shift, to a particularly large increase in productivity because this waste would be reduced. This effect on the rate of increase of productivity should diminish as the shift to price regulation is completed.

Empirical verification of this hypothesis is not easy. Accounts of these forms of waste in individual firms, or even whole industries, were frequent in Israeli newspaper reporting of the economic scene during the early 1950s. The feeding of chickens with bread (which was always kept cheap and in abundant supply) or the presence of rusted machinery lying in the backyards of plants became almost popular symbols of that period.[12] These, however, suggest the flavor of the time but give little indication of the extent of waste and inefficiency.

TABLE 6-4

Productivity of Resources, 1951–65
(annual percentage rate of increase)

Year	Total Economy	Total Excluding Housing and Public Sector	Manufac- turing	Agricul- ture	Transpor- tation
1951	7.9	5.5	4.2	−11.5	22.8
1952	−2.3	−3.4	−20.6	11.8	−1.0
1953	−3.4	−3.6	−1.4	—	−8.5
1954	12.2	15.8	0.8	15.6	28.9
1955	6.8	10.0	6.6	−7.4	−1.0
1956	2.4	3.6	2.2	15.7	7.6
1957	1.8	2.8	−1.1	2.7	6.6
1958	2.0	3.4	6.7	12.3	2.0
1959	6.2	8.0	7.0	12.0	9.4
1960	2.8	3.6	3.8	1.0	7.0
1961	2.8	4.0	4.8	3.1	0.6
1962	3.5	4.8	−0.8	4.7	6.6
1963	3.4	4.5	5.9	11.0	2.9
1964	3.7	4.6	6.6	7.4	2.7
1965	0.6	1.2	6.2	−4.1	1.0
Annual averages					
1951–52	2.8	1.1	−8.2	0.2	10.9
1953–55	5.2	7.4	2.0	2.7	6.5
1956–65	2.9	4.1	4.1	6.6	4.6
1951–65	3.4	4.3	2.1	5.0	5.8

SOURCE: Calculated from A. L. Gaathon, *Economic Productivity in Israel* (New York: Praeger, 1971), Table A-12.

Table 6-4 is an attempt not to derive any precise estimate of productivity, but to test the hypothesis described above. The measure presented in the table was constructed by A. L. Gaathon, along Kendrick lines, to estimate productivity of total resources of the economy.[13] The period from 1951 to 1965 (the earliest and latest years for which data about change in productivity are available) is divided into three subperiods: 1951–52—the peak time of the QR system; 1953–55—the main years of transition to price regulation; and 1956–65—the years following.

Among the series in Table 6-4, the most pertinent to the purpose at hand are those given in columns 2 and 3. These data, relating to a selected part of the economy, are more appropriate than those in column 1, which cover the economy as a whole, since the former exclude residential housing (which cannot be neatly included in a meaningful estimate of productivity) and the public sector, in which productivity estimates are largely arbitrary. Among the major sectors of the economy, the factors affecting productivity and efficient allocation of resources are more likely to have an important impact in manufacturing (column 3) than in agriculture (column 4) or transportation (column 5). Agriculture during the earlier years was heavily affected by weather conditions; up to 1958, years of good and poor harvest alternated; and as it happens, the three-year period 1953–55 contains two years of poor harvest, greatly reducing the estimated average rise of productivity in these years. In transportation, on the other hand, estimates for the earlier years may be technically correct, but devoid of much meaning. For instance, the very impressive increase (23 per cent!) in productivity in this sector from 1950 to 1951 is obtained without taking into account the long lines and waste of time of consumers, with which much of this rise of productivity was involved.[14]

From most of the data in Table 6-4, particularly in columns 2 and 3, the impression gained is indeed in conformity with the postulated effect of QRs; namely, the rate of increase of productivity rose markedly from 1951–52, the peak period of QRs, to 1953–55, the period of rapid transition to the price mechanism as a means of regulating imports as well as other activities in the economy. For the economy as a whole (excluding housing and the public sector), the rate of increase of productivity was not as fast in the decade from 1956 to 1965 as in the transitional years, 1953–55—though this is not true for the manufacturing sector; and it was faster than in the period of controls, 1951–52. It should be recalled, moreover, as was emphasized in Chapter 2, that in the transitional period, 1953–55, the level of imports evidenced only a slight rise; in fact, there was a rather substantial decline in the ratio of imports to output. The rapid increase in productivity in those years thus can*not* be explained by the removal of bottlenecks through an increased supply of imports.

It thus seems that these data conform to a-priori expectations about changes in productivity as the nature of the exchange system changed. It is tempting to go further and state that the causal connection between the two is thus verified or substantiated. This, however, would be a rather dubious inference, since the Israeli economy during its earlier years underwent fast and radical changes in size and structure. It should be recalled that the huge wave of immigration had subsided by late 1951. It is possible that increases in productivity in the first few years following this date occurred because immigrants, who made up a large fraction of the population, may have been placed in jobs they were not suited to during the period of mass immigration, and later sought and found more appropriate occupations. In this, the newcomers were aided by their acquisition of the basic elements of the language and by their growing acquaintance with the organizational principles of the country, its institutions, etc., which at first they did not grasp at all. For the same reasons, those who did not relocate but stayed in the same plant or occupation were likely to increase their efficiency very rapidly in the first few years after migration. Factors other than adjustment of the labor force were also likely to work in the same direction. Thus, it is most probable that those who entered Israel during the period of the large wave of immigration found an economy with a very inadequate infrastructure, but this was rapidly corrected in the first few years after the wave subsided, thus removing important bottlenecks and facilitating the efficient use of resources. It may also be argued that the reason the economy could produce more in the period 1953–55 with fewer imports, may have been that the pattern of investment in earlier years was adjusted to the scarcity of imports.

For all these reasons, productivity should have been expected to rise rapidly in the years 1953–55 even without a change in the QR regime. Therefore, it cannot be claimed that the whole of the rapid rise which actually took place in those years should be attributed to the change in the exchange system. Unfortunately, there is no feasible way of distinguishing the various factors which contributed to the increased productivity of that time. Thus, it may only be stated that the hypothesis that a shift from QRs to price regulation of the economy leads to faster growth through increased productivity is at least not contradicted by the facts of the Israeli experience. More generally, it may perhaps be stated that the rapid growth of productivity during the transitional period was due to a "learning-by-doing" process; and that as part of this process the shift from QRs to price regulation represents a "collective" learning, reflected in the changing policy patterns.

iv. THE EXCHANGE RATE IN THE GROWTH PROCESS

The effects of growth on the exchange rate may be expected to be particularly strong in an economy with Israel's specific attributes—limited size, meager resources and, above all, the role played in it by capital imports and by the import surplus. We shall be concerned here not with the *structure* of the exchange-rate system, that is, with its discriminatory nature with respect to different industries and products, but rather with the over-all (i.e., average) level of the exchange rates for exports and imports.

There is some ground for expecting that economic expansion relative to the world as a whole leads to, and is conditioned upon, an increase in the price of foreign exchange relative to domestic prices. If growth is "neutral" (neither export nor import biased), the terms of trade of a relatively expanding economy are expected to deteriorate. If, as is often assumed, with considerable justification, foreign demand for a country's exports is less elastic than foreign supply of its imports, the terms-of-trade effect of a devaluation would be expected to be negative (that is, the price of exports would fall relative to the price of imports), and the "required" worsening of the terms of trade could be achieved through a devaluation.

In Israel's case, probably due to the small size of its economy, no deterioration of the terms of trade took place, despite the rapid economic expansion (as mentioned in Chapter 1) which certainly surpassed that of the world as a whole and that of Israel's major trading partners. This result is apparent from the aggregate data on export and import prices presented in Table 6-5. These, it should be noted, are far from being perfect estimates; they are particularly deficient for the early and mid-1950s. Furthermore, they refer only to trade in goods and hence exclude services. Yet the general impression gained is probably reliable. It appears that the terms of trade of the country have been fairly stable, with fluctuations concentrated mainly in the early 1950s—the time of the Korean crisis and the years immediately following. There seems to be hardly any discernible trend, certainly not from 1954 on: the terms-of-trade index in the late 1960s and early 1970s is about at the level of the mid-1950s. Even the prices of exports in which Israel plays an important role in the world market—mainly citrus fruits and polished diamonds—appear not to have fallen in relation to the country's import prices (though this detail is not shown in Table 6-5), probably because the income elasticities of demand for these exports are rather high.

If both export and import prices rise to the same extent, the terms of trade are not affected, but the real value of any given size of a unilateral capital inflow is thereby reduced. Consequently, the country suffers a real loss and a deterioration of the over-all terms of its international transactions.[15] Since import prices have actually increased over the period surveyed, this deterioration has indeed occurred. But, it should be noted, this deterioration is not in any way causally related to the process of growth. Also, the loss of the purchasing power of capital imports due to the increase in prices, although of some substance, is not very significant in relation to the main role played by capital imports for the problem at hand. This role deserves a few additional words of explanation.

Israel started out with an inflow of capital that was very high in proportion to the size of its economy. Suppose that the economy's growth, from that point on, is "neutral" in both production and consumption; that, with unchanged prices, the proportions of saving and of domestic investment do not change (i.e., are independent of the scale of the economy); and that the ex-

TABLE 6-5

Israel's Terms of Trade, 1950–71

(indexes of prices in dollars, 1950 = 100)

Year	Export Prices (1)	Import Prices (2)	Terms of Trade (ratio: col. 1 to col. 2) (3)
1950	100	100	100%
1951	107	120	89
1952	105	121	86
1953	99	108	92
1954	106	101	104
1955	111	109	102
1956	117	115	101
1957	121	124	98
1958	119	110	108
1959	107	107	101
1960	104	107	97
1961	105	103	102
1962	104	101	103
1963	109	102	106
1964	109	105	104
1965	113	107	106
1966	120	109	111
1967	118	109	108
1968	117	107	110
1969	123	112	110
1970	121	113	107
1971	125	115	108

NOTE: Discrepancies between figures in column 3 and ratios calculated directly from columns 1 and 2 are due to rounding.

SOURCE: 1950–55—Michael Michaely, *Foreign Trade and Capital Imports in Israel* (Tel Aviv: Am Oved, 1963; in Hebrew), Table 38.

1956–71—*Statistical Abstract of Israel*, various years.

ternal position of the country is initially in equilibrium. The economy will then remain in external equilibrium, with given relative prices, only if autonomous capital inflow grows at the same rate as the rate of expansion of the economy. If capital imports fail to rise to this extent, the economy's growth pattern must move toward either an increase of exports (beyond the rate of growth of the economy) or import substitution, or a combination of both, so that the excess of the economy's demand for imports over its supply of exports will fail to expand at the same rate as the economy's growth. A policy which leads to a growth process biased in this way must be based on an increase in the relative price of foreign exchange. This may, of course, be done in a variety of ways: through a formal change of the rate, through manipulation of nonformal components, through measures such as QRs, governmental subsidies to investment in tradable industries, etc.

As is shown in Table 6-6, autonomous capital imports have indeed failed to expand in Israel as much as the economy's real product.[16] With some substantial year-to-year fluctuations, this trend of relative decline seems to be quite obvious.[17] For the external position of the country to remain in equi-

TABLE 6-6
National Product and Autonomous Capital Inflow, 1950–66

Year	GNP (1950 = 100) (1)	Autonomous Capital Inflow (1950 = 100) (2)	Col. 2 as Per Cent of Col. 1 (3)
1950	100	100	100
1951	130	139	107
1952	138	156	113
1953	136	139	102
1954	163	206	126
1955	185	168	91
1956	202	175	87
1957	220	161	73
1958	235	195	83
1959	265	199	75
1960	283	239	84
1961	312	282	90
1962	343	316	92
1963	382	299	78
1964	419	334	80
1965	457	296	65
1966	462	257	56

SOURCE: App. A, Tables A-2 and A-14.
Columns 1 and 2 are in constant prices; column 2 is derived by deflating current-dollar flows by the index of import prices in Table 6-5, column 2.

librium—or, alternatively, to stay at the same level of disequilibrium throughout the period—the relative price of the foreign exchange should have been
rising throughout the period.

As may be seen from Table 6-7, which includes some data from the last
chapter, the relative level of effective exchange rates did indeed go up very
considerably over the period covered: by 1971 the level for both exports and
imports was roughly two and one-half times that of 1950. It should be noted,
however, that this trend of increasing PPP-adjusted EERs was not uniform
throughout the period; on the contrary, two fairly distinct subperiods may be

TABLE 6-7

Effective Exchange Rates Adjusted for Purchasing Power Parity, 1950–71
(1950 = 100)

Year	PPP-adj. Export Rate (1)	PPP-adj. Import Rate (2)	Weighted Average of Cols. 1 and 2 (3)
1950	100	100	100
1951	103	95	96
1952	136	130	131
1953	159	139	142
1954	202	201	201
1955	212	247	241
1956	227	240	237
1957	243	246	245
1958	235	223	226
1959	231	223	225
1960	235	224	227
1961	220	206	210
1962	226	258	249
1963	215	245	235
1964	208	234	227
1965	196	224	215
1966	198	215	209
1967	210	215	213
1968	230	234	233
1969	235	242	240
1970	240	234	236
1971	244	244	244

SOURCE: Export and import rates are from Table 5-6. Weights for last column are annual
data for value added of exports and imports for domestic use.

distinguished. The rates went up until the mid-1950s—1955 in the case of imports and 1957 in the case of exports—and from then on remained at a rather constant level, despite some fluctuations, which sometimes persisted for periods of several years each. By and large, this division into subperiods is consistent with the movement of the data in Table 6-6 on autonomous capital inflow.[18] It may be seen there that the decline in the ratio of capital inflow to GNP went on from the beginning of the period until 1957.[19] From then on until 1964, the ratio shows a few large fluctuations, but no downward trend; and only in 1965 and 1966 does the downward movement reappear.

A change in the price of foreign exchange will, of course, achieve the purpose of adjusting the economy to changes in the relative size of autonomous capital inflows only if it has a corresponding effect on the relative size of the import surplus. As will be recalled from the preceding chapter, and as can be seen in column 1, Table 6-8, below, this indeed has been the case: the relative size of the import surplus declined substantially during the 1950s and, with sometimes considerable year-to-year fluctuations, remained at a constant level in later years. On the basis of analysis in the preceding chapter, there is reason to believe that these trends were primarily due to changes in the relative level of the rate of foreign exchange.

v. EXPORT GROWTH AND IMPORT SUBSTITUTION

At least as interesting as the performance of the import surplus is the development of its separate components—imports and exports. Specifically, it is useful to determine how much of the reduction of the import surplus was achieved by reducing imports and how much by increasing exports. For a country in Israel's position, that is, starting out its economic expansion with a very large import surplus, such an investigation would provide a means of determining whether the process of growth was biased toward or against foreign trade. A related question, of course, is whether any bias that is found could be attributed to the operation of the foreign-exchange system.

Table 6-8 contains estimates of value added in exports (column 3) and imports for domestic use (column 5), obtained by assuming that the amount of each will be in the same ratio to GNP in the current year as it actually was in the preceding year. The figures in columns 2 and 4 are the actually observed values of these aggregates. The excess of actual exports over their "expected" value is a contribution to the reduction of the ratio of the import surplus to GNP; and the opposite is, of course, true of imports. These contributions are presented in columns 6 and 7 in absolute amounts and in columns 8 and 9 as ratios to GNP.[20]

It appears from these figures that the period can be divided into two subperiods: the 1950s up to and including 1959, and the 1960s and early 1970s up to and including 1971. In the 1950s, most of the contribution to the relative reduction of the import surplus came from the import side; the contribution due to the rise of exports was also positive, but much less significant in size. The dominance of imports in their impact on the development of the import surplus was, however, simply due to their overwhelming size in comparison with exports. In relation to their own size, as is shown by the data in columns 10 and 11, the contributions of exports and imports to the decline of the import surplus were quite similar—even slightly higher in exports than in imports. In this period, then, both exports and imports were involved in the process of reducing the import surplus.

During the 1960s, the relative increase in exports continued as before. The contribution of exports to the relative reduction of the import surplus was, on average, in the same ratio to the national product as it was in the 1950s. However, since the relative size of exports was gradually increasing, this meant a lower ratio of exports themselves, as may be seen in column 10. Imports, on the other hand, exhibited a relative *rise;* that is, they contributed to an increase of the import surplus rather than to its reduction. This trend was not as substantial as the opposite trend of the 1950s, but its existence cannot be doubted: from 1959 to 1971, imports rose over the increase which would have maintained the ratio of imports to GNP constant from year to year by about 6 per cent of GNP; or, put in a different way, the relative annual increase of imports over this period (average of the 1960–71 figures in column 11) was about 2 per cent of imports.

Looking back at columns 1 and 2 of Table 6-7, it seems that the difference in import trends between the 1950s and the 1960s could be explained by the difference in movement of the EERs. The remarkably large increase in the import rate until 1955 was sufficient to overcome the effect of relaxing the QRs and still have a substantial negative impact on the size of imports. It could be assumed, moreover, that the effect of such a substantial price rise on imports is not quickly consummated, but is spread gradually over several years. Thus, the relative decline of imports during the 1950s could well have been due to the increase in import exchange rates in the first half of the decade. In the 1960s, on the other hand, import rates remained fairly constant, with a few substantial year-to-year fluctuations. If relative prices of imports were the only determinant of imports, the size of imports (in relation to GNP) should have been about constant over this period. The slight increase in the ratio of imports to GNP over this period could conceivably be explained by the liberalization of the 1960s; but it could also be due to changes in taste or to above-unity income elasticity of demand for imports. As yet, not enough research on this issue is available to substantiate any conclusion.[21]

The performance of exports during the 1950s was also in line with the

TABLE 6-8

National Product and the Import Surplus, 1950–72

Israeli Pounds in Millions in 1955 Prices

Year	Ratio of Import Surplus[a] to GNP (1)	Value Added in Exports[b]		Imports for Domestic Use[b]		Contribution to Import Surplus[c]		Ratio of Contribution to GNP		Ratio of Contribution to Expected Size	
		Actual (2)	Expected[d] (3)	Actual (4)	Expected[d] (5)	Exports [(2) less (3)] (6)	Imports [(5) less (4)] (7)	Exports [(6)/GNP] (8)	Imports [(7)/GNP] (9)	Exports [(6)/(3)] (10)	Imports [(7)/(5)] (11)
1950	42.5%	38		504							
1951	43.8	48	50	677	660	−2	−17	−0.1%	−1.2%	−4.0%	−2.6%
1952	32.5	64	52	565	727	+12	+162	+0.8	+10.5	+23.1	+22.3
1953	25.9	80	65	484	571	+15	+87	+1.0	+5.6	+23.1	+15.2
1954	19.5	124	97	496	590	+27	+94	+1.4	+4.9	+27.8	+15.9
1955	20.6	117	139	557	556	−22	−1	−1.0	0	−15.8	−0.2
1956	21.1	154	127	642	605	+27	−37	+1.2	−1.6	+21.3	−6.1
1957	22.2	185	167	747	700	+18	−47	+0.7	−1.9	+10.8	−6.7
1958	19.3	200	202	733	816	−2	+83	−0.1	+3.0	−1.0	+10.2
1959	14.6	247	225	704	830	+22	+126	+0.7	+4.0	+9.8	+15.2

Year										
1960	13.8	320	267	788	761	+53	−27	+1.6	−1.8	+19.9	−3.5
1961	15.4	359	355	937	872	+4	−65	+0.1	−1.7	+1.1	−7.5
1962	13.4	477	405	1,043	1,058	+72	+15	+1.7	+0.4	+17.8	+1.4
1963	11.2	563	533	1,089	1,165	+30	+76	+0.6	+1.6	+5.6	+6.5
1964	16.1	560	619	1,396	1,202	−59	−194	−1.1	−3.7	−9.5	−16.1
1965	13.7	646	599	1,408	1,491	+47	+83	+0.8	+1.5	+7.8	+5.6
1966	11.5	708	659	1,360	1,437	+49	+77	+0.9	+1.4	+7.4	+5.4
1967	8.6	772	717	1,266	1,377	+55	+111	+1.0	+1.9	+7.7	+8.1
1968	11.4	936	876	1,682	1,439	+60	−243	+0.9	−3.7	+6.8	−16.9
1969	14.9	949	1,046	2,038	1,881	−97	−157	−1.3	−2.1	−9.3	−8.3
1970	15.6	1,146	1,017	2,368	2,184	+129	−184	+1.6	−2.3	+12.7	−8.4
1971	9.4	1,615	1,247	2,415	2,575	+368	+160	+4.3	+1.9	+29.5	+6.2
1972	9.6	1,751	1,777	2,655	2,657	−26	+2	−0.3	+0.02	−1.5	+0.1

NOTE: For details of construction and sources, see accompanying text.

SOURCE: Tables A-10 and A-13.

a. Excludes imports of military goods.

b. Obtained by subtracting the import component in exports from both exports and imports.

c. Positive sign denotes contribution to relative improvement of the surplus; negative sign, deterioration.

d. Assuming it was in the same ratio to GNP as in the previous year.

trend that would be expected in view of the movement of PLD-EERs for exports: an increase of exports accompanying a sharp rise of export rates. As with imports, the continued rise of exports in the late 1950s could possibly be explained by the rise of export rates a few years earlier: the latter rose sharply until 1954, and then mildly until 1957. The persistent rise of exports during the 1960s, however, can by no means be explained by price changes: just as with imports, the level of export rates was not rising during this period. It might be argued that the continued rise of exports in the 1960s was still a lagged effect of the rate increases of the 1950s. But this is most doubtful, on two grounds. First, it is unlikely that events of this kind would still be influential three to as long as fifteen (!) years later. And second, if the effect of the rate had persisted over this long period, it should have been reflected in imports as well as in exports, since there is no apparent reason for it to do otherwise.

One possible explanation of the development of exports during the 1960s may be the use of various measures of export encouragement which are not taken account of in the estimate of PLD-EERs for exports, either because they could not be quantified or because they are not constituents of the rate (since they do not depend on the size of exports). Some of these are devices used to encourage exports of goods produced in existing facilities. But mainly, these are measures which affect the allocation of new investment in favor of industries with high export potential.

The share of industries of varying export intensities in total manufacturing investment is shown in Table 6-9.[22] It appears that the share of relatively export-intensive industries rose during the period from 1958 to 1969. An appropriate point of separation between "low-export" and "high-export" industries seems to be an export proportion of 10 per cent. Thus, the first ten industries listed are classified as low export, and the remaining eight, as high export.[23] In this classification, the share of the high-export industries in investment seems to have risen substantially during the years presented. But the trend of development is not uniform over the period and the selection of another dividing line for classification might have shown a weaker trend.[24] Such a trend may, of course, be due to measures or factors other than the government's investment policies, but it is difficult to find alternative explanations.

In summary, it appears that a distinction should be made between *levels* of protection of exports and import substitutes and *movements* of these levels. There seems to be no doubt that, even in the late 1960s and early 1970s, the level of protection afforded by the exchange system was considerably higher for import substitutes than for exports (see Chapter 4, section 3). In this sense, the government's policy, as expressed in the exchange system, has been biased toward import substitution. When policy changes over the years are considered, on the other hand, it appears that exports and import

TABLE 6-9

Share of Industries in Investment, 1958–69

(per cent)

Industry	Share of Exports in Industry's Sales, 1965	Share of Industry in New Investment (two-year averages)					
		1958–59	1960–61	1962–63	1964–65	1966–67	1968–69
1. Electrical and electronic equipment	1.8	2.6	1.6	2.2	2.7	6.0	4.9
2. Transport equipment	1.9	5.7	7.5	5.1	6.6	8.9	8.7
3. Metal products	2.6	4.8	4.1	3.9	5.2	4.7	7.8
4. Nonmetallic mineral products	4.1	4.1	7.6	7.5	8.5	7.9	2.9
5. Printing and publishing	4.3	2.8	1.8	2.0	2.6	1.3	2.3
6. Leather and leather products	4.9	0.5	0.3	0.3	0.6	0.7	0.5
7. Paper, cardboard, and their products	5.5	10.7	2.7	1.6	1.8	3.9	2.6
8. Basic metals	5.7	11.5	7.9	2.6	2.6	1.3	2.4
9. Food products	7.4	16.5	13.6	14.4	16.5	18.5	13.8
10. Wood and wood products	8.2	2.6	4.1	3.4	3.3	2.5	2.8
Total, lines 1–10		61.8	51.2	43.0	50.4	55.7	48.7
11. Chemicals	12.2	10.8	7.3	7.1	9.6	7.7	6.2
12. Machinery	12.7	2.1	2.2	2.1	2.7	3.8	6.3
13. Textiles	14.5	13.0	19.7	16.1	11.1	11.8	17.6
14. Rubber and plastic products	15.2	4.6	3.8	2.9	3.9	4.2	5.8
15. Clothing	16.4	0.9	0.7	0.9	0.7	1.0	1.7
16. Miscellaneous manufacturing	33.7	0.8	0.8	1.1	0.7	0.8	1.2
17. Mining and quarrying	49.1	5.8	14.0	26.4	20.7	14.5	12.2
18. Polished diamonds	99.0	0.2	0.3	0.4	0.2	0.5	0.3
Total, lines 11–18		38.2	48.8	57.0	49.6	44.3	51.3
Total, all industries		100.0	100.0	100.0	100.0	100.0	100.0

SOURCE: Yoseph Tawil, "Effective Exchange Rates and Investment in Manufacturing Exports" (M.A. diss., Hebrew University, 1973; in Hebrew), calculated from data in App. 1B.

substitutes were similarly encouraged during the 1950s. In the 1960s, the direction of policy change must have been biased toward exports: the growth process was biased toward trade.[25] This is probably explained, at least in part, by nonprice elements in the trade and exchange system. The slight relative increase in imports during these years, with rather stable EERs (as they are actually estimated), may possibly be due to the gradual relaxation of quantitative restrictions on imports, which during the 1950s had provided an added motivation for import substitution, particularly of finished consumer goods. Similarly, measures taken by the government in its budgetary and long-term credit policies to direct investments toward export industries may provide an explanation of the growth of exports, during the 1960s, in addition to the encouragement resulting from relative changes in the exchange rate.

NOTES

1. See the discussion of "imports without payment" in Chapter 2.
2. This conclusion is supported by data on proceeds from tourist expenditures in Israel, the tourist inflow being also dependent to a large extent, it may be assumed, on the country's security position. These proceeds, as recorded in the balance-of-payments estimates, amounted to about $5 million to $6 million annually until 1957. In 1958, they increased to $12 million; in 1959, $16 million; 1960, $27 million; 1961, $30 million; 1962, $38 million; 1963–66, $50 million–$55 million. The Six-Day War of 1967 materially changed the nature of tourism in Israel, leading to a jump in proceeds from this item in subsequent years.
3. An excess of the import surplus over domestic (net) investment is thus recorded as negative savings in the economy: this has been the case in most of the years recorded in Table 6-2 as well as in later years.
4. This is not true of households, for which consumer surveys find the patterns in the ratio of savings to disposable income to be rather similar to those observed in other middle- and high-income economies. It should be noted, however, that disposable income includes personal transfer payments from abroad, such as German restitution payments, which are not included as income in the national accounts. Consequently, personal consumption spending out of these transfer payments is recorded as dissaving. This treatment results in ratios of savings to GNP which are very low or even negative (cf. Table 6-2).
5. An important exception of the most recent years is U.S. military assistance, given in the form of long-term loans for the purchase of military equipment in the United States. *Technically,* these receipts too are recorded in the development budget, but there is no doubt that *causally* they are related to the size of military expenditures, which are part of the current budget.
6. The late Amotz Morag was first to point out this effect on the allocation of governmental income between the two parts of the budget. This is discussed rather extensively in his *Public Finance in Israel: Problems and Development* (Jerusalem: Magness Press, 1966; in Hebrew), Chap. 4.
7. It will be recalled that on an earlier occasion the highest among the major export rates was used in this study to represent the equilibrium level, an assumption which, although also arbitrary, could be better defended.
8. The downward bias is partly offset by an element of government saving that is pointed out at the end of this section.
9. Once more, an obvious case in which this procedure was *not* followed is that pointed out in note 5, above: U.S. military assistance of recent years is definitely not regarded as a contribution to the development budget, although the revenue is recorded there; technically, this is reflected in transfers from the development to the current budget.

10. The most important exception was probably the transfer of capital through the imports-without-payment market, which was discussed in Chapter 2. Another, less significant, arrangement for transferring capital at above the formal exchange rate, which was carried out mainly in the 1950s, was through the purchase of "blocked accounts" in Israel, which were then released for investment. It was also possible to transfer capital by buying Development bonds below par in the New York market and selling them to the Israeli Treasury at their face value at the formal rate, but little use was made of this technique.

11. This analysis should not be taken as exhaustive of the government's policy in the area of foreign investment. Over most of the period, the government applied specific measures to encourage foreign investment that were independent of the foreign-exchange system. Most important was the "law of encouragement of (foreign) investment," under which an "approved" investment enjoyed certain rights, primarily accelerated depreciation and reduced corporate income tax, as well as a governmental commitment to permit the unhindered repatriation of invested capital and the transfer of profits.

12. A few illustrative case studies of the waste can be found in Alex Rubner, *The Economy of Israel* (London: Frank Cass, 1960), particularly the appendixes.

13. See A. L. Gaathon, *Economic Productivity in Israel* (New York: Praeger, 1971). The productivity measure is constructed to compare changes in real output with changes in real inputs, the latter being weighted by their respective shares in national income.

14. This is a well-known deficiency of estimates of productivity of the services sector in Soviet-type economies: disregard of the consumer's time leads to the relatively high measures of productivity normally found in these sectors in Soviet-type countries compared with free-market economies.

15. This would not be true to the extent that the nominal value of unilateral transfers may be assumed to rise with price rises; an obvious example is gifts in kind.

16. Table 6-6 contains data only through 1966, since the Six-Day War of 1967 has led to a radical transformation in this respect. Autonomous capital inflow has grown very substantially since 1967; but at the same time, an equally large increase of defense expenditures, to a large extent in foreign exchange, may be said to have led to a substantial structural change of the economy. An analysis starting with the assumption of "neutral" growth is, therefore, obviously inapplicable to these years.

17. It should be remarked that in 1950 and 1951, autonomous capital imports were actually higher than the figures on which the data in column 1 of Table 6-6 are based. As was mentioned earlier, in those two years, freed sterling reserves of roughly $100 million were used. Since formally this is a use of short-term assets, they were not counted as autonomous capital imports, although for present purposes they should be so regarded. If those balances are taken into consideration, the relative decline of capital imports (column 3) over the period is even greater than indicated in the table. Using the same base as in the table, i.e., with the sterling-financed inflow excluded, the average relative inflow for 1950 and 1951 including the sterling inflow would be 128; the corresponding average for the figures in column 3 is 104.

18. Some portion of the relative rise of the foreign-exchange rate in the first subperiod (1950–57) may be explained as a correction of an existing overvaluation of the currency at the start of the period. But in 1950, the degree of disequilibrium of the rate could not yet have been high enough to account for any major share of the increase in the relative rate of almost 150 per cent between 1950 and 1957.

19. It should again be recalled that the indices for 1950 and 1951 were in fact higher because of the availability in those years of freed sterling balances (the indexes for 1950

and 1951 would be, respectively, 131 and 126). It should also be remarked that the increase of the ratio in 1954 is misleading: as was mentioned earlier, a large volume of short- and medium-term loans was raised in the United States in that year to build some foreign-exchange reserves and repay hard-pressing short-term loans. But since this "consolidation loan" was not raised directly by the Israeli government but by the Jewish communities in the United States, it is recorded as a unilateral transfer of capital to Israel. If these items are taken into account, the downward trend of the ratio from 1950 to 1957 is sharper than it appears to be.

20. In principle, the summation of the export and import figures of columns 8 and 9 for each year should yield the same result as the year-to-year changes which may be derived from column 1. The slight differences between the two are due to rounding.

21. In a study in progress conducted by Yehezkel Guttman, at the International Trade Workshop of the Hebrew University, a slight *decline* in the ratio of imports to income as income rises was observed in cross-sectional data.

22. These intensities are measured by the proportion of exports in the industry's product in a given year, 1965; but use of the 1968 proportions yields basically similar results.

23. Although use of the 1968 export intensities would somewhat change the ranking of industries, use of the 10 per cent dividing line would leave precisely the same industries in each class as the 1965 intensities.

24. The problem of arbitrariness of the classifications can be overcome by using Lorenz curves to compare the entire distribution year by year. Using this procedure, Tawil found evidence of the trend—Yoseph Tawil, "Effective Exchange Rates and Investment in Manufacturing Exports" (M.A. diss., Hebrew University, 1973; in Hebrew).

25. A bias toward trade development is indicated also in Halevi, "Devaluation," and Weinblat, "Effect of the Effective Exchange Rate."

Chapter 7

A Concluding Note: Increasing Reliance on the Price Mechanism

Comprehensive quantitative restrictions of imports, as the major component of a system of price control and rationing, were practiced and intensified in Israel during the years 1949–51. This was the period in which the country, which was just emerging from the War of Independence, about doubled its population through immigration. It was argued then that under such unusual conditions a market mechanism could not be expected adequately to fulfill the tasks of an economic system—the determination of production, consumption, and distribution. In particular, it was believed that establishing equilibrium in the balance of payments by raising the rate of exchange enough to allow freedom in international transactions would lead to a socially unacceptable structure and distribution of imports.

In what way a rationing plan would be more effective than the market mechanism was not usually very well specified. But presumably, the former was intended to fulfill two objectives: One was to achieve a more equal income distribution than a market mechanism would provide; and the other was to increase savings and investment as proportions of income. Since these targets could also be reached by a market mechanism plus taxes and subsidies, it may be inferred that the QR system was judged to be a better, or perhaps more *feasible,* means of implicit taxation than the conventional methods of explicit taxation. For a while, the QR system seemed indeed to achieve some equalization of income, by adding a price in "rationing points," distributed equally among the population, to the conventional money price. It apparently also produced, for some two years, a significant rate of "forced" savings. But the Israeli experience has shown that the QR system could be maintained, and

177

its targets achieved, only for a short while and only insofar as it caused no major deviations from what would have been the result of free market forces. Since the price control and QR systems were combined, during these years, with a very expansionary monetary-fiscal policy, it soon became unsustainable. By 1951, the degree of disequilibrium became high enough to lead to a disintegration of the system—to very intensive shortages and scarcities, widespread absenteeism of labor, and the rapid overtaking of the system by the black market. From a political point of view, too, the system, which was presumably thought to be more acceptable than explicit taxation, became untenable. The Israeli lesson from the period of 1949–51 is clear: a QR system probably fulfills the task of distributing some essential goods from a given stock better than any other system; but a comprehensive scheme of controls and rationing cannot replace the market mechanism, once the degree of disequilibrium in the system becomes substantial, unless a full shift is made toward a centrally planned economic regime.

The degree of failure of administrative controls probably contributed much to the fact that, once a shift to the use of the price mechanism was begun in early 1952, it progressed virtually without any relapse. In this shift, again, the foreign-exchange rate and import prices were the focal points of the system as a whole. The switch was sudden and of overwhelming proportions. Within a period of less than three years, the rate of exchange increased fivefold; and although domestic prices, too, rose very fast, with the gradual relaxation of controls, the PLD-EER more than doubled. By the latter half of 1954, when this process was completed, the exchange rate and the balance of payments were close to equilibrium, as were most other prices and quantities in the economy. During this period of three years, despite a short period of increased unemployment resulting from a restrictive monetary-fiscal policy, the increase in the economy's productivity was particularly high and the economy's growth particularly fast.

Once restriction of imports had been imposed due to balance-of-payments considerations, however, inevitably there were protective effects as well. Thus, when equilibrium in the balance of payments was restored, in the mid-1950s, the economy had already acquired patterns determined by the protection until then afforded to import substitutes. While the correction of a very high degree of balance-of-payments disequilibrium required only a few years, the removal of the protective aspects of the QR system has not been completed even at present, close to twenty years after the balance-of-payments motivation for the restrictions had disappeared. Removal of the QRs proved to be easy, and was performed quite rapidly, for imports of raw materials and semimanufactured intermediate goods. Since these were not produced in Israel, and could not potentially be produced within a relevant price range, liberalization of such imports did not effectively reduce protection to any local industrial branch. Indeed, such liberalization increased the effective protection granted to local industries using these intermediate inputs and was therefore welcomed by those industries. When, however, an import good did compete with a local industry, and the effect of its liberalization was to lower effective protection, the situation was radically different. Such liberalization of imports competing with local industries—mainly imports of finished consumer goods—started only much later, and by a much more gradual and protracted process. In fact, total protection of import substitutes by QRs remained in force some seven or eight years after the restoration of the balance-of-payments equilibrium. Only with the second New Economic Policy, in 1962, did the progressive relaxation of these restrictions start. Even then, for some seven years the change was primarily in the *form* of protection: quantitative restrictions were replaced by the price mechanism, that is, by appropriate tariffs designed to grant each industry roughly the same protection it had enjoyed under the QR regime. In this sense, then, the shift from the use of QRs to reliance on the price mechanism was completed not in 1954 but only some fourteen years later, in 1968. Since 1969, a gradual reduction in the level of effective protection of the industries formerly enjoying QR protection has been underway. And by present forecasts, over twenty years are anticipated to pass between the time the original balance-of-payments motivation for QRs disappeared and the time when most of the protection afforded by this system will have been removed. The lesson drawn from this experience in Israel is that once comprehensive QRs of imports are imposed, and the economy's structure adjusts to them, the protective aspect of the system is not easy to remove. Liberalization of QRs is easy and speedy where it leads to an increase in effective protection to local import-using industries; but when, to the contrary, it lowers protection, the liberalization process must be gradual and protracted. The process is likely to be helped by a shift in the method of protection from QRs to tariffs, even though at first such a shift may be purely a nominal liberalization, leaving the level of protection unaffected.

The degree of protection has throughout been much less uniform, and on the average higher, for import substitutes than for exports. This was obvious under the QR regime, when the importation of almost anything that competed with existing or potentially feasible local production was in fact banned, leading sometimes to extremely high levels of protection in import-substitution industries, whereas no similar policy of producing at "any cost" was applied to exports. When QRs were replaced by tariffs designed to afford each branch the same protection as the QRs, the level and dispersion of protection of import substitutes remained, of course, largely unchanged. But even regardless of the QRs, and abstracting from the tariffs that were designed to replace them, effective protective rates appear to have been higher and, primarily, much more diversified for import substitutes than for exports.

Several factors could explain this difference between import substitutes and exports. One is a tendency toward a policy of autarky, which apparently prevailed during the 1950s. Another is the *size* of the two sectors: exports being, particularly in the earlier years, a very small segment of total trade, they carried relatively little weight in the policymaking process. Still another factor, certainly not one confined to the case of Israel, was that protection to import substitutes could be hidden to some extent: protection afforded not by QRs but by tariffs even yields a revenue to the government, whereas export subsidies are mostly a governmental expenditure. Another factor, apparently specific to the case of Israel, was the early recognition by the government that protection should be measured by its effect on the price of the value added rather than the price of the final good: ever since the mid-1950s this view has been almost universally accepted in Israel and has been applied to exports in particular. Effective protective rates in exports were thus considered and determined *directly,* and not as a chance by-product of decisions about nominal rates of subsidy, a fact which certainly contributed to the uniformity of these rates. In imports this principle was not generally applied, probably because high import duties (unlike export subsidies) had existed before the effective protective principle was recognized, and because tariff duties also fulfill other functions besides protection. In the stage of nominal liberalization of the 1960s the effective protection principle was most probably applied in the determination of import duties; but in this case, it was designed to maintain the nonuniform degrees of protection introduced by the QR system rather than to lead to a uniform level. The progressive lowering of protection since 1969, on the other hand, has been aimed at achieving uniformity of effective protection in import substitution.

The combination of the relatively large size of the import-substituting sector and the large dispersion in the degree of protection granted to the various industries involved must have resulted in a significant loss of productive capacity due to misallocation of resources. The loss from protection of exports, on the other hand, could not be of a substantial size, even in recent years, when the export sector has grown in importance.

The process of devaluation, which started in 1952, has proceeded ever since, either through large-scale formal devaluations or small changes in nonformal components of the exchange rate, such as import tariffs and export subsidies. Both the size of the several devaluations, however, and their degree of success, varied considerably. The formal devaluation of 1952–54 could be termed an unqualified success, and was probably an example rarely repeated in other countries. As mentioned, the PLD-EER more than doubled within less than three years. During this period, not only was the QR system largely scrapped and the severe shortage of imports largely eliminated, but the quantity of imports also declined, while the national product increased at a very fast rate. Exports, too, rose during the period at a record rate. Other devaluations, on the other hand, notably the formal devaluation of 1962, fared much less well, and the benefits were dissipated within only a few years. As discussed in the concluding section of Chapter 5, the major factor which accounts for the difference in performance between the devaluation of 1952–54 and other devaluations was the nature of the accompanying demand policy: this was restrictive during most of the period of 1952–54, and expansionary during other episodes of devaluation.

The contrast in fiscal and monetary policies between 1952–54 and subsequent devaluations may probably be explained mainly on two grounds. One is that the first devaluation was undertaken under emergency conditions, when the country's external reserves were nil and a general feeling of collapse was pervasive, whereas the other devaluations were undertaken in more secure circumstances. The other difference lies in the strong, automatically expansionary impact the later devaluations had on money and liquidity in the economy, owing to the existence and accumulation of external and exchange-rate-linked assets. The lesson which may be drawn from the history of the devaluation process in Israel is that although a restrictive demand policy is essential to the success of a devaluation, it is particularly difficult to undertake when strong automatic forces lead in an expansionary direction and when no sense of emergency prevails in the population or among policy-makers.

One indicator of the success of the various steps in the process of devaluation is the movement of the level of the PPP-adjusted EER, which shows the relative change in the price of tradables (exports and imports) versus other prices. The level of this rate increased considerably (by close to 150 per cent) from the time just before promulgation of the 1952 New Economic Policy to the mid-1950s. Since then, however, the rate has been stable over the long run, with the various acts of devaluation leading only to temporary fluctuations in its level.

Two major forces seem to have motivated the devaluation process, both operating mainly in the early and mid-1950s. One, mentioned earlier, was the need to overcome the consequences of the system of controls and restrictions of 1949–51, and to replace this collapsing system by a workable price mechanism. The other was the need to reduce the dependence of the economy on capital imports, and to provide for the economy's continuous growth in face of a relative decline in the inflow of foreign capital. Indeed, the second target has been achieved just as well as the first: there has been almost continuous full employment and an almost uninterrupted rapid growth; and the dependence of the economy on capital imports, as measured by the ratio of the import surplus to the GNP, has sharply declined. Reduction of this dependence took place almost entirely during the 1950s: in later years, there are large fluctuations, but the long-term trend is only slightly downward.

It is interesting to note that this drastic (relative) reduction of the import surplus altered only slightly the importance of foreign trade for the economy. This may be illustrated by the following comparison of the beginning and end pairs of years of the period under review. In 1950–51, the ratio of the import surplus (excluding imports of military goods) to GNP was about 43 per cent; in 1971–72, it was less than 10 per cent. Yet, the combined ratio of value added in exports and of imports for domestic use (again, excluding military imports) to GNP declined merely from about 50 per cent in 1950–51 to 47 per cent in 1970–71. Despite the overwhelming decline of the import surplus, the economy retained almost the same degree of openness as before; that is, the declining gap between imports and exports was provided chiefly by export expansion rather than by a contraction of imports. This process, again, did not follow a uniform course over the years. During the 1950s, it was primarily a reduction of imports which contributed to the decline in the import surplus. In later years, on the other hand, imports not only ceased declining but even increased slightly, while exports expanded substantially.

This performance stands in sharp contrast to the prevailing view in Israel during the first few years after the establishment of the state, which leaned toward autarkic development. Based on something like an "absolute advantage" theory, the common argument made was that a country in Israel's position, with almost no raw materials and little industrial skill, could become competitive in only a very few goods. Having little to offer to the outside world, it therefore had to turn inward, producing for itself whatever it possibly could. In illustration of the extent to which Israel's actual growth process has deviated from this dim projection, it may be noted that by the early 1970s, value added of Israel's exports exceeded its 1950 GNP. Given the substantial change in relative prices introduced in the 1950s, rapid growth has thus been consistent with the drastic reduction of the economy's dependence on the import surplus and with maintenance of an open economy.

Appendixes

Appendix A

Basic Statistical Data

TABLE A-1
Population, 1948–72

	Population		Civilian Labor Force[a] (annual aver.; thous.) (3)	Natural Increase (rate per thous.) (4)	Migration Balance (thous.) (5)
	Number of Thousands (end of year) (1)	Per Cent Increase Over Preceding Year (2)			
1948	867.0				104.4
1949	1,173.9	35.4	343		234.9
1950	1,370.1	16.7	450	27.4	160.1
1951	1,577.8	15.2	545	27.2	166.9
1952	1,629.5	3.3	584	25.7	10.7
1953	1,669.4	2.4	599	25.4	−1.6
1954	1,717.8	2.9	608	22.5	11.1
1955	1,789.1	4.2	619	23.1	31.2
1956	1,872.4	4.7	646	22.2	43.8
1957	1,976.0	5.5	690	21.6	61.1
1958	2,031.7	2.8	698	20.7	14.5
1959	2,088.7	2.8	714	20.8	14.7
1960	2,150.4	3.0	736	20.9	17.8
1961	2,234.2	3.9	774	19.3	37.5
1962	2,331.8	4.4	818	18.6	54.9
1963	2,430.1	4.2	840	18.9	53.2
1964	2,525.6	3.9	884	19.4	47.3
1965	2,598.4	2.9	912	19.5	22.8
1966	2,657.4	2.3	943	19.2	8.2
1967	2,776.3[b]	4.5	927[b]	17.6	3.0
1968	2,841.1	2.3	970	18.3	11.6
1969	2,919.2	2.7	990	19.2	21.9
1970	3,001.4	2.8	1,001	20.1[c]	22.5
1971	3,095.1	3.1	1,033	21.2	29.0
1972	3,201.8	3.4	1,076	19.9	43.3

Notes to Table A-1

Source:

Col. 1—For 1948, *Statistical Abstract of Israel*, 1949–50, Table B/1; for 1949–71, ibid., 1972, Table II/1; for 1972, ibid., 1973, Table II/1.

Col. 3—For 1949–56, Avner Hovne, *The Labor Force in Israel* (Jerusalem: Falk Project for Economic Research, 1961; in English), pp. 12–13; for 1957–72, *Statistical Abstract of Israel*, various years.

Col. 4—For 1950–60, ibid., 1962, Table 21, p. 62; for 1961–71, ibid., 1972, Table III, p. 63; for 1972, Bank of Israel, *Annual Report*, 1973, Table IX/1, p. 206.

Col. 5—For 1948–64, *Statistical Abstract of Israel*, 1965, Table B/2; for 1965–71, ibid., 1972, Table II/2; for 1972, ibid., 1973, Table II/2.

a. Persons aged 14 and over.

b. As of June 1967, includes population of East Jerusalem.

c. As of 1970, includes East Jerusalem.

TABLE A-2
Gross National Product, 1950–72

	In Millions of 1955 IL			Per Capita[a] (1955 IL)	
	In Current Prices (mill. IL) (1)	Amount (2)	Per Cent Change Over Preceding Year (3)	Amount (4)	Per Cent Change Over Preceding Year (5)
1950	460	1,096		865	
1951	700	1,435	30.9	960	11.0
1952	1,063	1,541	7.4	959	−0.1
1953	1,335	1,560	1.2	945	−1.5
1954	1,764	1,902	21.9	1,126	19.2
1955	2,129	2,134	12.2	1,219	8.3
1956	2,543	2,317	8.6	1,267	3.9
1957	2,947	2,528	9.1	1,310	3.4
1958	3,420	2,766	9.4	1,383	5.6
1959	3,916	3,130	13.2	1,518	9.8
1960	4,393	3,383	8.1	1,598	5.3
1961	5,283	3,741	10.6	1,708	6.9
1962	6,256	4,225	12.9	1,845	8.0
1963	7,544	4,715	11.6	1,981	7.4
1964	8,741	5,204	10.4	2,098	5.9
1965	10,456	5,558	6.8	2,165	3.2
1966	11,500	5,678	2.2	2,158	−0.3
1967	11,972	5,750	1.3	2,096	−2.9
1968	14,026	6,539	13.7	2,324	10.9
1969	15,801	7,317	11.9	2,531	8.9
1970	18,666	7,842	7.2	2,633	4.0
1971	23,357	8,529	8.8	2,771	5.2
1972	28,958	9,365	9.8	2,946	6.3

SOURCE:

Col. 1—*Statistical Abstract of Israel*, 1973, Table VI/1, p. 154.

Cols. 2 and 4—For 1950–68, Don Patinkin, "The Economic Development of Israel" (unpublished; January 1970), Appendix Tables 5, 6, and 7; for 1969–71, *Statistical Abstract of Israel*, 1972, p. 152; for 1972, calculated from ibid., 1973, Table VI/1.

a. Based on mean of population data for each year.

TABLE A-3
Consumption and Savings, 1950–72

	Private Consumption (1955 IL)			Gross Savings[b] as Per Cent of GNP (5)	Net Savings[c] as Per Cent of NNP (6)
	In Millions (1)	Per Capita[a] (2)	Per Cent Change Over Preceding Year of Col. 2 (3)		
1950	930	734		7.2	3.4
1951	1,140	763	3.9	13.4	9.8
1952	1,225	762	−0.0	7.7	1.3
1953	1,268	768	0.8	5.2	−3.3
1954	1,458	863	12.4	7.2	−1.2
1955	1,576	900	4.3	6.1	−2.3
1956	1,722	942	4.7	0.2	−9.0
1957	1,841	953	1.2	6.2	−2.6
1958	2,028	1,013	6.3	8.6	0.4
1959	2,227	1,080	6.6	10.4	2.6
1960	2,381	1,125	4.2	10.8	2.8
1961	2,642	1,206	7.2	11.8	3.8
1962	2,918	1,275	5.7	8.1	−2.2
1963	3,209	1,348	5.7	9.5	−0.8
1964	3,553	1,434	6.4	10.4	0.4
1965	3,843	1,500	4.6	11.0	1.3
1966	3,949	1,502	0.1	8.4	−1.7
1967	4,004	1,475	−1.8	2.2	−8.6
1968	4,511	1,608	9.0	4.5	
	4,426[d]	1,577[d]		4.3[d]	−6.1[d]
1969	4,874	1,693	7.4	3.7	−6.5
1970	5,012	1,694	0.1	2.7	−7.8
1971	5,259	1,727	1.9	7.7	−2.3
1972	5,723	1,820	5.4	10.6	0.6

SOURCE: *Statistical Abstract of Israel*, 1973, Table VI/1, p. 154; except for data on depreciation, which are from Bank of Israel, *Annual Report*, various years.

a. Computed from mean of population data for each year.

b. Computed from current-price data; gross savings = GNP less consumption.

c. Computed from current-price data; net savings = GNP less (consumption + depreciation).

d. Revised estimates.

TABLE A-4

Capital and Investment, 1950–72

(at 1955 prices)

	Gross Fixed Capital Stock[a] (mill. IL) (1)	Domestic Investment		
		Amount (mill. IL) (2)	As Per Cent of GNP (3)	As Per Cent of Resources (4)
1950	2,147	606	55	33
1951	2,691	716	50	33
1952	3,344	615	40	29
1953	3,869	515	33	24
1954	4,304	574	30	24
1955	4,777	707	33	26
1956	5,346	669	29	22
1957	5,955	783	31	25
1958	6,631	841	30	25
1959	7,340	919	29	25
1960	8,125	965	29	25
1961	8,936	1,151	31	26
1962	9,940	1,269	30	26
1963	11,092	1,314	28	25
1964	12,243	1,588	31	27
1965	13,574	1,596	29	21
1966	14,851	1,338	24	18
1967	15,921	1,038	18	13
1968	16,733	1,534	23	16
1969	17,871	1,898	26	18
1970	19,336	2,111	27	18
1971	20,960	2,492	29	19
1972	23,077	2,716	29	20

SOURCE:

Col. 1—For 1950–66, A. L. Gaathon, *Economic Productivity in Israel* (New York: Praeger, 1971), Table A-31; for 1967–72, Bank of Israel, *Annual Report*, 1972, Table V/17, p. 134.

Col. 2—*Statistical Abstract of Israel*, 1973, Table VI/2, pp. 154–155.

Col. 3—Table A-2, above.

Col. 4—For 1952–64, *Statistical Abstract of Israel*, 1969, Table E/2, p. 138; for 1965–72, ibid., 1972, Table VI/2, p. 154.

a. Beginning-of-year figures.

TABLE A-5

Composition of Investment, 1952–72

(millions of Israeli pounds at current prices)

	Building and Construction			Machinery and Equipment			
	Dwellings (1)	Non-residential Buildings (2)	Other Con-struction Works (3)	Transport Equip-ment (4)	Machinery and Other Equipment (5)	Change in Livestock Inventory (6)	Total Invest-ment (7)
1952	127.3	43.0	68.0	13.9	70.2	4.3	326.7
1953	133.4	49.0	92.3	10.1	83.3	7.5	375.6
1954	179.4	58.7	115.0	19.2	99.4	7.8	479.5
1955	241.1	82.8	138.6	35.8	130.5	7.7	636.5
1956	235.0	99.6	142.5	40.6	171.2	11.6	700.5
1957	299.4	116.3	180.8	86.5	168.1	19.3	870.4
1958	300.2	150.7	177.7	62.5	223.9	26.3	941.3
1959	337.1	178.2	204.3	56.2	244.6	15.8	1,036.2
1960	348.9	188.9	212.5	107.4	262.1	5.7	1,125.5
1961	474.0	229.2	258.1	168.6	335.4	10.6	1,475.9
1962	688.9	292.6	330.5	167.9	481.4	9.6	1,970.9
1963	728.2	366.5	389.5	190.3	529.5	0.2	2,204.2
1964	867.7	475.8	425.4	356.5	620.7	2.4	2,748.5
1965	976.8	549.9	451.1	275.7	678.8	2.1	2,934.4
1966	787.2	501.8	399.9	184.3	612.6	1.2	2,487.0
1967	532.3	401.6	411.5	128.7	500.0	13.0	1,987.1
1968	666.7	490.3	530.6	354.0	843.1	4.1	2,888.8
1969	1,082.1	617.7	607.7	383.6	1,212.0	6.8	3,909.9
1970	1,735.8	772.2	542.5	503.7	1,426.3	9.2	4,989.8
1971	2,400.9	952.6	742.6	1,058.4	1,840.0	15.8	7,010.3
1972	3,492.7	1,316.2	947.5	783.7	2,577.7	16.0	9,133.9

SOURCE: For 1952–64, *Statistical Abstract of Israel*, 1971, Table F/11, pp. 160–161. For 1965–72, ibid., 1973, Table VI/7, pp. 166–167.

TABLE A-6
Public-Sector Investment, 1952–72
(per cent)

	Share of Investment Undertaken by Public Sector			Share of Investment Financed by Public Sector			
	Total Invest- ment (1)	Total Non- dwelling Investment (2)	Dwelling (3)	Agri- culture and Irrigation (4)	Industry and Con- struction (5)	Mining and Quarry- ing (6)	Total Fixed Invest- ment (7)
1952	34						
1953	45						
1954	50						
1955	59		41				
1956			39	72	39	93	52
1957			51	61	43	84	57
1958	45		47	74	42	75	53
1959	38		45	72	32	71	52
1960	41		40	84	39	50	53
1961	45		44	81	36	10	43
1962	49	49	47	75	24	11	41
1963	42	45	38	83	24	21	40
1964	43	46	37	90	10	13	39
1965	41	44	36	92	7	24	40
1966	42	47	33	89	11	55	48
1967	45	53	29	91	52	100[a]	67
1968	41	46	24	91	34	100[a]	57
1969	42	48	25	100	30		47
1970	36	38	28				
1971	38	42	32				
1972	38	44	29				

SOURCE:

Cols. 1, 2, and 3—For 1952–59, Don Patinkin, *The Israel Economy: The First Decade* (Jerusalem: Falk Project for Economic Research, 1960; in English), Table 32; for 1960–72, Bank of Israel, *Annual Report*, various years, Table V/3.

Cols. 4 through 7—For 1956–64, Nadav Halevi and Ruth Klinov-Malul, *The Economic Development of Israel* (New York: Praeger, 1968), Table 71; for 1965–68, Bank of Israel, *Annual Report*, 1968, Table V/11; for 1969, ibid., 1969, Table V/13.

a. In 1967 and 1968, government loans to firms engaged in mineral extraction exceeded their actual investment.

TABLE A-7
Share of Manufacturing and Agriculture in Net Domestic Product[a]
and Employment, 1950–72
(per cent)

	Share of Agriculture[b] in Net Domestic Product (1)	Share of Manufacturing[c] in Net Domestic Product (2)	Share of Agriculture in Employment (3)	Share of Manufacturing in Employment (4)
1950			17.3	21.2
1951			16.7	20.9
1952	11.4	21.7	17.4	20.1
1953	11.4	22.8	17.2	21.0
1954	12.1	22.4	17.1	21.9
1955	11.2	22.4	17.5	21.5
1956	11.5	22.1	16.9	21.5
1957	12.8	21.8	16.3	22.5
1958	13.2	22.1	17.6	22.4
1959	12.1	23.0	17.6	22.6
1960	11.6	23.9	17.3	23.2
1961	11.0	24.6	16.5	24.2
1962	10.3	24.6	15.5	25.1
1963	10.3	24.6	14.4	25.8
1964	9.1	24.3	13.9	25.9
1965	7.9	23.7	13.3	25.5
1966	7.7	21.8	12.4	26.1
1967	8.4	22.5	12.6	24.6
1968	7.6	24.8	10.4	24.0
1969	7.0	24.1	9.7	24.0
1970	6.4	24.2	8.8	24.3
1971	6.5	23.6	8.5	24.1
1972	6.2	23.5	8.0	23.8

SOURCE:

For 1972, ibid., 1973, Table IV/9.

Cols. 1 and 2—For 1952–68, *Statistical Abstract of Israel*, 1971, Table F/13; for 1969–71, ibid., 1972, Table VI/8; for 1972, ibid., 1973, Table IV/9.

Cols. 3 and 4—For 1950–65, A. L. Gaathon, *Economic Productivity in Israel* (New York: Praeger, 1971), Table A-24; for 1966–67, *Statistical Abstract of Israel*, 1968, Table K/10; for 1968–71, ibid., 1972, Table XII/11; for 1972, Bank of Israel, *Annual Report*, 1972, Table IX/10.

a. Net domestic product at factor cost, computed from current-price data.

b. Agriculture includes forestry and fishing.

c. Manufacturing includes mining.

TABLE A-8

Census Value Added in Manufacturing, 1959–70

(millions of Israeli pounds at market prices)

	1959	1960	1961	1962	1963	1964	1965	1966	1967	1968	1969	1970
Mining and quarrying	25.8	26.9	40.7	57.2	59.3	97.2	118.4	104.0	99.2	113.9	148.4	155.9
Food, beverages, and tobacco	164.4	182.4	231.8	284.2	342.1	366.8	417.7	470.2	526.0	553.9	675.9	757.2
Textiles	87.7	96.0	138.3	159.0	190.4	227.8	274.1	278.3	294.0	391.8	327.0	397.3
Clothing	21.3	20.4	37.2	33.1	51.0	50.7	61.8	60.5	68.7	91.2	184.0	237.6
Leather and leather products	15.6	12.4	18.5	20.0	26.0	25.3	32.8	31.0	32.9	35.0	41.6	44.0
Wood and wood products	46.3	44.5	67.7	78.1	114.0	116.9	134.1	137.7	110.3	155.7	151.0	176.5
Paper and paper products	17.0	20.1	29.9	40.7	45.9	50.6	55.0	58.5	68.4	92.7	94.3	117.1
Printing and publishing	22.9	38.4	48.6	52.1	67.8	85.3	100.7	100.3	101.7	129.9	150.9	164.1
Rubber and plastic products	26.7	30.2	44.1	63.0	71.9	87.8	103.1	93.1	22.9	177.7	209.6	239.4
Chemicals and oil products[a]	69.9	72.0	88.4	111.5	131.2	164.5	189.8	187.2	227.5	277.6	291.5	355.9
Nonmetallic mineral products	84.8	97.8	124.1	150.6	172.5	199.0	221.5	204.5	172.0	218.7	256.8	311.8
Basic metals		23.9	41.7	47.9	62.6	77.5	86.4	80.0	76.2	120.9	168.9	172.6
Metal products	80.5	71.6	79.7	83.5	109.1	134.0	174.9	143.7	195.1	268.6	405.8	505.1
Machinery	43.2	54.1	75.4	94.4	115.2	141.9	164.8	128.4	150.1	215.4	242.0	273.7
Electrical and electronic equipment	27.6	33.1	48.8	58.9	82.8	90.4	110.5	106.3	134.1	203.2	352.2	399.7
Transport equipment	63.7	71.2	93.0	107.9	154.0	168.6	239.4	224.8	223.7	274.1	269.5	406.9
Diamonds	13.0	16.9	21.8	39.8	49.3	60.1	68.7	87.2	94.6	154.1	132.2	121.8
Miscellaneous	13.2	12.8	17.8	21.7	28.8	27.9	31.7	37.1	35.8	47.8	53.1	63.3
Total	833.8	924.7	1,244.5	1,500.6	1,873.9	2,163.3	2,585.3	2,532.8	2,733.2	3,522.5	4,154.7	4,899.9

NOTE: Data are for budget years (April to March); census data cover establishments having five employed persons or more.

SOURCE: *Statistical Abstract of Israel*, various years.

a. Establishments engaged in the production of edible oils were included in "chemicals" until 1961–62; for 1962–63 on they are included in "food."

TABLE A-9

Industrial Production, by Industry, 1958–71

(index: average 1958 = 100)

	1958	1959	1960	1961	1962	1963	1964	1965	1966	1967	1968	1969	1970	1971
Total	100	114	129	149	169	193	220	242	245	237	306	356	393	442
Mining and quarrying	100	132	156	172	184	210	253	314	331	313	371	392	467	467
Manufacturing	100	115	128	148	168	192	218	239	242	234	303	354		
Food, beverages, and tobacco	100	105	112	125	135	143	162	172	183	193	220	238	251	275
Textiles	100	109	128	160	188	214	246	271	285	268	345	393	441	486
Clothing	100	117	129	140	160	181	212	264	272	268	348	407	454	601
Wood, wood products, and furniture	100	119	121	144	182	219	260	299	306	285	403	477	503	529
Paper, cardboard, and their products	100	105	131	153	169	201	236	250	265	293	350	361	389	434
Printing and publishing	100	118	134	150	158	180	202	220	242	285	323	338	341	323
Leather and leather products	100	110	118	131	155	164	170	190	183	162	199	225	235	245
Rubber and plastic products	100	121	133	160	186	225	271	301	312	310	448	547	629	738
Chemicals	100	112	131	153	171	193	222	261	287	301	384	437	508	571
Nonmetallic mineral products	100	116	123	137	159	182	197	207	193	144	182	203	228	252
Diamonds	100	133	165	192	244	304	313	335	373	350	426	444	435	542
Basic metals	100	125	146	175	202	227	242	261	242	202	294	349	341	341
Metal products	100	113	124	137	161	186	209	219	210	179	246	296	318	375
Machinery	100	122	133	158	173	209	233	247	224	198	279	332	394	403
Electrical and electronic equipment	100	117	143	175	199	240	271	306	291	246	421	677	727	800
Transport equipment	100	112	130	152	170	187	220	229	204	202	285	372	477	567
Miscellaneous manufacturing	100	118	176	193	173	184	226	242	223	248	333	403	425	556

SOURCE: For 1961–69, *Statistical Abstract of Israel*, 1970, Table 49; for 1970–71, ibid., 1972, Table XIV/9.

TABLE A-10

Exports, Imports, and the Import Surplus,[a] 1950–72
(millions of dollars at current prices)

	Exports				Imports				Import Surplus	
	Goods (1)	Services (2)	Total (3)	Yearly Per Cent Change in Col. 3 (4)	Goods (5)	Services[b] (6)	Total (7)	Yearly Per Cent Change in Col. 7 (8)	Total (9)	Yearly Per Cent Change in Col. 9 (10)
1950	35	11	46		299	29	328		282	
1951	45	22	67	45.7	380	46	426	29.9	359	27.3
1952	44	42	86	28.4	323	70	393	−7.7	307	−14.5
1953	56	46	102	18.6	282	83	365	−7.1	263	−14.3
1954	88	47	135	32.4	292	81	373	2.2	238	−9.5
1955	89	55	144	6.7	334	93	427	14.5	283	18.9
1956	110	68	178	23.6	367	168	535	25.3	357	26.1
1957	141	81	222	24.7	432	125	557	4.1	335	−6.2
1958	139	96	235	5.9	417	152	569	2.2	334	−0.3
1959	176	110	286	21.7	427	175	602	5.8	316	−5.4
1960	210	149	359	25.5	491	205	696	15.6	337	6.6
1961	238	187	425	18.4	574	283	857	23.1	432	28.2
1962	271	232	503	18.4	614	344	958	11.8	453	4.9
1963	337	270	607	20.7	647	364	1,011	5.5	404	−10.8
1964	350	306	656	8.1	800	425	1,225	21.2	569	40.8
1965	404	345	749	14.2	794	475	1,269	3.6	520	−8.6
1966	475	397	873	16.6	795	522	1,317	3.8	444	−14.6
1967	518	412	930	6.5	729	727	1,456	10.6	526	18.5
1968	598	534	1,132	21.7	1,057	755	1,812	24.5	680	29.3
1969	679	587	1,265	11.7	1,259	929	2,188	20.8	923	35.7
1970	717	644	1,361	7.6	1,372	1,277	2,649	21.1	1,288	39.5
1971	900	914	1,814	33.3	1,759	1,323	3,082	16.3	1,268	−1.6
1972	1,082	1,037	2,119	16.8	1,895	1,327	3,222	4.5	1,103	−13.0

SOURCE: For 1950–64, balance-of-payments data in Nadav Halevi and Ruth Klinov-Malul, *The Economic Development of Israel* (New York: Praeger, 1968), Tables 50, 51, 52, 54, and 56. For 1965–72, Bank of Israel, *Annual Report*, 1972, Table 3-1.

a. Imports c.i.f.; exports f.o.b.

b. Transportation revised (c.i.f. recording of commodity imports).

TABLE A-11

Composition of Exports, by Major Commodity Group, 1950–72
(per cent of annual total)

	Citrus Fruits (1)	Other Farm Prod. (2)	Citrus Products (3)	Other Food-stuffs (4)	Dia-monds (5)	Textile Prod. (6)	Chem-icals (7)	Tires and Tubes (8)	Mine and Quarry Prod. (9)	Other Industrial Prod. (10)	Total (11)	Over-All Growth Rate of Total (12)
1950	47.2	0.6	3.9	4.8	24.7	11.0	1.4	—	0.3	6.2	100	
1951	35.5	0.4	7.1	3.3	26.1	14.5	2.9	—	0.2	9.8	100	27.6
1952	37.9	0.5	7.1	1.8	26.4	11.0	1.4	—	0.9	12.9	100	−2.9
1953	37.5	0.9	4.3	1.0	22.2	9.4	2.6	1.6	2.6	17.9	100	32.4
1954	38.8	2.7	3.2	1.4	18.2	5.3	3.1	2.7	3.6	21.0	100	49.8
1955	35.5	2.9	2.4	1.5	22.8	6.2	3.3	2.9	3.3	19.4	100	3.1
1956	37.7	3.2	3.6	2.2	23.2	5.3	3.6	3.5	3.5	14.4	100	19.7
1957	34.5	4.3	2.7	2.8	25.2	5.7	5.4	3.5	2.9	13.1	100	31.5
1958	34.8	6.0	4.1	2.1	23.9	6.7	4.3	4.2	1.7	12.3	100	−0.7
1959	26.0	6.9	3.0	3.4	25.6	6.4	4.9	3.7	3.7	16.4	100	26.8
1960	22.1	7.9	1.3	3.4	26.7	8.6	4.9	3.7	3.3	18.1	100	19.8
1961	16.9	9.2	3.3	3.3	27.3	10.2	5.2	3.5	2.6	18.2	100	13.2
1962	18.1	7.1	3.7	3.3	30.3	11.1	4.3	3.6	2.4	16.1	100	13.5
1963	22.1	4.2	3.8	3.4	30.7	9.2	4.0	2.6	2.2	17.8	100	24.6
1964	15.0	3.8	5.1	3.6	33.6	11.3	4.9	2.4	3.6	16.7	100	4.0
1965	17.5	3.9	4.6	3.5	32.5	10.0	6.1	2.2	3.4	16.4	100	15.4
1966	15.7	4.1	4.0	3.3	34.5	9.5	5.2	2.0	4.0	17.6	100	18.4
1967	16.5	4.3	4.6	2.5	30.5	10.1	7.0	1.8	5.6	17.1	100	8.5
1968	14.7	4.1	4.4	2.9	32.4	10.4	7.1	1.8	5.4	16.9	100	16.4
1969	13.3	4.0	4.8	4.4	31.3	12.1	6.3	1.9	5.3	16.6	100	14.4
1970	11.4	6.1	4.8	3.8	27.6	13.6	7.2	2.2	5.6	17.6	100	6.1
1971	12.4	4.5	4.7	3.9	28.9	13.5	5.9	2.0	4.6	19.8	100	25.7
1972	10.9	4.4	5.1	3.7	34.7	11.9	5.5	2.9	4.0	16.9	100	20.4

SOURCE: Bank of Israel, *Economic Review*, April 1973, statistical tables.

TABLE A-12
Distribution of Imports of Goods, by End Use, 1950–72
(per cent of annual total)

	Consumer Goods (1)	Raw Materials (2)	Investment Goods (3)	Fuel and Lubricants (4)	Unclassified Goods (5)	Total Imports (6)	Over-All Growth Rate of Total (7)
1950	25.3	39.9	27.0	7.4	0.5	100.0	
1951	25.0	43.6	22.1	9.2	0.1	100.0	26.7
1952	21.6	43.6	20.3	12.2	2.4	100.0	−15.3
1953	20.3	48.8	20.2	10.7	—	100.0	−12.9
1954	16.7	56.6	16.7	10.0	—	100.0	2.9
1955	14.8	56.5	18.4	10.2	0.1	100.0	16.0
1956	13.4	53.7	21.7	11.0	0.2	100.0	12.4
1957	12.1	53.3	22.4	12.1	0.2	100.0	14.9
1958[a]	12.9	54.9	22.7	9.5	0.1	100.0	
	11.5	61.0	18.0	9.5	—	100.0	−2.7
1959	9.5	65.0	17.4	8.1	0.2	100.0	1.7
1960	8.8	63.4	20.9	6.9	0.1	100.0	16.8
1961	7.7	61.1	25.4	5.8	0.1	100.0	17.8
1962[a]	7.9	58.8	26.9	6.3	0.1	100.0	
	7.0	64.1	22.5	6.3	—	100.0	7.2
1963	8.6	63.9	20.8	6.6	—	100.0	5.9
1964	9.9	61.0	23.6	5.6	—	100.0	24.6
1965[b]	9.9	62.4	21.4	6.4	—	100.0	−0.2
1966	10.8	65.6	16.6	7.0	—	100.0	0.3
1967	9.8	66.3	16.8	7.1	—	100.0	−7.2
1968	9.9	63.7	20.8	5.6	—	100.0	44.1
1969	10.6	62.6	21.5	5.3	—	100.0	18.7
1970	9.8	61.5	23.8	4.8	—	100.0	9.3
1971	9.8	56.6	28.6	4.9	—	100.0	24.2
1972	10.4	60.7	23.6	5.3	—	100.0	2.2

SOURCE: Bank of Israel, *Economic Review*, April 1973, statistical tables.
a. New classifications.
b. Since 1965, includes imports of nonmonetary gold.

TABLE A-13
The Import Surplus, 1950–72

	In Millions of Israeli Pounds		As Per Cent of		
	At Current Prices (1)	At 1955 Prices (2)	Total Uses (at 1955 prices) (3)	Domestic Investment (at 1955 prices) (4)	Value of Imports of Goods and Services (at current prices) (5)
1950	102	715	39.5	118.0	86.0
1951	129	747	34.2	104.3	84.3
1952	215	607	26.6	98.7	78.1
1953	185	545	24.0	105.8	72.1
1954	339	506	19.1	88.2	63.8
1955	509	579	19.5	81.9	66.3
1956	643	690	21.0	103.1	66.7
1957	603	623	17.9	79.6	60.1
1958	601	644	17.0	76.6	58.7
1959	569	579	13.7	63.0	52.5
1960	607	570	12.4	59.1	48.4
1961	1,296	762	14.5	66.2	50.4
1962	1,359	790	13.5	62.3	47.3
1963	1,607	687	10.8	52.3	40.0
1964	1,212	877	12.4	55.2	46.4
1965	1,707	815	10.8	51.1	41.0
1966	1,560	665	8.7	49.7	33.7
1967	1,332	744	9.3	71.7	36.1
1968	1,841	1,061	11.2	69.2	37.5
1969	2,380	1,342	7.0	70.7	42.2
1970	4,508	1,639	13.8	77.6	48.6
1971	5,009	1,645	12.7	66.0	41.1
1972	4,633	1,614	11.7	59.4	34.2

SOURCE:
Col. 1—Value of the import surplus in dollars, from Table A-10, col. 9, above, converted to values in Israeli pounds by use of the formal rate recorded in Table 5-1, above.
Col. 2—Don Patinkin, "The Economic Development of Israel" (unpublished; January 1970), Appendix Table 5; extended for 1970–72 by using the rate of change of the import surplus derived from (foreign-price) deflated import and export values.
Col. 3—Col. 2 divided by aggregate of itself and GNP size in Table A-2, col. 2.
Col. 4—Col. 2 divided by data on domestic investment in Table A-4, col. 2, above.
Col. 5—Table A-10, above: col. 9 divided by col. 7.

TABLE A-14

Sources of Autonomous Capital Imports, 1950–71

(millions of dollars, except column 13)

	From U.S. Govt.		From German Govt.		Unilateral Transfers from World Jewry		Independence and Development Bonds of Israeli Govt.
	Grants-in-Aid (1)	Loans (2)	To Israeli Govt.[a] (3)	To Households (4)	To Israeli Govt.[a] (5)	To Households[b] (6)	(7)
1950	—	—	—	—	74	20	—
1951	14	—	—	—	84	39	55
1952	86	—	—	—	89	16	46
1953	47	—	40	—	75	11	36
1954	39	—	80	6	123	17	29
1955	21	32	83	19	53	35	32
1956	7	41	79	26	93	36	47
1957	25	26	76	45	61	35	45
1958	17	46	70	65	75	37	34
1959	10	45	66	71	74	30	35
1960	14	47	76	98	87	37	28
1961	10	42	88	111	92	45	32
1962	8	45	47	134	74	68	33
1963	6	50	28	139	85	92	23
1964	—	53	—	134	80	96	24
1965	—	42	—	113	94	98	33
1966	—	41	—	110	97	84	11
1967	—	36	—	123	325	84	171
1968	—	35	—	143	165	134	79
1969	—	54	—	138	181	152	63
1970	—	343	—	204	290	172	136
1971	—	262	—	231	264	297	184
Total, 1950–71	304	1,240	733	1,910	2,635	1,635	1,176

(continued)

TABLE A-14 (*concluded*)

	Other Long- and Medium-Term Loans (8)	Direct Private Investment (net) (9)	Total Unilateral Transfers (10)	Total Transfers on Capital Account (11)	Total Capital Imports (12)	Col. 12 in Mill. IL at Formal Rate of Exchange[c] (13)
1950	47	21	94	68	162	58
1951	36	42	137	133	270	96
1952	39	30	191	115	306	306
1953	12	22	173	70	243	243
1954	23	19	265	71	336	336
1955	5	14	211	83	294	529
1956	−20	17	241	85	326	587
1957	−14	18	242	75	317	571
1958	6	8	264	94	358	644
1959	15	13	251	108	359	646
1960	2	43	312	120	432	778
1961	21	52	346	147	493	887
1962	52	82	331	212	543	1,629
1963	−29	125	350	169	519	1,557
1964	60	143	310	280	590	1,770
1965	62	83	305	230	535	1,605
1966	60	71	291	183	474	1,422
1967	88	8	532	303	835	2,505
1968	138	9	442	260	702	2,457
1969	103	29	481	215	696	2,436
1970	85	29	668	593	1,259	4,406
1971	210	101	791	757	1,548	6,115
Total, 1950–71	1,001	979	7,226	4,371	11,597	31,584

SOURCE: Balance-of-payments data from *Statistical Abstract of Israel* and Bank of Israel, *Annual Report*, various years.

a. Including national institutions.
b. Including transfer by immigrants, etc.
c. Formal rate from Table 5-1, above.

TABLE A-15
Public Finance, 1950–72

	Public Expenditures on Goods and Services (mill. IL)		Government Revenues (mill. IL)	
	Amount (1)	Ratio to Total Uses (2)	Amount (3)	Ratio to National Product (4)
1950			60	13.0
1951			97	13.9
1952			163	15.4
1953			232	17.4
1954			327	18.6
1955			456	21.4
1956			561	22.1
1957			729	24.7
1958	559	12.2	823	24.1
1959	661	12.7	919	23.5
1960	908	15.5	1,098	25.0
1961	1,036	14.6	1,365	25.8
1962	1,566	16.9	1,644	26.3
			1,594a	25.5a
1963	1,884	17.3	1,908	25.3
1964	2,149	17.0	2,179	24.9
1965	2,217	15.3	2,571	24.6
1966	2,618	16.7	2,962	25.8
1967	3,487	21.0	2,855	23.8
1968	4,312	20.8	3,637	26.5
1969	4,912	20.1	4,593	29.1
1970	6,575	22.7	5,909	31.7
1971	7,827	21.4	8,230	35.2
1972	9,006	20.0	10,361	35.8

SOURCE:

Col. 1—"Public" = central government and national institutions (Jewish Agency), and excludes local authorities; "expenditures" = purchases on both current account and capital account. Data are from Bank of Israel, *Annual Report*, various years.

Col. 2—Total uses for 1958–64 from *Statistical Abstract of Israel*, 1969, Table E/1; for 1965–72, from ibid., 1973, Table VI/3.

Col. 3—"Government" = central government; "revenues" = receipts from taxes and other compulsory payments. Data for 1950–62 are from Amotz Morag, *Public Finance in Israel: Problems and Development* (Jerusalem: Magnes, 1966; in Hebrew), Table 8/13; for 1963–72, from Bank of Israel, *Annual Report*, various years.

Col. 4—GNP at current prices from Table A-2, above.

a. These figures for 1962 are given in the source used for 1963–72.

TABLE A-16
Money Supply, 1950–72

	Total (annual average; mill. IL) (1)	Yearly Rate of Increase (per cent) (2)	Col. 1 as Per Cent of Annual GNP (3)
1950	170		37
1951	224	31.8	32
1952	247	10.3	23
1953	290	17.4	22
	263[a]	6.5	20
1954	328	24.7	19
1955	395	20.4	19
1956	465	17.7	18
1957	558	20.0	19
1958	642	15.1	19
1959	724	12.8	18
1960	820	13.3	19
1961	970	18.3	18
1962	1,126	16.1	18
1963	1,474	30.9	20
1964	1,679	13.9	19
1965	1,826	8.8	17
1966	1,963	7.5	17
1967	2,344	19.4	20
1968	2,815	20.1	20
1969	3,015	7.1	19
1970	3,167	5.0	17
1971	3,876	22.4	17
1972	5,034	29.9	17

SOURCE:

Col. 1—For 1950–53, Don Patinkin, *The Israel Economy: The First Decade* (Jerusalem: Falk Project for Economic Research, 1960; in English), Table 39; for 1954–71, *Statistical Abstract of Israel*, 1972, Table XIII/1; For 1972, ibid., 1973, Table IX/1.

Col. 3—GNP at current prices from Table A-2, above.

a. New series.

APPENDIX A

TABLE A-17
Price Indices, 1950–72
(annual averages; annual 1964 = 100)

	Consumer Prices (1)	Wholesale Prices (2)	GNP Price Deflator[a] (3)
1950	22.9	n.a.	21.7
1951	26.1	n.a.	25.4
1952	41.3	n.a.	36.9
1953	52.9	n.a.	47.2
1954	59.3	n.a.	52.0
1955	62.8	n.a.	55.1
1956	66.9	n.a.	60.3
1957	71.2	n.a.	64.3
1958	73.6	n.a.	69.7
1959	74.7	n.a.	70.8
1960	76.4	n.a.	74.5
1961	81.5	n.a.	81.3
1962	89.2	n.a.	87.5
1963	95.1	n.a.	94.7
1964	100.0	100.0	100.0
1965	107.7	103.9	109.7
1966	116.3	108.9	119.3
1967	118.2	110.2	121.6
1968	120.7	112.7	123.9
1969	123.7	114.9	126.9
1970	131.2	122.7	138.4
1971	147.0	134.0	157.7
1972	166.0	149.5	178.8

n.a. = not available.
SOURCE:
Col. 1—*Statistical Abstract of Israel*, 1973, Table X/3.
Col. 2—Ibid., Table X/1.
Col. 3—Ibid., 1972, Table VI/1.
a. GNP at current prices divided by GNP at 1964 prices.

Appendix B

Calculation of Effective Exchange Rates (EERs) and Effective Protective Rates (EPRs)

My purpose in this appendix is to discuss the main principles involved in the construction of estimates of EERs and EPRs for the years 1949–62. The estimates for later years (1963–71) were based on similar principles, although the instruments used in export promotion (from 1966 on) were somewhat different from the methods pursued in earlier years, thus leading to some differences in estimating procedures.

ESTIMATES OF EFFECTIVE EXCHANGE RATES IN EXPORTS

Rates for Value Added and Total Value.

The data on effective exchange rates in this volume are for *value added* in exports, not for total value. For economic analysis, this is the only useful concept in the case of Israel. Through a slight transformation, which is explained below, it yields the effective rate of protection in production for exports. This would also be the concept to use for time-series analyses of factors affecting the size of exports in comparisons with, for instance, time series of GNP prices or wage levels, etc.

The value-added rate does not yield the local price of finished export goods. But a separate calculation of the effective exchange rate for total value, designed to correct this omission, would not be warranted in the case of Israel. For the most part, sales of potential export goods in the local market constitute only a small fraction of total sales in that market; the higher the degree of aggregation in the classification of goods, the more evident this is. The local market price is thus a function of the exchange rate for *imports* of the good rather than for its exports.[1] This does not hold for the two large, traditional export goods—citrus fruits and polished diamonds. But there, too, the exchange rate for total value would be mostly irrelevant for the purpose of determining the local price. In the case of diamonds, this is because there are practically no local sales of the product (in the government's handling of the industry, it is always assumed that all of the imported raw material— the unpolished diamonds—is re-exported). In citrus fruit, on the other hand, local sales are primarily dictated by physical factors which determine the fraction of the crop which, due to its quality, cannot be exported, that is, exports and local sales are not of exactly the same product. Economic forces are not absent here altogether: some substitution does exist, and so the level of export prices does marginally affect the fraction exported. Still, the home price and the export price diverge radically from each other.

It should be pointed out that the combined use of the drawback system in exports (which has been in force all along, except for the special import levy of August 1970) and the premium-payment plan of 1956–61 for net value added, leads to the establishment of a shadow exchange rate for the import component in exports which is equal to the exchange rate for value added. Thus, under such a system, the exchange rate for *total* value will also be equal to the exchange rate for value added. This may be explained as follows: Suppose the producer maintains a given level of exports, but reduces the level of imported input by one dollar, thus increasing value added by this amount. This would yield him a saving of expenditure on imports equal to the value of the formal exchange rate for imports *and* an increase in premium receipts equal to the size of the premium rate. Thus, the net revenue created by the reduction of imports valued at one dollar would be equal to the formal exchange rate plus the premium rate; that is, to the effective exchange rate for value added in exports. The same result follows symmetrically if we suppose that imported input is *increased* by one dollar.[2]

Let

X = exports (total value in dollars);
M_X = import component in exports (value in dollars);
R_F = formal rate of exchange (Israeli pounds per dollar);
R_P = rate of export premium (Israeli pounds per dollar of value added);
Y = revenue from export transaction (Israeli pounds).

$$Y = (X - M_X)(R_F + R_P) + M_X R_F$$
$$= X(R_F + R_P) - M_X R_P$$

It appears, therefore, that the revenue is the same as if the exporter received the effective exchange rate per value added for his *total* exports (X) and was fined by a payment at the premium rate (R_P) on the import component. That is, the effective exchange rate for value added in exports is the shadow price for the import component, and this equals the formal rate plus the premium rate (the rate of the "fine"). In other words, this method is entirely equivalent to one in which an existing uniform rate is used for exports and the import component in exports, and which equals the effective exchange rate for value added in exports.

Rates of Exchange Using Pamaz Rights.

As was stated in the text, the effective exchange rate implied by taking account of the compensation of exporters in the local market was not estimated systematically and was not incorporated into the exchange rate calculations. The most important compensating device was created by the Pamaz plan, during the period 1953–59. For the years 1956–59, however, when both the Pamaz plan and the comprehensive premium plan were in effect, this omission is only slightly relevant if the effective exchange rate has to be estimated *at the margin,* as it would be for most purposes in economic analysis.

It will be recalled that during those years, exporters who were entitled to Pamaz rights could opt, instead, for premium payments. If rational behavior is assumed, an exporter would be expected to use his Pamaz rights up to the point at which the marginal revenue derived from use of this right is equal to the premium, and to sell the rest of his export proceeds (i.e., of his value added) to the Treasury, at a price equal to the formal rate plus the premium rate. If an exporter avails himself at all of the premium plan, this would mean that at the margin the effective exchange rate, using the Pamaz right, equals the premium rate. The data indicate that in the large majority of export industries, some use of the premium plan was indeed made. In the estimates, it was assumed that the effective rate involved in the use of Pamaz rights was equal to the effective rate created in selling the receipts to the Treasury. This, then, is not a gross distortion of the correct estimate so far as the rate at the margin is concerned.

ESTIMATES OF EFFECTIVE EXCHANGE RATES IN IMPORTS: TARIFF DUTIES

Two alternative methods can be used to estimate the exchange rate element involved in the tariff level for each good. One is to divide tariff revenue by the dollar value of imports, thus obtaining tariff duties in Israeli pounds per dollar of imports. The other is to apply the formal exchange rate to the tariff rates specified in the tariff schedule, thus again yielding the tariff in pounds per dollar. In the estimates constructed here, the second method was used rather than the first, for two reasons.

One is the well-known problem of timing. Tariff revenues are recorded when the duties are paid, not when the dutiable imports arrive; that is, they are recorded on a cash rather than an accrual basis. Dividing the revenues recorded in one calendar year by the imports recorded in the same year would thus not be justified in principle; and when long intervals of time elapse between clearance and payment and the value of imports is not constant—circumstances which are the rule rather than the exception—the error may be considerable.

But even were there no timing problem, the two alternative methods would not have yielded the same result, because some imports of dutiable goods enter duty free. As was explained in the text, this applies to two categories: imports destined for use in export production (which are entitled to drawbacks, and on which in effect no duty is charged to begin with) and imports (such as those of the government, or certain institutions, during parts of the period) that enjoy "conditional exemption." If the first method of estimating the tariff level were used, it would have yielded the *average* tariff imposed on all three categories: "normal" imports for domestic use, imports for exports, and duty-free imports under conditional exemption. The inclusion of imports for exports would patently be a wrong procedure: this category should not be included in this estimate just as it is not in the estimate of the effective exchange rate in exports. As was just shown, under the plan in effect during part of the period the shadow rate of exchange applying to this category was equal to the effective exchange rate for value added in exports rather than to the formal rate of exchange, as would be implied by including this category and assigning it a zero tariff rate. Inclusion would make the estimates invalid for use in economic analysis. Similarly, imports subject to conditional exemption should be excluded if the purpose of the estimate is, as it should be, to obtain the rate *at the margin*. For an analysis of protection, for instance, it is of no consequence that an institution has been granted the right to import some goods free of duty, as long as *these are not resold* in the local market, a condition that has usually been fulfilled.

The estimates used here refer, therefore, only to "normal" (i.e., non-duty-free) imports for domestic use. For this reason, as well as the timing problem, the method adopted for estimating was based on tariff schedules. In aggregating, the weight given to each good was determined by the level of non-duty-free imports only; these data were available for most of the period. When tariff schedules changed within a calendar year, annual averages were computed by using as weights not imports within each subperiod of the year, but the length of time to which each schedule applied. This was done as a short cut, and because monthly data on imports are not fully reliable and weekly data do not exist at all. The error involved in this procedure is probably small.

For most other components of the import exchange rate (except the formal rate), the *first* method—that of using actual, recorded revenue or expenditure—was followed. This is because these components are not usually based on any given, predetermined schedule: the profit or loss of the government's commercial account, for instance, could not be replaced by some schedule of profit or loss margins; no such ex-ante schedule is to be found. Thus, these estimates necessarily suffer from the discrepancies introduced by the timing problem.

TRANSFORMATION OF EFFECTIVE EXCHANGE RATES INTO EFFECTIVE RATES OF PROTECTION

Effective exchange rates for exports refer directly, as has just been explained, to value added. For import-competing goods, effective exchange rates for value added have been derived in the way explained in the text; that is, by use of input-output data, which include import components in each industry detailed by import group, and data on exchange rates for total value (i.e., value of final good) of each import group. The exchange rate for value added in industry j (R_{vj}) is obtained as follows:[3]

let

a_{ij} = coefficient of import i in industry j;
R_i = exchange rate for total value (final good) of import i;
R_j = exchange rate for total value of import j.

Then

$$R_{vj} = \frac{R_j - \sum_i a_{ij} R_i}{1 - \sum_i a_{ij}}$$

These are the values presented in the import-substitution columns in Table 4-6 in the text. As is explained in the text, the values arrived at in this way, through the use of aggregated input-output data, suffer from a few deficiencies. In particular, they are biased downward, probably to a substantial degree.

The transformation from the effective exchange rate for value added to effective rates of protection is technically simple; but it rests on a crucial assumption. If g_j is the effective protective rate for value added in industry j, and R_{vj} is the effective exchange rate for value added in j (whether for exports or in import substitution), then:

$$g_j = \frac{R_{vj}}{\overline{R}} - 1$$

or

$$g_j = \frac{\left(\dfrac{R_j}{\overline{R}} - 1\right) - \sum_i a_{ij} \left(\dfrac{R_i}{\overline{R}} - 1\right)}{1 - \sum_i a_{ij}}$$

The crucial assumption concerns the definition and size of $\overline{R}$. If this is taken as the formal rate of exchange, the outcome could have little meaning. If a positive g_j should indicate the existence of positive protection, then $\overline{R}$ must be the equilibrium rate of exchange, or, in practice, as good an approximation of the equilibrium level as can be conceived. If elasticities were known, $\overline{R}$ could be estimated from the data on the system of exchange rates, by calculating an average weighted by both the size of exports or imports of each good and its price elasticity of domestic supply or demand (assuming, as could probably be done for Israel without much distortion, fixed foreign prices).[4] In fact, these elasticities are not known; and making arbitrary assumptions about them would yield an estimate which is more arbitrary and less defensible than the one yielded by the procedure adopted here.

It is assumed here, instead, that the government continuously determines an exchange rate system for exports such that it will yield just the amount of foreign exchange at which, at the margin, the market value of imports of a unit of foreign exchange equals the domestic cost of obtaining that unit. On this assumption, the equilibrium rate of exchange is always the highest exchange rate (for value added) granted to exporters. However, it is obvious that some particularly high rates were accorded to individual industries on specific and particular grounds, rather than being motivated merely by the wish to obtain foreign-exchange proceeds for the economy. Therefore, in this calculation, the value actually selected in each year to represent the equilibrium foreign exchange rate was the highest rate granted to a significant part of total exports.[5] The rates thus taken as equilibrium levels were as follows: 1956, IL 2.40 per dollar; and 1957–60, IL 2.65 per dollar.

It should be noted that this derivation of EPRs involves two deviations from the appropriate definition and estimate of the concept. The a_{ij}'s stand for the fractions of total (direct and indirect) import components, whether the indirect component is an input to a tradable or to a nontradable input, whereas only the latter should have been included. On the other hand, they stand for coefficients of *imports* rather than of *tradables;* that is, they exclude inputs of exportable materials. It may be assumed that in the case of Israel, these errors of commission and omission do not affect the result in a significant manner.

NOTES

1. Were products completely homogeneous, no product could be both exported and imported in a country like Israel, where local transportation costs are very low in comparison with international transportation costs. No classification of goods is, however, detailed enough to lead to complete homogeneity; and certainly not a classification, such as the one used here, of all goods into eighty groups.

2. This presentation, as well as the explanation, is based on David Pines, *Direct Export Premiums in Israel, 1952–1958* (Jerusalem: Falk Project for Economic Research in Israel, 1963; in Hebrew), pp. 78–79.

3. The coefficient a_{ij} is from Michael Michaely, *Israel's Foreign Exchange Rate System,* Part III, *Appendixes* (Jerusalem: Falk Institute, 1970; in Hebrew), pp. 152–159. The data were prepared by the research department of the Bank of Israel on the basis of the 1958 input-output estimates.

4. See the discussion in W. M. Corden, "The Effective Protective Rate, the Uniform Tariff Equivalent, and the Average Tariff," *Economic Record* 42 (June 1966): 200–216.

5. A somewhat broader discussion of this procedure, in a different context, may be found in Michael Michaely, *Israel's Foreign Exchange Rate System* (Jerusalem: Falk Institute, 1971; in English), pp. 66–70.

Appendix C

Definition of Concepts and Delineation of Phases

DEFINITION OF CONCEPTS USED IN THE PROJECT

Exchange Rates.

1. *Nominal exchange rate:* The official parity for a transaction. For countries maintaining a single exchange rate registered with the International Monetary Fund, the nominal exchange rate is the registered rate.

2. *Effective exchange rate (EER):* The number of units of local currency actually paid or received for a one-dollar international transaction. Surcharges, tariffs, the implicit interest foregone on guarantee deposits, and any other charges against purchases of goods and services abroad are included, as are rebates, the value of import replenishment rights, and other incentives to earn foreign exchange for sales of goods and services abroad.

3. *Price-level-deflated (PLD) nominal exchange rates:* The nominal exchange rate deflated in relation to some base period by the price level index of the country.

4. *Price-level-deflated EER (PLD-EER):* The EER deflated by the price level index of the country.

5. *Purchasing-power-parity adjusted exchange rates:* The relevant (nominal or effective) exchange rate multiplied by the ratio of the foreign price level to the domestic price level.

Devaluation.

1. *Gross devaluation:* The change in the parity registered with the IMF (or, synonymously in most cases, de jure devaluation).

2. *Net devaluation:* The weighted average of changes in EERs by classes of transactions (or, synonymously in most cases, de facto devaluation).

3. *Real gross devaluation:* The gross devaluation adjusted for the increase in the domestic price level over the relevant period.

4. *Real net devaluation:* The net devaluation similarly adjusted.

Protection Concepts.

1. *Explicit tariff:* The amount of tariff charged against the import of a good as a percentage of the import price (in local currency at the nominal exchange rate) of the good.

2. *Implicit tariff* (or, synonymously, tariff equivalent): The ratio of the domestic price (net of normal distribution costs) minus the c.i.f. import price to the c.i.f. import price in local currency.

3. *Premium:* The windfall profit accruing to the recipient of an import license per dollar of imports. It is the difference between the domestic selling price (net of normal distribution costs) and the landed cost of the item (including tariffs and other charges). The premium is thus the difference between the implicit and the explicit tariff (including other charges) multiplied by the nominal exchange rate.

4. *Nominal tariff:* The tariff—either explicit or implicit as specified—on a commodity.

5. *Effective tariff:* The explicit or implicit tariff on value added as distinct from the nominal tariff on a commodity. This concept is also expressed as the effective rate of protection (ERP) or as the effective protective rate (EPR).

6. *Domestic resources costs (DRC):* The value of domestic resources (evaluated at "shadow" or opportunity cost prices) employed in earning or saving a dollar of foreign exchange (in the value-added sense) when producing domestic goods.

DELINEATION OF PHASES USED IN TRACING THE EVOLUTION OF EXCHANGE CONTROL REGIMES

To achieve comparability of analysis among different countries, each author of a country study was asked to identify the chronological development of his country's payments regime through the following phases. There was no presumption that a country would necessarily pass through all the phases in chronological sequence.

Phase I: During this period, quantitative restrictions on international transactions are imposed and then intensified. They generally are initiated in response to an unsustainable payments deficit and then, for a period, are intensified. During the period when reliance upon quantitative restrictions as a means of controlling the balance of payments is increasing, the country is said to be in Phase I.

Phase II: During this phase, quantitative restrictions are still intense, but various price measures are taken to offset some of the undesired results of the system. Heightened tariffs, surcharges on imports, rebates for exports, special tourist exchange rates, and other price interventions are used in this phase. However, primary reliance continues to be placed on quantitative restrictions.

Phase III: This phase is characterized by an attempt to systematize the changes which take place during Phase II. It generally starts with a formal exchange-rate change and may be accompanied by removal of some of the surcharges, etc., imposed during Phase II and by reduced reliance upon quantitative restrictions. Phase III may be little more than a tidying-up operation (in which case the likelihood is that the country will re-enter Phase II), or it may signal the beginning of withdrawal from reliance upon quantitative restrictions.

Phase IV: If the changes in Phase III result in adjustments within the country, so that liberalization can continue, the country is said to enter Phase IV. The necessary adjustments generally include increased foreign-exchange earnings and gradual relaxation of quantitative restrictions. The latter relaxation may take the form of changes in the nature of quantitative restrictions or of increased foreign-exchange allocations, and thus reduced premiums, under the same administrative system.

Phase V: This is a period during which an exchange regime is fully liberalized. There is full convertibility on current account, and quantitative restrictions are not employed as a means of regulating the ex ante balance of payments.

Index

Agorah, 146
Agriculture: contribution to employment, 12; contribution to GNP, 12; cooperatives, 3; exports, 17, 148; immigrants, 2, 12; imports, 65–66; liberalization, 65, 67, 76; productivity in, 161–162
American Jewry, 53
Amiel, Valery D., 93, 114
Autarky, 180, 182. *See also* Openness

Bank of Israel: and credit expansion, 128, 130; establishment of, 2; financing of exports by, 88; lending to government by, 2, 147; monetary policy techniques of, 128, 146
Barkai, Haim, 25, 80
Baruch, Joseph, 102, 114, 117
Beham, Miriam, 148
Ben-Shahar, Haim, 105, 117
Bilateral clearing agreements, 50, 54–55
Black market for commodities, 41–43, 48, 57, 133–134, 178. *See also* Rationing
Black market for foreign exchange: general description, 41, 45, 57; and "imports without payment," 37–39; prices in, 43, 45–46
Blocked accounts, 175

"Branch funds," 85–86, 91. *See also* Premiums
British mandatory government: budget of, 2; equalization funds use, 83–84; and exchange rate, 119; foreign-exchange policy of, 22; foreign trade policy of, 24, 27
Broken cross-rate. *See* Pound sterling
Budget: under British mandate, 2; and defense expenditures, 147; deficit in, 20; development of, 155–158, 174, 202; foreign-exchange, 28–33, 37, 55–56; and lending from central bank, 2, 147. *See also* Government sector

Capital: and domestic savings, 153–159; imports of, 12–18, 33–34, 53, 121, 130, 150–151, 155, 164, 166, 175, 200–201; physical, 11, 15, 20, 190; and private foreign investment, 150–153, 159; and repatriation, 151–152
Cartels: and liberalization policy, 64; and subsidies on exports, 91, 115
Central Bank. *See* Bank of Israel
Central Bureau of Statistics, and the price index, 41
Central planning, and quantitative restrictions, 178

215